Getting Started in

CHART
PATTERNS

The *Getting Started In* Series

Getting Started in

CHART PATTERNS

Thomas N. Bulkowski

WILEY

John Wiley & Sons, Inc.

Published by John Wiley & Sons, Inc., Hoboken, New Jersey.
Published simultaneously in Canada.

For general information on our other products and services or for technical support, please contact our
Customer Care Department within the United States at (800) 762-2974, outside the United States at (317)
572-3993 or fax (317) 572-4002.

Wiley also publishes its books in a variety of electronic formats. Some content that appears in print may
not be available in electronic books. For more information about Wiley products, visit our web site at
www.wiley.com.

Library of Congress Cataloging-in-Publication Data:

Bulkowski, Thomas N., 1957-

Getting started in chart patterns / Thomas N. Bulkowski.
     p. cm.
   Includes index.
   ISBN-13: 978-0-471-72766-8 (pbk.)

1. Stocks—Charts, diagrams, etc. 2. Commodity futures—Charts, diagrams, etc. 3. Investment analysis.
I. Title.
  HG4638.B853 2006
  332.63'2042—dc22   2005017555

10 9 8

To Mary Schramski
I found the answer to your question, "What is creative nonfiction?"

Contents

Chapter 8

Chapter 9

Chapter 10

Chapter 11

Chapter 12

Preface

I read that a chartist becomes world class after he views a million chart patterns. If you analyze one pattern per chart on 250 stocks each trading day, it'll take fifteen years to reach a million. Fifteen years! We don't have that much time. I'm asking for only a few hours.

Before we go any further, look at the cover of this book. See where it lists the price? If you buy this book and make one profitable trade because of it, that money will be well spent. That's cheap education, but I'm going to give you much more.

Chart patterns are the *footprints* of smart money. The smart money leaves false trails. So if you're like a close friend who looked at everything but the road when driving, you're going to pick up bad habits. Those habits may cause you to freeze when trading so that you get in late or exit early. The million bucks you dream about will be just that—a dream. My chapter on trading psychology keeps your eyes focused on the road ahead.

After that, we make music discussing chart patterns, one by one, starting with the basics: trendlines, support and resistance, special situations—all geared to the beginning investor or trader, but it comes with tips and techniques that will delight and inform professionals, too. I show you the top 10 bullish performers and then discuss the band members. Those band members are the chart patterns everyone knows. They are your backup vocals. Together, they help you perform like a rock star. No performance would be complete without an audience, and that's where event patterns come in. They are the audience, and I show you how to make money from them.

When fans scale the fences trying to get into the concert free, I discuss tactics to handle the busted chart patterns. Often, they represent the best profit opportunities.

Once you have met your band members and the stage is ready, then it's time for rehearsal. I discuss trades that I made throughout this book, but I dedicate an entire chapter to them. Study them. Learn what I did and consider what you would have done differently. Pull up the charts on your own computer so that the patterns become familiar to you.

The statistics I mention throughout this book are not guesses but the results of studies that I conducted on over 38,500 chart and event patterns. Each statistic represents the performance of hundreds of patterns *traded perfectly*, *without* commissions or fees. You won't be able to achieve those returns, but these numbers provide a basis for comparison. I've included a table of performance statistics at the back of the book with the chart and event pattern's performance rank—so pick the patterns you like. I also provide an index of chart patterns to help with identification.

Let's meet Jake. He's a character all right, but a fictional one. I use him as a literary device to highlight actual trades, the points I want to make, or just to keep things lively. If his trade mentions specifics— shares traded and the cost—then *it is an actual trade that I made with my own money in the stock market.*

When the crew comes to pack up the gear for the next gig, I provide trading checklists so that you won't forget anything. After that, you'll be on your own, but in case your concert tour needs help, this book should remain at hand.

Buy it.
Read it.
Make money.

THOMAS N. BULKOWSKI
September 2005

Acknowledgments

I would like to thank the talented efforts of Pamela van Giessen, editorial director at John Wiley & Sons, senior production editor Mary Daniello, and assistant editor Jennifer MacDonald. These three make publishing a book easy and fun. Almost. Thanks to Bernice Pettinato at Beehive Production Services for proofreading the book. I am indebted to Lt. Colonel James Bulkowski for acting as my support group. Thanks brother. And keep your head down in Iraq should you find yourself there.

Regarding Serious Inquiries

If you would like to contact me, e-mail me at tbul@hotmail.com. Make sure you fill in the subject line with something like "Chart pattern question" so that I don't mistake it for spam and delete it unread. I'll try to reply, but your patience will be appreciated. My web site address is http://mysite.verizon.net/resppzq7/.

T. N. B.

The Smart Money's Footprints

J ake was here to rob me.

How he got near my office undetected was anyone's guess, but my hand shot to one of the panic buttons I have hidden. I didn't press it; something held me back. He reminded me of Clint Eastwood with white hair, tall and thin, yet with an inner strength stronger than granite and a dimple that etched his chin when he smiled.

"Sorry about that," he said. "I didn't mean to startle you. I'm Murphy. Jake Murphy."

His name meant nothing to me. My finger caressed the sandpaper top of the panic button, shaking slightly, my body tense, adrenaline pumping—my breath a pressure cooker waiting for release.

"Have you ever heard of Murphy's Law?" He smiled and pointed a finger at himself. If he was telling the truth, I was going to trade the opposite of everything he did. "I e-mailed you last week about learning to trade."

I started breathing again. My hand went to my chest and felt for my heart, but then a polite tone and a flashing green symbol on the computer screen caught my attention. I held up my fist, index finger extended.

Wait one . . .

Jake froze.

My hand returned to playing the keyboard, dancing over it with the skill of an accomplished musician.

Thirty seconds later, having relieved someone of several thousand dollars, I looked back at Jake. "Please." I waved him to the chair beside mine, seated at the feet of computer monitors staring at us like eyeballs. I had a special air-conditioning system installed just to keep those eyeballs and their bodies from frying. Computers are the cooking utensils of a trader.

"I'm not trying to embarrass you Jake, but I want the truth. Did you use stops on every trade?"

He paused for a moment, and his face took on the color of a stop sign. "No." His voice sounded apprehensive, in contrast to the Clint Eastwood growl through clenched teeth that I expected.

"Did you buy near the yearly high to surf upward momentum?"

He shook his head.

"Did you look at the market averages and industry-related stocks before trading to see which way they were headed?"

He looked down but said nothing.

I felt like I was questioning my own father, but this torture chamber had no bright light shining in his eyes, just padded chairs like those in a NASA control room. "Forget it," I said touching his shoulder and then pointing at the computer eyeballs staring at us. "What do you see?"

He put on reading glasses and his head moved closer, examining every pixel, and then he backed away. The glasses disappeared into his pocket so quickly that I knew the specs were more than just a tool. An embarrassment, perhaps? A sign that he was growing older and refusing to accept it? I discarded this clue about Jake Murphy.

"You're looking at the smart money. They know everything there is to know about that stock or any stock. Yet they have a weakness. Do you know what it is?"

He raised his eyes in thought and then snapped them back level. But he said nothing.

"They can't hide their tracks." I pointed at one monitor. "Those tracks are not squiggles on the screen. They're footprints of the smart money. String enough footprints together and they form chart patterns. Those chart patterns give buy and sell signals. If you trade using those signals, you can make money." I leaned back in my chair, hands clasped behind my head, eyes cycling between Jake and the monitors, scanning for trading signals. "You *do* want to make money, don't you?"

His eyes lit up and he nodded.

"What's your story?"

He cleared his throat and leaned forward in the chair. "I'm a self-employed engineer nearing retirement, and I trade between jobs. I started trading using fundamental analysis, but when the fundamentals said 'buy,' nothing happened to the stock for months or even years. I got tired of waiting. I started looking at technical analysis. I tried moving averages. I tried Elliott wave. I tried cycles and candlesticks and indicators and black box systems. Nothing worked.

"I want to afford health insurance. I want to have enough money to feel secure in my retirement. It's not hard to meet expenses. They're everywhere!"

Then Jake dropped his eyes and turned away. I knew he wasn't telling me everything.

2

Trading Psychology

"**W**hat aren't you telling me?"

Jake looked down at his shoes and rubbed one against the back of his pants, polishing it even though it didn't need polishing. If he were standing, I'm sure he'd be shuffling his feet with embarrassment. After a lengthy pause, he admitted, "I want to have enough money to do things that I couldn't do when I was younger. I want to *live!*"

"A midlife crisis? I had mine when I was 30. I kept asking myself, 'What am I here for?' and not finding an answer. It took almost a decade to understand that I'm here to make a difference. But let's talk about trading. You mentioned a telecom trade in your e-mail."

He started wringing his hands as if he were nervous or embarrassed talking about it. "I worked as a computer technician once, so I knew all about the telecom." He researched the company's fundamentals as best he could, but solid information was scarce. The rumors, however, were like ants at a picnic.

"They're going to lay enough fiber to circle the earth four times!" someone said at a conference.

"I heard that insiders are buying like crazy," said another. "Four bought in the last month, six this quarter."

"I drove by HQ last week and the lights were on at three in the morning," said a third. "I'm thinking: takeover."

"A friend of mine knows someone who knows someone who used to work there. He said that two of the Baby Bells are interested. This stock isn't a buy. It's a steal!"

Jake shook his head and rolled his eyes. "I bought 600 shares. Cost me a grand."

Two weeks after he bought, apparently the rumors turned out to be true because the stock moved up 30% to $2 a share. Everyone was talking about the company, how the stock was going to Pluto at warp 10.

Then the stock stopped going up. It dropped a dime one day, then a nickel. Two weeks later, it was down to his purchase price. "I thought: it'll come back. I'll just hang on until it reaches its old high and then sell."

The word in the chat room was that "The Company has a buyback plan in place. They're forcing the stock down so the company can buy it back on the cheap." Another said, "I heard that they're planning to take the company private. Management's no dummy. They know a good opportunity when they see it. Buy more."

The stock eased down a little each day—no skydiver plunge, just slow torture.

Then the chat rooms were aflame with a new rumor, sworn to be true. "The company declared bankruptcy."

Was this an example of Murphy's Law for traders? The obituaries confirmed it. Trading at 50 cents, the stock gapped lower to a dime and flatlined like a dead animal.

"Why didn't you sell on the way down?" I asked him.

His dimple appeared in a strained smile, and he shrugged his shoulders. "It wasn't the first time, either." He flew an airline stock into the ground, receiving pennies instead of dollars for his investment when it, too, went bankrupt.

"Why didn't you sell the second time?" Good question. This chapter takes a closer look at why traders make such mistakes and how to avoid them.

Trading Psychology

Let's tackle Jake's problem first by conducting an experiment. Suppose you had the choice of selecting Door Number One, which contains $500, or Door Number Two that holds either $1,000 or nothing. Which door do you choose?

Next, consider another two doors. Selecting Door One means you will owe $500, and selecting Door Two means you will owe either $1,000 or nothing. Which door do you choose?

In the first question, most people will select the $500 gain (Door One), but when it comes to losses, they prefer to take a chance on a larger loss by selecting Door Two. In the investment world, that means they cut their profits short and let their losses run—the exact opposite of what they should do.

"What can I do about it?" Jake asked.

Use a *stop-loss order*. It sounds simple, doesn't it? Without a stop in place when the trade begins to go bad, you have a choice to make: to sell or not to sell. That's when the fear of taking a loss appears. The pain of loss is two and a half times as strong as the joy of making a profit, according to Gerald Butrimovitz, a behavioral finance expert. That means traders will take even greater risks to avoid losses. Having a stop in place takes the agonizing decision out of your hands. Either you're stopped or you're not. Chances are a properly placed stop will give you a smaller loss than if you try to manage the trade without a stop. Unwillingness to use a stop is what separates an amateur trader from a professional. If you want to make money in the markets, then use stops on every trade.

> **stop or stop-loss order**
> an order to sell at a price below or to buy at a price above the current price.

Raise the stop as prices climb. After I started using stops consistently and raised them as prices climbed, my *average* loss decreased. I no longer suffer from seeing large paper gains turn into losses when the trend changes. The stop locks in a profit.

> **average**
> the sum of the scores divided by the number of scores.

If you feel you're going to be stopped out, close out the trade. When the stock drops and a voice inside whispers, "I'm about to be stopped out," then don't wait. Sell immediately at the higher price and save yourself some money. Wishing and hoping will not change the direction of the stock. I know. I've tried.

The Basics

The longer you trade, the more likely you are to develop trading habits, some good and some bad. Bad trading habits are like termites: If you see one coming out of a hole in the wall, then you have a serious problem.

By knowing ahead of time what to expect, you can head off the development of bad habits.

Let's brush up on the basics. No system is perfect, including chart patterns. Let's say that you expect your trades to work 80% of the time but the trading system you've just bought or invented works just half the time. Your expectations do not match reality and you are destined for failure and disappointment. In fact, many traders will tell you that their win/loss ratio ranges between 40% and 60%.

Jake nudged me. "What's your win/loss ratio?"

"Forty-nine percent, but that's over a lifetime. It's been higher in recent years. What's yours?"

"Don't know, but my total cholesterol is 198." He laughed and his dimple made its requisite appearance.

Here are some tips.

Match your expectations to reality. A woman e-mailed me saying that she wanted to move from being an entrepreneur of a successful business to trading securities. She had dabbled in the market for years with *some* success and wanted to do it full time. She wanted to pull $2,000 a week out of the market, or 100 grand in the first year. That's certainly possible if you believe some book titles, but the odds of it happening are against you. Be excited if you're profitable the first year.

Select good tools, a winning system. To be a successful trader, you need two things: a winning system and the ability to follow it. It doesn't matter whether the system is a mechanical one where you just buy and sell when it tells you to, or a discretionary one where you decide whether the signal is worth trading. If it's a winning system, following it will make you money.

Follow the system. I read of a trader that marketed his trading system. After the system had a *winning* year, he polled the people that bought his system and found that just 5% were still using it. Think about that the next time you consider paying big bucks for a trading system.

Keep costs low. If you think that trading losses are more important than commissions, then you may have a problem. Like commissions, losses are just the cost of doing business. It's like the retailer that has a pile of wool sweaters going into summer. He's going to have to sell his inventory for a loss. The question is will he do better next time? Will he take the time to study the market and learn from his mistakes?

Do research; learn from mistakes. "I remember when I bought 1,000 shares of JLG Industries for 14.60 per share," Jake said. "Then, the company released earnings that were better than expected and the stock climbed 15% in one session, topping out at 16.54. At the peak, on paper, I made almost $2,000."

"Did you sell?"

"Yup. But first I did research." The stock was in the process of making an inverted dead-cat bounce that I discuss in Chapter 8 (see Figure 8.5). "I found that 46% of the stocks made a higher high the next day after a large gain, and that was the highest high in the coming month. But two days later, the stock closed higher—Murphy's Law." He shrugged his shoulders, palms pointed toward heaven.

"You traded the probabilities," I said. "That's always the smart move. Besides, you made money."

Curing Negative Thoughts

Close your eyes and listen to the sounds around you. In my dining room, as I write this, I can hear the refrigerator running. I have a fan on the counter blowing cool air in the summer heat. The grandfather clock in the far corner is ticking loudly; every 15 minutes it tolls. The cardinal in the bushes outside my window has a distinctive high-pitched chirp that tells his mate where he is and that he's still alive. The bearings in my windmill are no longer smooth; as the propeller spins, it rivals the grandfather clock in its ticking.

Focus on the positive. Just by thinking about it, I can shift my focus from sound to sound, emphasizing one and diminishing others. Why not do the same with your thoughts? Instead of dwelling on how the trade that you are about to make will lose money, visualize a winning trade. Think of how you will feel watching the stock double in price. Focus on what you *want* to happen. Visualize how great you'll feel with a big winner and how awful you'll feel if you miss the opportunity.

Be patient. Positive thoughts bolster your confidence and help remove barriers that may color your perception of the markets. Instead of hesitating getting into a trade, you will jump right in. Don't expect changes overnight. This technique takes at least three weeks before you will see a difference. That is how long it takes your subconscious to accept it.

When my dad died, my mom had trouble coping. She had a confidence problem. I told her to repeat the phrase "I can do it" several times a day. After three weeks, her confidence returned, and she was able to move on with life. You can do the same with your trading by visualizing what you want to happen and by focusing on the positive aspects of each trade. Practice it every day.

The Comfort Zone

Fearful about placing a trade because you might lose money? Getting nervous that an upward price trend is topping out? These are warning signals that you are moving out of your comfort zone. Everyone wants to stay in their comfort zone and let the profits tumble in without having to make trading decisions. Successful traders tell you that they push the comfort zone, trying to expand it so every trade feels good. Learn to push the envelope. Make earning millions feel as comfortable as when you were making thousands. Make earning thousands as comfortable as when you earned hundreds.

Remember when you first started driving, how you gripped the steering wheel, how you dutifully checked each mirror every 15 seconds? Now, the radio blares, a cell phone covers your ear, and you don't even think about keeping the car centered in the lane. Driving has become rote, just as trading should be.

Ignore profits. I have noticed that once profits move into four figures, I get nervous about protecting them. I move out of the comfort zone. Instead of letting the profits grow, I micromanage the trade and soon sell.

How did I fix the cutting-profits-short problem? Let me give you an example. I bought Lam Research at the bottom of a rounding turn on the weekly scale. That pattern will take months to complete. Because I'm looking for price to return to the left lip high, I can ignore the daily fluctuations and watch for a significant trend change. Focusing on a longer-term trade (the weekly scale) is one way of fixing the selling-too-soon problem.

Focus on price behavior. Another tip is to concentrate not on how large the profits are, but on price action. If I don't see that I've made $2,000, I won't be inclined to sell. I can focus on how the stock is behaving, not on some artificial need to lock in a gain. I have tamed the comfort zone.

Get used to making too much money. A related problem is being a trading saboteur. A trader begins to sabotage his trades once he reaches a certain income level. He (or she) may feel that he doesn't deserve to earn that much money. Perhaps his parents held multiple jobs and worked long hours to achieve success. He feels that he doesn't work as hard as they did and shouldn't earn as much money. Everyone has a comfort zone for the income that they create and going outside that zone can cause problems.

Recognize that you have a problem if you feel uneasy about your trading, have a stagnant income level, or have an inability to stick to a trading plan despite the knowledge that doing so would boost your income.

Next, visualize what you want to happen with your trades. See yourself placing trades without worrying about the outcome, living with an income that is higher than you have experienced, placing trades on time and at the correct price. Whatever the problem you have identified, see yourself overcoming it without stress or worry.

Fish or cut bait? Trade to make money. Have you heard of the trader who spends months refining a trading system? Instead of using it to trade, he continues tweaking it. He enjoys tuning the system, adding bells and whistles to the extent that he has forgotten the point of the exercise: to make money using the system. Locked inside of the comfort zone, he is unwilling to bust out and play the game.

Another trader perceives himself as a successful trader. He takes profits early. Instead of aggressively moving into a trade, he hesitates. If he doesn't trade, he can maintain his winning image by not losing.

There was a point in my trading career when I would log a chart pattern into the system so that each time I looked at the stock, the pattern appeared. Sometimes I would identify a pattern too late to trade and other times I would find it well ahead of the breakout. But I didn't trade the pattern. I just watched it form and watched price take off.

I did two things to fix this. First, I programmed my computer to recognize chart patterns *before* the breakout. That way, I can analyze price behavior and plan the trade. Second, when I get a buy signal, I don't ask if I should trade the stock. I ask what is preventing me from taking a position. The number of trades I have made has grown substantially and so have the profits.

The Sell Signal

Not long after meeting Jake, price broke out downward from a symmetrical triangle in Questar Corporation. Then it closed there. That was the sell signal. The next day, I sold for a $300 loss. Two days after I sold, the stock started to recover. Price shot out the top of the triangle, moved 15% higher in about a week, and continued climbing.

I wondered if Jake's bad luck was starting to rub off on me. Then I started laughing. This was the perfect busted trade—when price moves down a small amount before shooting out the other side of the pattern. Did I sell too soon? If I held on longer, the trade would have worked out just as I expected, but I know from experience that this was a fluke. When price breaks out downward, sell immediately and don't look back. There are other chart patterns begging for your attention like abandoned puppies in an animal shelter.

What would have happened if I decided to hold on? By ignoring a sell signal and having a winning trade, I would be reinforcing negative behavior. I would question each sell signal and my losses would grow in step with trading anxiety.

Obey the signals. Obey your trading signals and don't let bad habits form. If you do make a mistake, don't dwell on it; just vow to do better next time. Close your eyes and visualize making the same trade, but this time obeying the signals.

Big losses usually come from small ones. "I watch a loss grow until I can't take it anymore," Jake said. "Then I sell two days before it bottoms."

If you use a stop, you won't have this problem. Don't let those small losses grow into big ones, and don't allow a profit to turn into a loss. Use a stop-loss order on every trade.

Plan the Trade and Trade the Plan

When you have a losing trade, you may wonder what you did wrong. Instead, try focusing on how well you executed the trade. Did you follow your plan? Did you even have a plan to follow? Did you buy in late or sell too soon?

Focus on the big picture. Are you in a streak so cold it makes Antarctica look like the sun's surface, producing losing trade after losing trade?

- Paper trade until you start winning again. Then jump back in using the techniques you refined when paper trading.

- Focus not on any one trade but on a series of trades. The small loss you took today pales next to the blockbuster gain you made a month ago.

- Recheck your trading system and see if tuning it gives better results. The market changes over time. Your trading system, whether mechanical or discretionary, needs to be able to cope with those changes.

Profit Barriers

Trading barriers come in many forms—I experienced one firsthand. The newspaper said that brokerage firms were reporting better than expected earnings. My broker announced earnings and the stock jumped up on the news. The company expected 2004 to be a good year. When the price eased back down, I bought. The stock waffled up and down. I felt confident that the price pattern would develop into an earnings flag and the stock would take off, so I doubled my position.

The general market turned down and sucked the life out of the stock. I was so confident in the stock performing that I lost 13%— about double the usual loss. The good news came when the market told me I was wrong—I sold. I followed my plan.

Avoid scenario trading. Some call this scenario trading—trading on an idea or story. Enthusiasm for the story drowns out the warning bells. You only hear the siren song seducing you into a trade that is destined to fail. You watch the business reports on television or read about them in the financial news or on the Internet. Scenarios are all around you, trying to make you believe a new trend is starting. Don't believe it. The trend is about to end.

"I was into gold mining stocks once," Jake said, "so I followed the price of gold. I read a columnist who cited numerous experts who claimed that gold had bottomed. But month after month, gold continued down. It took almost two years to reverse, but by then . . ." He stood up and showed me his empty pockets. "I didn't contribute to my IRA that year because what little I had left over went to pay for health insurance." His hands turned into two fists, clenched so his knuckles turned white. "I hate insurance companies."

Ignore rumors and chat. Following the chat room chat and buying a pump-and-dump stock is another mistake traders make. Someone of perceived authority says buy ABC because his Already-Been-Chewed gum is the best there is. The stock is selling for pennies and it will go to five bucks in a heartbeat. He might be right. What he doesn't tell you is that he'll sell you his shares when the time is right, just before the stock crashes. Don't listen to the chat room chat. Make up your own mind. And when you do make a mistake, sell quickly.

Set price targets. Not having a profit or loss target is a trading barrier to success. How will you know when to get out? Sometimes setting a profit target means you call the top exactly. A loss target tells you when you are wrong and a stop takes you out. If you don't set a profit target, raise your stop until price takes you out when the trend changes.

Decide what's more important, being right or making money? For some people, making money in the market is less important than being right. Think of those traders who hold on to a stock, riding it down, holding it regardless of the paper loss so that they can sell it when it crosses the threshold back into profitability. They can brag that they have never had a loss or that their win/loss ratio is 90%. Don't be afraid to sell. Losses are the cost of doing business.

Avoid emotional trading. "Winning streaks are another problem I have," Jake said. "I get so elated that I buy anything. Then, someone comes along with a rolled-up newspaper and swats me down. I lose all that I made and more. But I feel good that I owe the government less money."

Don't trade when you're emotionally stressed (too excited or too upset). Sometimes you feel you have to double your bet so that you can get back to breakeven sooner. You're angry and it's time for payback. You haven't had a winning trade in so long you're sure this one is going to be the big winner. You buy large and pump additional money into the position, tying to prop up the stock single-handedly. I've tried supporting a stock. It doesn't work because the market has other plans.

I turned to Jake. He was fidgeting in the chair because he knew what I was going to ask.

The Truth about Trendlines

"**H**ere's that financial statement you asked for," Jake said. His hands shook as he held it out to me. His veins bulged. When I tried to take it, he wouldn't let go. His fingers seemed tipped with glue. I pried it from his hand and then scanned the document.

"Budgets are a way to go broke methodically." He slumped lower in the chair. "I can't go on losing money like this."

"I'll help you out. Which way did you come in?" I smiled at the joke but Jake didn't. "Sorry. Before you make your next trade, run it by me."

Trading stocks is a lot like fishing—patiently waiting for a chart pattern to appear and excitement when the chase begins. If you're lucky, the sweetness of success will overcome the bitter taste of failure. You will have both, but trendlines can help.

A Trendline Example

Jake's finger hovered over the keyboard when I snuck up behind him and asked, "Is that the trade?"

He jumped and then yelled "Jeez!" I wondered if he was going to have a coronary. He released his chest, took a deep breath, and then pointed at the screen. "I'm going to buy that puppy."

"Do you like losing money?" I said in my best Clint Eastwood imitation.

He swung around in his chair and looked at me.

"That trade is good for at most seven points, maybe as little as two."

He frowned then looked back at the screen, wondering how I knew. Figure 3.1 shows what he was looking at. The two lines surrounding the falling wedge slope downward, joining at the wedge apex sometime in the future. Volume also slopes downward as it does in many chart patterns. Breakout day volume—the day price closes above the top pattern line—is high, but not worth writing home about. The upward breakout confirmed the falling wedge as a valid chart pattern and signaled a buy. Or did it?

Jake turned back to me. "I don't see it."

"The falling wedge predicts that 70% of the time price will rise to at least the top of the wedge. If the rise stops there, the trade would be

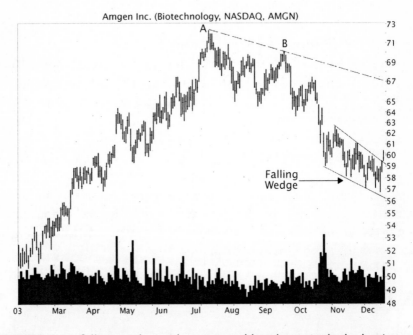

FIGURE 3.1 A falling wedge with an upward breakout marked a buying opportunity until a trendline, drawn along the tops connecting points A and B and extended down, warned that price might stall when it reached the trendline.

worth only two points. More likely, though, is that price will push higher until it hits a trendline connecting these two tops." I pointed to peaks A and B. "With a declining price trend, the chances are good that prices will rise to meet the trendline and then plummet faster than a hot air balloon out of propane." I leaned closer to the screen. "If you trade the stock *perfectly*, you'd make 10%, but with Murphy's Law at the wheel . . ." I shrugged my shoulders.

Out of spite, Jake placed the trade anyway. In early February 2004, the stock reached a high of 66.88, one point above the downsloping trendline before the stock reversed and sank to a low of 52 and change.

Jake read the manuscript over my shoulder. "I should have listened."

I turned around to face him. "How much did you lose that time?"

"Enough money to pay for groceries for three years, or a month's worth of health insurance premiums. Those bloodsuckers . . ." His jaw tightened and his voice was a rattler hissing. "Tell me everything you know about trendlines."

Trendlines: External, Internal, and Curved

If you look at almost any price chart, your eyes will find prices that zigzag but still follow an imaginary path. That path is called a "trend." If you draw a line connecting the peaks or valleys along that trend, you get a trendline. A trendline can outline a chart pattern as it does in Figure 3.1 (the falling wedge), or it can show a price trend (trendline A and B). Trendlines indicate buying or selling opportunities when price crosses them.

External Trendlines

Trendlines come in three flavors: external, internal, and curved. External trendlines are straight lines drawn so that the line rests on the peaks or grips the bottom of valleys. Figure 3.2 shows an external trendline. Upsloping trendlines *connect the valleys of a rising price trend*. That way, when price crosses the trendline, it is an indication of a possible trend change from up to down. In the stock market, knowing when the trend will change is worth big bucks. Notice that prices zigzag as they move higher, but they still follow the straight trendline.

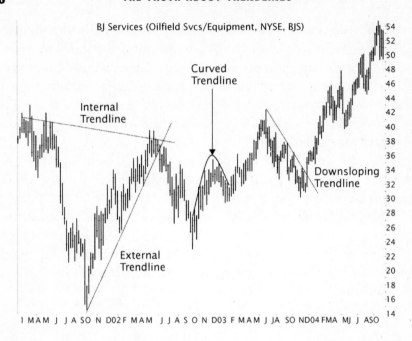

FIGURE 3.2 Shown on the weekly scale are the three types of trendlines: external, internal, and curved. The curved trendline highlights an ascending and inverted scallop chart pattern.

The downsloping trendline beginning in mid 2003 is also an external trendline, but it rests on the price peaks. *Draw downsloping trendlines along the price peaks* to indicate a possible trend change from down to up. Notice that both external trendlines in Figure 3.2 do not cut through prices but rest along the tops or bottoms of the peaks or valleys. Cutting through prices is what differentiates an internal trendline from an external one.

Internal Trendlines

Internal trendlines are lines of trend drawn so that they rest on the flat portion of peaks or valleys—and frequently cut through prices. If the price peak were a hill, an internal trendline would rest on the ground. An external trendline, by contrast, would only connect the tops of the tallest trees. Figure 3.2 shows one example of an internal trendline. Notice how the line cuts through prices instead of resting on them.

"Why would someone want to use that?" Jake asked and pushed his reading glasses higher on his nose.

One technical analyst argues that the line better represents the trading behavior of the masses, whereas external trendlines show the behavior of just a few traders, the ones that traded at the price extremes.

Most chartists use external trendlines, especially when drawing chart patterns, and that is my personal preference. Sometimes I'll use an internal trendline to highlight a trend better, especially an unusually long one, or a chart pattern with a few price outliers.

Curved Trendlines

Occasionally, the price trend is not straight, but curved as Figure 3.2 shows. Draw a curved trendline along the peaks or valleys to highlight the price pattern. The curved line in the figure shows a chart pattern called an "ascending and inverted scallop."

Sometimes traders get excited about a stock and push prices up (or down) at faster and faster rates. The price trend moves up at a good clip (30 to 45 degrees) and then starts curving upward in a parabolic arc. These vertical climbs can be both exciting and scary because prices move higher than you expect, but you know that the rise is going to stop eventually. Then, everyone races for the exits, forcing prices to plummet. When price closes below a rising but curved trendline, that is the sell signal, and it can help you be one of the first out the door. A sharp reversal often follows the breakout from a parabolic or steep trendline.

For all three varieties of trendlines—external, internal, and curved—traders simply refer to them as *trendlines*. Whether you use an internal or external trendline is a matter of personal preference.

Touch Spacing

When I wrote *Trading Classic Chart Patterns* (John Wiley & Sons, 2002), I conducted research on trendlines and proved what others had merely speculated. I looked at about 200 trendlines with narrow and wide touch spacing and found that larger price moves occurred after a breakout from a trendline with widely spaced touches.

Figure 3.3 shows line AC has four trendline touches and the line is five months long. On average, the touches are widely spaced. Trendline AB has five trendline touches; four of the touches are just a day apart. That trendline has narrowly spaced touches.

FIGURE 3.3 Trendlines with widely spaced touches perform better than do ones with narrow touches.

I found that when the average spacing between touches was less than the median 29 days in a downsloping trendline, the resulting price rise after an upward breakout averaged 36%. Trendlines with touches spaced wider than 29 days showed prices climbing 41%. The same applies to upward sloping trendlines. There, the median was 28 days between touches and narrow trendline touches gave declines averaging 14%, but widely spaced touches showed declines averaging 19%. The results from these tests are for *perfect trades without any fees*, so don't expect to replicate them in actual trading.

If you are considering trading a trendline with four touches in a month compared to a longer trendline with four touches each one month apart, trade the one with wider spacing. It will be more reliable, meaning that price is less likely to pierce the trendline and reverse (a false breakout).

"Let me see if I understand," Jake interrupted. "Trendline AB has widely spaced touches (see Figure 3.1), so I should have viewed it as a concrete wall."

"That's right. Price bounced off it and turned down. But there's more."

Trendline Touches

I also looked at the number of times price touched a trendline. Experienced traders say that the more times price touches a trendline, the more significant becomes a breakout from the trendline. I proved that true.

For example, I look at 85 downsloping trendlines that had price touching the trendlines three times. After an upward breakout, price climbed an average of 33%. Then I compared it to 40 trendlines with five touches and found that the postbreakout rise averaged 57%.

To check this result, I split the trendlines into those with four touches or fewer. They showed gains averaging 35%. Those trendlines with more than four touches climbed an average of 48%. Again, those trendlines with more touches led to better performance after the breakout.

I conducted the same research using upsloping trendlines and found similar results, but the performance difference was closer.

Trendline Length

Of all trendline features, length is one of the important ones. Do long trendlines perform better than short ones after breakout? Yes. I found that the median length for downward sloping trendlines that I used was 139 days. Trendlines shorter than the median saw price climb an average of 33% after the breakout, but long trendlines soared 43%.

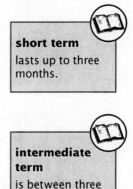

short term lasts up to three months.

As a check, I used another method and sorted the trendline length into three categories: *short term* (0–3 months), *intermediate term* (3–6 months), and *long term* (more than 6 months). Short-term trendlines had postbreakout rises averaging 34%. Intermediate- and long-term trendlines had gains averaging 35% and 46%, respectively. I found similar results for upsloping trendlines.

intermediate term is between three and six months.

Trendlines are like diving boards: You get a better bounce from a longer diving board than a shorter one.

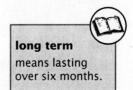

long term means lasting over six months.

Trendline Angles

Another important consideration is the angle that the trendline makes with the horizontal. The steeper the trendline, the worse the performance. That's the conclusion I reached when I researched trendline angles. I measured the angle from the horizontal and sorted the trendlines by the angle they made. For both up- and downsloping trendlines, the distance that prices moved decreased the steeper the trendline became after a breakout. (For upsloping trendlines, a trendline breakout means a close below the trendline; for downsloping trendlines, it's a close above the trendline.)

"How do I use that?" Jake asked.

"Look for trendlines that slope 30 to 45 degrees. Trendlines with those angles can last a long time. However, if the trendline slopes upward at, say, 60 degrees or more, then you'd better tighten your stop." That means adjusting your stop-loss order often, moving it closer to the current price. The price may continue soaring, but when the turn comes, the resulting decline will likely be rapid. A tight stop limits the dollars you give back.

Jake's fingers were laced together and his thumbs were twiddling, making small circles that chased each other. "Are we done yet?"

"Not as exciting as driving a racing car?"

His eyes lit up and his mouth opened to speak.

"No," I said before he could regal me with his latest exploit. "We're not even halfway through trendlines and it's important. You want to make enough money to pay for your health care, don't you?"

Jake became a model student.

Trendline and Breakout Volume

Does volume influence how far price will move after a trendline breakout? Yes. Let's take trendline volume first. I did a study of volume and trendlines and found that upsloping trendlines that had volume trending upward over their length resulted in a decline averaging 19% after a downward breakout. When volume receded over the length of the trendline, the decline averaged just 14%.

For downsloping trendlines, when volume climbed over the course of the trend, price climbed 30% after the upward breakout. A receding volume trend had prices climb by 45%. In short, here's what I found:

- Expect a larger price decline after a breakout from an upsloping trendline if volume is *trending up*.

- Expect a larger price decline after a breakout from a downsloping trendline if volume is *trending down*.

> **breakout volume**
> is the volume level on the breakout day.

What about breakout day volume? I compared volume on the day prices staged a breakout to the three-month average and found the following to be true:

- Upsloping trendlines with heavy (above average) *breakout volume* mean a larger decline—19% versus 16%.

- Downsloping trendlines with light (average or below average) breakout volume mean a larger rise—39% versus 36%.

Because the performance difference is not massive, don't bet that a large price change will occur, and *don't* think that price will rise by 39%. As I mentioned, the statistics in this chapter are for comparison purposes only because they result from 200 *perfect* trades. They represent the price rise or decline after a breakout to the ultimate high or low, respectively.

Measure Rule for Trendlines

When price closes below an upsloping trendline, how far will it fall? One answer to that question comes from the *measure rule*. Figure 3.4 shows an upsloping trendline. The measure rule is a tool used to help predict how far prices will decline after a breakout. To use the rule, find the breakout where

> **measure rule**
> varies from pattern to pattern but is usually the pattern height added to (upward breakouts) or subtracted from (downward breakouts) the breakout price. The result is the predicted price target. Price often falls short of the target, so use half the height in the measure rule computation.

price closes below the trendline (point D). Then look for the widest distance between prices and the trendline until the last time price touched the trendline. The last touch happened at point C, so the widest vertical distance is between points A and B. The price difference between those two is 20.75 points in this example. Subtract the difference from the breakout price (point D, the point where price intersects the trendline) to get the target price, which turns out to be 12.25. Price reaches the target (not shown) in September 2001.

"What happens if the prediction is a negative number?" Jake asked.

At least he's paying attention, I thought. "In that case, either the company is about to go bankrupt or the trend is about to change. Probably the latter."

FIGURE 3.4 Use the distance from the trendline to the price high (A–B), measured vertically then projected downward from the breakout (D) to get a postbreakout price target. This is the measure rule for trendlines, but it only works between 63% (upsloping trendlines) and 80% (downsloping trendlines) of the time.

That's the good news. The bad news is that this method works only 63% of the time, according to my tests. You can apply this technique to downsloping trendlines in the same manner. Find the widest distance between price and the trendline from the breakout to the prior trendline touch and project the difference upward from the breakout price. For downsloping trendlines, the method works 80% of the time. Thus, when predicting a target, be conservative and assume that prices will fall short of the target.

Drawing Trendlines

Now that we've explored trendline features, what's left? Answer: Figuring out how to draw them. Some analysts argue that it's harder than just connecting several peaks or valleys. It's not, unless you are searching for a trend change. I'll discuss that in a moment.

If you see several peaks that line up, then draw a trendline across them. The same goes for valleys. Sometimes you'll want to draw both and form a channel—two parallel trendlines with prices bouncing between them. Think of the channel as a price conduit. When price reaches the bottom of the channel, buy the stock, and sell when it shows signs of turning at the top of the channel. If price fails to reach the top (bottom) of the channel, that may signal a weakening (strengthening) trend and time to sell (buy). The odds increase—but not guarantee—that when price reaches the bottom (top) of the channel, prices will stage a downward (upward) breakout and punch through the trendline.

"What have we learned, Jake?"

"We learned that two peanuts were walking down the street. One was *assaulted*. Get it? A salted? Sorry. Please continue."

1-2-3 Trend Change Method

By definition, when price closes below an upsloping trendline, price is no longer trending up. The same applies to downsloping trendlines. A close above the trendline means price is not trending down. But that does not mean price has changed trend.

"I'm confused," Jake said.

trend change

when price goes from trending up to down or horizontal, or horizontal to up or down.

Price usually moves in a zigzag fashion, like climbing stairs, so price may pierce the trendline, rebound, and continue rising. The 1-2-3 *trend change* method takes the guesswork out of determining a trend change. Here are the three rules for upsloping trendlines:

1. Draw a trendline from the lowest valley *before* the highest peak and leading to the highest peak on the chart such that the trendline does not overwrite any prices between them. Look at Figure 3.5. I show a dashed line AB connecting the lowest valley to the highest peak. Notice how the line overwrites prices. Swivel the line from point B to the right until the line touches but does not overwrite prices. I show the trendline as line AC1. Point 1 is the breakout. Incidentally, this method of drawing a trendline is a good one to learn for all of your trendlines.

2. Price should retest the high after the trendline break. That means price should attempt to climb back to the price level of the highest

FIGURE 3.5 Shown is the 1-2-3 method of detecting a trend change. Point 1 is the breakout from an upsloping trendline. Point 2 is a test of the high, and point 3 is near a close below a recent low.

peak but not exceed it by much, if any. I show this attempt at point 2.

3. Finally, price must *close* below the lowest valley between points 1 (the breakout price) and 2 (the retest of the high). I mark this valley with a horizontal line ending at point 3.

When all three conditions become true, then the trend has changed from up to down.

How well does this method work for upsloping trendlines? By my definition, a trend change is a 20% decline in prices after the breakout. I tested the 1-2-3 trend change method on 67 trendlines that obeyed the above conditions. I found that the average decline was 21% after the breakout, which is higher than the 17% decline for all trendlines that ignored the 1-2-3 approach. Unfortunately, only 43% of the 67 trendlines accurately predicted a decline of at least 20%. Before you draw conclusions about this method, note that the sample size is small and there are ways to improve the sell signal that I ignored during testing called the *2B method.* (For more information, see Victor Sperandeo, *Trader Vic: Methods of a Wall Street Master,* John Wiley & Sons, 1991.)

You can use the 1-2-3 trend change method for downsloping trendlines to denote a trend change. Here are the steps:

1. Draw a downsloping trendline from the highest peak to the lowest valley such that it doesn't intersect prices until *after* the lowest valley.
2. Price should retest the low after the trendline break.
3. Price must rise above the highest peak between the breakout and the retest.

In Figure 3.5, assume that point 1A is the highest peak on the chart. Step 1 says draw the trendline downward to the lowest valley such that it doesn't intersect prices until after the lowest valley. I show the line as 1A2A, with the lowest valley being point D. Along the way, the trendline touches but doesn't cross prices between points 1A and 2A until *after* point D.

Step 2 says prices should retest the low. That happens at 2A when they approach but do not exceed the valley low at D. Finally, step 3 says look for a rise above the peak between the breakout (a close above the trendline, shown directly below 3) and the retest (2A). I show that as the horizontal line 3A. When price closes above that line, it signals a trend change.

How often does the 1-2-3 trend change method work for downsloping trendlines? Again, I classify a trend change as a rise of 20% after the breakout, and 73% of the 101 trendlines I tested that matched the three steps in the 1-2-3 method showed an average rise of 35%. While the 73% rate I consider good, the 35% result falls short of the 38% average rise posted by all trendlines excluding those used in the 1-2-3 test. Nevertheless, for both up- and downsloping trendlines, I consider the 1-2-3 trend change method to add value.

Sample Trade Using Trendlines

Jake plopped into the chair beside me, smiling. "Are you telling them about my trendline trade? I'm thinking of spending the profits from it on a pilot's license for a hot air balloon."

Figure 3.6 shows a trade he made with two trendlines giving the buy and sell signals. On the weekly price chart, using a logarithmic scale, he bought the week after price broke out upward from the ascending, broadening wedge (ABW).

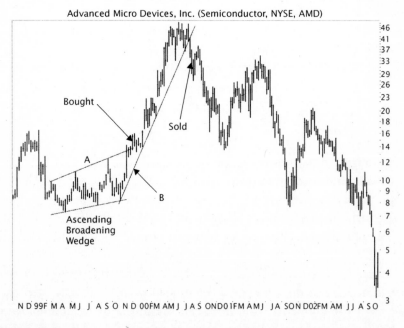

FIGURE 3.6 In the sample trade, Jake traded this trendline to double his money.

The ABW is a chart pattern with two trendlines that widen over time, but both tilt upward. A close above top trendline A occurred the week before he bought, and it is the buy signal.

Prices followed trendline B higher until late July. That's when price closed below the trendline for the first time.

"I sold the next week and doubled my money."

"You were lucky," I said. "Did you know that the weekly scale gives reliable selling signals? If the stock punches through on the weeklies, then the chances improve that price will continue moving down."

"I knew that," Jake said.

"Did you know that the logarithmic scale signals a trendline pierce earlier than the arithmetic scale?"

Advanced Trendline Tactics

Here are some interesting trendline trivia that you may not know but may prove useful:

- When price moves away from the trendline, momentum is increasing. When price moves toward the trendline, momentum is decreasing. When price rides along the trendline, the rate of change is constant.

- Trendline mirrors: Sometimes, a price bump on one side of the trendline reflects across the other side of the line as a dip, and vice versa.

- When price pierces a steep trendline, it often moves up at a slower pace, following a new trendline.

- When price pierces a downsloping trendline and makes a higher peak (note: this is the second, higher peak), connect the two peaks with an upsloping trendline. Then, draw a new line parallel to the original trendline starting at the low between the two peaks. The lower trendline will show where price is likely to reverse.

pullback
occurs after a *downward* breakout when price returns to, or comes very close to, the breakout price or trendline within 30 days. There must be white space between the breakout point and the pullback low. The white space rule prevents the pullback term being applied to prices clustering near the breakout price. Contrast with throwback.

throwback

occurs after an *upward* breakout when price declines to, or comes very close to, the breakout price or the chart pattern trendline within 30 days. There must be white space between the hooking price action of the throwback and the breakout price. Contrast with pullback.

intraday

within a single trading day.

- Expect a *pullback* (downward breakout) or *throwback* (upward breakout) after price pierces a trendline. Figure 3.4 shows an example of a pullback, when price returns to the trendline before continuing down. In Figure 3.5, point 2 is a pullback to trendline AC1 (extended into the future) and point 2A represents a throwback to line 1A2A.

- During strong uptrends, price may pierce the trendline and head down for about a month before resuming the uptrend at nearly the same angle. This stair-step rise is a chart pattern called a measured move up. The reverse also applies and forms a measured move down.

- When prices pierce the trendline, look at the prior day's close. For upsloping trendlines, if the prior close was at or near the intraday high, the chances increase that the downward breakout is false (because profit taking got carried away, forcing price down). If the close was near the intraday low, then chances increase that the breakout is valid.

I found that last gem in Barbara Rockefeller's book, *Technical Analysis For Dummies* (John Wiley & Sons, 2004), so I decided to test it. I used 202 upsloping trendlines and split the trading range the day before the trendline breakout into thirds and then placed the closing price that day within one of the thirds. Those with prices within a third of the intraday high performed worst after the breakout, just as the theory predicted. I also found the same behavior for downsloping trendlines. A close near the intraday high the day before the breakout suggested a less powerful move.

Trendline Review

For further review, see also the suggested chapter section in the list entries that follow:

- Draw upsloping trendlines along the valleys. When price closes below the trendline, it indicates a possible trend change. See *External Trendlines*.

- Draw downsloping trendlines along the peaks for the same reason to spot a possible trend change. See *External Trendlines*.

- Draw internal or external trendlines as needed. Sometimes, an internal trendline will better represent the trend and trading behavior of the masses. However, most chartists use external trendlines. See *Internal Trendlines*.

- A sharp reversal often follows the breakout from a steep trendline. See *Curved Trendlines*.

- Look for trendlines with widely spaced touches. See *Touch Spacing*.

- Select trendlines with many price touches. See *Trendline Touches*.

- Long trendlines are more reliable than short ones. See *Trendline Length*.

- Shallow trendlines are more reliable than steep ones. See *Trendline Angles*.

- When trendline volume follows the slope—up for upsloping trendlines, down for downsloping ones—the breakout is likely to send prices farther. See *Trendline and Breakout Volume*.

- Upsloping trendlines accompanied by heavy breakout volume and downsloping trendlines accompanied by light breakout volume give the best postbreakout performance. See *Trendline and Breakout Volume*.

- Use the measure rule to predict a price target. See *Measure Rule for Trendlines*.

- A channel is two parallel trendlines that bound price. See *Drawing Trendlines*.

- When price fails to reach the top of the channel, a downward breakout may occur. The reverse is also true for price failing to reach the bottom of the channel. An upward breakout may occur. See *Drawing Trendlines*.

- Use the 1-2-3 trend change method to determine when the price trend changes. See *1-2-3 Trend Change Method*.

- Draw trendlines on the weekly scale for reliable trading signals. See *Sample Trade Using Trendlines.*

- Use the log scale to signal a trendline pierce sooner than an arithmetic scale. See *Sample Trade Using Trendlines.*

I use trendlines often to exit a trade as they reliably get me out when the trend changes. But what if the trend doesn't change? It won't matter because I've moved on to the next trade.

Jake walked in and his face lit up the room like a floodlight on a moonless night.

"Look at this!" He waved the confirmation notice in front of my face. "I made almost six grand! And I'm thinking of doing something I've never done before—bungee jumping. Want to come?"

Chapter 4

Support and Resistance
The Most Important Chart Patterns

Jake stomped into the office and kicked the nearest chair. Fortunately, it didn't slide very far on the plush carpet. The last thing I needed was for him to crash it into one of my computers. He combed his fingers backward through his thinning white hair and then wrung his hands like a dishrag. I kept quiet as he paced the room and dug a trench in the rug. He would tell me what was bothering him when he was ready.

He returned the chair back to the desk and then plopped down on it. "The health insurance company is raising my monthly premium by forty percent. *Forty percent!* That's just three months since they raised it the last time by twenty-five percent. Can you believe that? What am I going to do?" He buried his face in his hands.

"Marry someone rich."

He looked up at me and his mouth dropped open in disbelief. How could I joke at a time like this?

I just made a killing in the market, so I was in a good mood. "Live it up but die before the money runs out?"

"That's not funny." The bloodsuckers at the insurance company were bleeding him dry a month at a time. "Do you know I'm paying almost $300 a year for a bunch of worthless coupons and services that I'll never use? They claim you have to join the stupid service to get the group rate. What a scam."

"Make enough money trading so you can buy the insurance company and fire the executives."

His eyes sparkled as if I had provided the key to a new life. It was a sign, a signal, a pathway to understanding how Jake Murphy worked, but I missed it. Instead, I talked about trading. "The next step is to learn about *support and resistance zones—SAR.*"

I consider SAR zones to be the most important chart patterns. Why? Because they show how much you are likely to make and how much you are likely to lose each trade. That's like playing poker and knowing the hands of your opponents. You won't always win, but it sure helps. Used intelligently, support and resistance zones guide you along a path to riches while avoiding the potholes.

What Is Support and Resistance?

SAR zones are locations where price stalls. Usually, SAR encompass a range of prices. A support zone, for example, is where overwhelming buying demand stops a decline. A resistance zone is where overwhelming selling pressure stops a rise.

If you bought a stock at 8 and watched it rise to 10 before dropping back to 8, you might say, "As soon as it gets back to 10, I'm selling." What will happen when others do the same? If the stock rises to 10, it'll hit a brick wall and bounce lower as you and others sell their holdings. Eventually, though, everyone who wanted to sell will have dumped their shares, allowing buying pressure to send the stock higher, piercing overhead resistance.

Have you ever wanted to buy a stock, but it soared away from you? Others feel the same way. They vow that as soon as the stock returns to their buy price, they are going to pounce. And they do. That puts a floor under the stock, supporting it, and pushing prices upward if buying demand is high enough. If sellers are determined, they will force the stock down and eventually dig through the floor, sending prices lower.

That's how support and resistance forms. It's supply and demand in action. The trick is to predict where SAR will occur. The remainder of this chapter explores the different types of SAR and what to look for.

Chart Pattern SAR

Remember the investor watching the stock move to 10, to 8, and back to 10 before price tumbled? That price pattern is called a "double top." Picture a capital letter M in your mind, and you'll know what a double top looks like. Chart patterns like the double top highlight support or resistance zones—places where price often pauses. Figure 4.1 shows examples.

On the left of the chart is a *triple top* marked Top 1, Top 2, and Top 3. The three peaks all stop near the same price, about 46. An invisible ceiling of resistance hovers over them, preventing price from climbing higher as the three peaks attest. When price drops below the lowest low between the peaks, it confirms the triple top as a valid chart pattern. This spells trouble for those holding the stock as price is destined to drop, sometimes substantially like that shown.

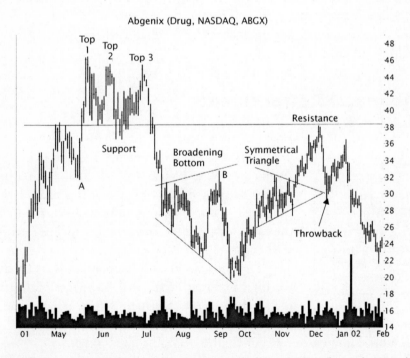

FIGURE 4.1 Chart patterns show support and resistance along the trendlines that form their borders.

Below the triple top is a support zone formed by the peak in May, and I show it as a long horizontal line. The valley between tops 1 and 2 stops at the support line. The support line in December changes into overhead resistance and repels the rise, causing a throwback to the symmetrical triangle's apex (where the two trendlines join). Notice that underlying support changes into overhead resistance as one trader's floor becomes another trader's ceiling. Support becomes resistance becomes support depending on which side price approaches.

The two trendlines of the broadening bottom show support (bottom trendline) or resistance (top trendline) as price moves to touch the lines and then rebounds like children in a water balloon throwing contest. After each toss, they step back and price takes longer to cross the chart pattern. Eventually, the water balloon explodes and soaks one of the children—sending price skittering off and breaking out of the chart pattern.

The symmetrical triangle is similar, only the children are far apart at the start of the contest and move a step closer after each toss. The two trendlines narrow over time and join at the triangle apex. The trendlines show where support and resistance zones lie and where you can expect them to occur in the future.

Fibonacci Retracements

retrace

after trending, prices give back some of their gains. That movement is called a "retrace" of the prior move.

Prices climb a wall of worry in steps, but you can predict this rise-*retrace* pattern and use it in your trading. Look at Figure 4.2, which shows the rise from A to B on the lower left (not the inset). If you split the rise into divisions of 38%, 50%, and 62%, then you get price levels where the stock is likely to stop declining.

For example, the low at point A is 65.88 and the high at B is at 76.07. A 62% retrace of this rise is a decline to 69.75, where I have drawn a horizontal line on the chart. I also show the 50% and 38% retracement levels. Notice how price turns at C after declining about 62%.

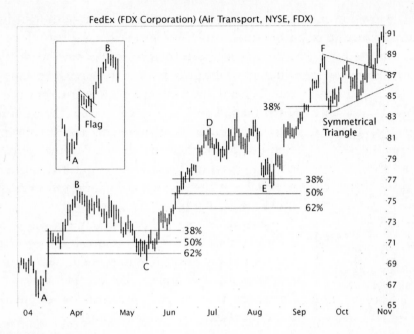

FIGURE 4.2 Price often stops between the 38% and 62% Fibonacci retracement of the prior move. The 62% retracement makes a good location for a stop-loss order.

The move from C to D shows support near the 50% retracement level, E. The move from E to F shows support at the bottom of the symmetrical triangle, 38% down from the peak at F.

Where did the 38%, 50%, and 62% numbers come from? The percentages are based on the Fibonacci summation series 1, 1, 2, 3, 5, 8, 13, 21, and so on. Each new number in the series is the sum of the prior two. The ratio of any two adjacent terms approaches 1.618 or 0.618, depending on whether you are moving backward (21/13 for example) or forward (13/21), respectively. The percentages come from manipulating those ratios. For example, 38% is 0.618/1.618. Robert Fischer and Jens Fischer, in *Candlesticks, Fibonacci, and Chart Patterns Trading Tools* (John Wiley & Sons, 2003), give a wonderful explanation of the Fibonacci series and how often it is found in nature. For our purposes, though, just know that they exist.

How do you use the retracement percentages? Look for straight-line runs—either up or down—then apply the percentages as I have done in the AB example. The retracement percentages don't always work, but they give you an indication of where price is likely to pause or reverse.

half-staff formation

chart patterns such as flags, pennants, and even members of the triangle family (ascending, descending, or symmetrical) sometimes appear midway in the price move.

When I am looking for a longer-term trade, I often place a stop a few cents below the 62% retracement value in an uptrend. If price hits my stop-loss order, then the chances are that price is going to continue lower. If the stop turns out to be a mistake, it doesn't matter because you never go broke taking a profit.

Figure 4.2 highlights two common chart patterns, *flags* (*half-staff* patterns because they often appear midway through a steep rise or decline) and a symmetrical *triangle*. The triangle apex is a known area of support or resistance as are the trendlines extended into the future.

Peaks and Valleys

Notice how the valley at E in Figure 4.2 stops at the price level of peak B; the bottom of the symmetrical triangle stops at the price level shown by the peak to the right of D. If you look at most any chart, you will see that price stops or pauses at prior peaks and valleys. Why does that happen?

A friend of mine invested $15,000 in a large mutual fund just before the crash of 1987. After that crash, her investment was worth just $11,500. Stung from the massive decline, she told me, "As soon as I get my money back, I'm selling." She was true to her word. Others did the same, and their selling caused the underlying stocks—and the mutual fund—to form a second peak, a double top.

If you see a peak or valley form on above average volume, then watch for price to reverse at those locations in the future. The reverse may be temporary, but it's a good guess that the trend will struggle there.

I studied SAR at peaks and valleys and found some interesting results. How I did it is complicated to explain, so I'll skip the details. However, I found that often prices stopped at a hilltop or valley after a breakout from a chart pattern. Table 4.1 lists the results.

**TABLE 4.1   How Often Prices Stopped Near Price
Peak or Valley after Breakout**

Breakout Direction	Stopped at Peaks	Stopped at Valleys
Up	26%	19%
Down	27%	27%

From 26% to 27% of the time, prices stopped near overhead resistance or underlying support setup by a prior peak or valley. The exception was 19% of the upward breakouts from chart patterns that stopped at the price level of a prior valley. How can prices, after an upward breakout, stop at a valley? Picture a downtrend when prices make several valleys, each lower than the last. When a chart pattern comes along and reverses the downtrend, prices climb until they hit the price level of one of those valleys. For example, in Figure 4.1, the top of the broadening bottom in August (B) hits valley A.

Horizontal Consolidation Regions

Horizontal consolidation regions (HCRs) are knots of price congestion. HCRs appear as prices with flat tops, flat bottoms, or both. Many times, price moves horizontally and shares a common price, but the tops and bottoms have an irregular shape. Figure 4.3 shows several HCRs. Below point A is a solid wall of horizontal price movement. It is not very tall or very long, and it forms at the price level of HCR1, a looser price structure. HCR2 is harder to see on this price scale; but many of the HCR's tops stop near the same price (about 29.50 in November and December). Several of the November price spikes also stop near the bottom line.

Now look at the head-and-shoulders bottom chart pattern. The two shoulder lows (LS and RS) are near the same price level, almost equidistant from the head, and the head is well below the shoulder valleys. A *neckline* connecting the armpits

consolidation
when prices move horizontally instead of trending upward or downward. A consolidation is an area of price congestion.

consolidation region
a solid block of prices or a region in which prices switch from trending to moving sideways.

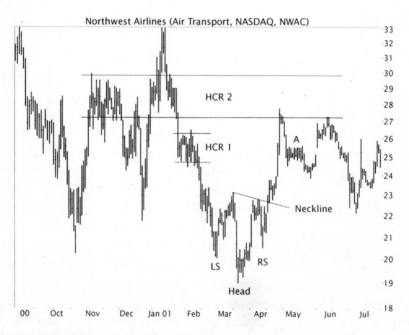

horizontal consolidation region

a horizontal, or almost horizontal, congestion area where prices share a common value for an extended time (usually weeks to months). Flat price tops or flat bottoms are the preferred appearance.

of the pattern represents a breakout when price closes above it. When a breakout occurs, the pattern becomes a valid head-and-shoulders bottom—and one worth trading . . . unless you see an HCR nearby.

How often does price stop within an HCR? After an upward breakout from a chart pattern, price reverses 30% of the time when reaching the level of a prior HCR. For downward breakouts, the effect is stronger with 35% stopping within an HCR. Thus, HCRs tend to stop prices more often than old peaks and valleys. *Always* look for nearby HCRs before trading.

Northwest Airlines (Air Transport, NASDAQ, NWAC)

HCR 2

HCR 1

A

Neckline

LS   RS

Head

00   Oct   Nov   Dec   Jan 01   Feb   Mar   Apr   May   Jun   Jul

FIGURE 4.3 Overhead resistance stops an upward breakout from a head-and-shoulders bottom chart pattern.

Notice that price stalls near 30 in November and December and finds support in October and February at 20, both round numbers.

Round Number SAR

Round number SAR is not one many people think about when trading stocks. When Jake started trading stocks, did he place an order to buy a stock at 9.97 or at 10? Did he put his stop-loss order at 34.93 or 35? He placed them at round numbers, just as we all did.

> **neckline**
> a trendline joining the valleys (head-and-shoulders top) or peaks (head-and-shoulders bottom). A close below or above the neckline, respectively, means a breakout.

What happens when everyone places a stop-loss order to sell at 10? When the price hits 10, the stop-loss orders become market orders. Depending on buying demand, the price may drop, triggering additional stops. This stop running or stop gunning, as it's called, doesn't happen very often. I never worry about it because I place my stop several cents below or above the round number.

By *round number* I mean numbers such as 10, 20, and 30, but I also include the fives: 15, 25, and 35. Prices often stall there.

Figure 4.4 shows a weekly chart where price stalls at round numbers (highlighted by the black circles, but not all areas are shown). Many of the prices do not touch the area exactly, but they come close. Round-number SAR is more like throwing grenades than horseshoes: You do not have to be dead-on to get results. Notice how support later changes into resistance, and vice versa. For example, underlying support at 40 in January and April 2001 turns into resistance until price pierces it decisively in late 2003.

How often does round number SAR work? A study I conducted revealed that 22% of the chart patterns with upward breakouts stopped within 50 cents of a round number, and a massive 42% stopped within a buck of a round number. Downward breakouts were similar with 20% stopping within 50 cents and 40% stopping within a buck of the round number. When I say *stopping*, I mean price reversed direction by moving at least 20% in the new direction.

I did another study using 38 stocks, marking all the peaks, valleys, and HCRs within those stocks from 1999 to 2004, covering both bull and bear markets. Then I researched how often a round number appeared within (near) those features. I found 56% of the valleys were located in round number SAR, 63% of the tops, and 73% of the HCRs.

What does this mean? It suggests that as price moves, expect it to bounce off round numbers.

Trendlines and Channels

Figure 4.5 features a broadening top chart pattern with a *partial decline* that predicts an upward breakout. Notice the way prices move up in the March channel, which is too steep to be sustainable. Price pauses (revolving around the dashed line in the chart pattern) at the broadening top and then continues moving up in a shallower channel. After peaking, prices drop following a downsloping channel.

Prices follow a trend, whether moving up in a channel or following the two trendlines of the broadening top. The trendlines show where price runs into support or resistance—buying demand or selling pressure.

SAR and Volume

If Jake wants to buy 850,000 shares of IBM for not more than 50, how loud will he scream if I buy ahead of him and push the stock up to 51? When the stock drops back to 50, he will be in there buying like crazy, putting a floor on the stock until he pockets his last share. Volume and SAR are related by trading psychology—but are SAR and high volume related? Yes, they are.

I took my 38 stocks with their peaks and valleys marked and compared the average volume surrounding the peaks and valleys with the prior 30-day average volume. I found that prices from 929 chart patterns (58% of the total) stopped at a

partial decline

after price touches a top trendline, it declines but does not touch (or come that close to) a lower trendline before forming a distinct valley and usually staging an immediate upward breakout. Partial declines must begin before the actual breakout and form after a valid chart pattern appears (in other words, after the minimum number of trendline touches, usually two, and any other criteria needed to establish a valid pattern). Applies to broadening patterns and rectangles.

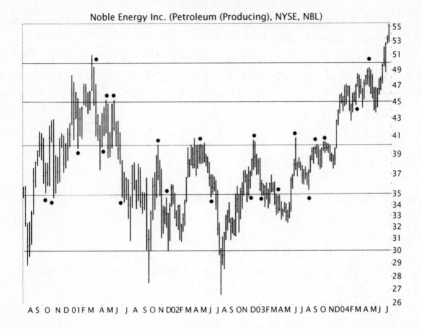

FIGURE 4.4 The black dots represent prices that approach a round number and stall there.

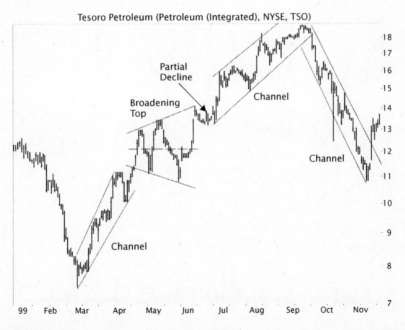

FIGURE 4.5 Prices follow trendlines and channels that highlight support and resistance.

price peak with high volume but only 662 (42%) stopped at a price peak that contained below average volume.

For bottoms, the results were better: 960 chart patterns (70% of the total) had prices reverse trend within a valley that contained above average volume but 417 (30%) stopped in a valley with below average volume.

Using SAR to Trade

I waved Jake over to look at the computer screen and the chart shown in Figure 4.6. "If the stock broke out upward from the descending triangle in October, would you buy the stock?"

"Um . . ." His index finger explored his dimple.

"Would it be time to sell it short or sell stock you owned if it broke out downward?"

To answer those questions, let's take apart the price landscape and see what grows beneath the topsoil. Towering like pines on a mountain top, price highlights a right-angled and ascending broadening formation.

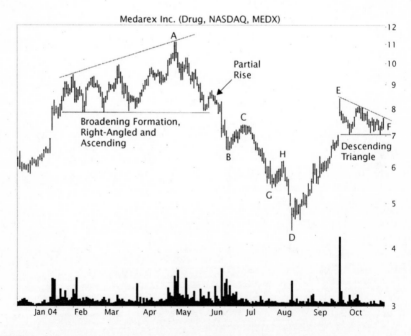

FIGURE 4.6 Several chart patterns set up overhead resistance.

After price touched the bottom trendline in May, it bounced, curled around, and plunged downward in a typical partial rise. A *partial rise* accurately predicts an immediate downward breakout 74% (*bull market*) to 79% (*bear market*) of the time. If you owned the stock at that time, you would sell it immediately.

Extending the bottom trendline toward point E (chart pattern SAR), you can see how prices climbed to the price level of the broadening formation bottom before withdrawing and forming a descending triangle. Sixty four percent of the 1,167 descending triangles I looked at broke out downward, so waiting for price to close outside the triangle trendlines is mandatory, especially if you hope the breakout is upward.

Notice that the bottom of the triangle supports prices (chart pattern SAR) and notice the volume spike at point E. With such high volume, we can expect price to stall there (peak and valley SAR, SAR and volume). However, since a climb from F to E is not far, I expect price to soar past it without pausing. It's just too close on a price basis to be of much worry.

However, if price were to decline after rising to 10 or higher, then I expect price to stall near the price of E. You will find that price often stalls 10% to 20% away from the breakout (most stop 15% away with 52% stopping within the 10% to 20% window). Nearby support or resistance, say 5% or less away, often sees prices punch their way through SAR without pausing.

Look at the volume surge around point A. You might expect price to stall at that price, especially since it is an old peak (peaks and valleys SAR). Coupled with the round number 10, I would expect an upward breakout to stall there (round number SAR).

partial rise
after price touches a lower trendline, it rises but doesn't touch (or come that close to) the upper trendline before forming a distinct peak and usually staging an immediate downward breakout. The partial rise must begin before the breakout and form near the end of a valid chart pattern (in other words, after the minimum number of trendline touches, usually two, and any other criteria needed to establish a valid pattern). A partial rise applies to broadening patterns and rectangles.

bull market
every date outside of the bear market from March 24, 2000, to October 10, 2002, as posted by the Standard & Poor's 500 Index.

bear market

I used the peak in the Standard & Poor's 500 Index on March 24, 2000, and the low on October 10, 2002, as the start and end of a bear market.

corrective phase

part of a measured move up or down, a region where prices retrace a portion of the prior move.

The price pattern ABCD forms a measured move down. The decline from C to D often mirrors the decline from A to B. The slope of the decline is often similar, too, just as it is here. The *corrective phase*, BC, sets up a support or resistance zone (chart pattern SAR) that price frequently struggles to pierce. What you commonly see happen is price declining to D and then rebounding to the corrective phase before stalling out. In this example, price jumps over the corrective phase on the way to E before reversing. Notice that the base of the triangle rests on the price level of the BC zone. Volume within that zone is also high, suggesting a potent support zone.

The move from C to D sets up its own measured move down, CGHD. If price breaks out downward from the descending triangle, will it reverse at GH? The volume level in corrective phase GH is unconvincing. Price might stall there, but it will probably push its way through. (It did, as you can see during the rise in late August.) The GH move is near the same price as the curving price trend in December 2003, which suggests there might be a support zone there.

There are two more chart patterns buried in the figure. The first is a high, tight flag. That pattern appears when price doubles in less than two months, as it does from D to E. Price forms a flag or, in this case, the descending triangle. Expect the upward move after F to be at least half the prior move. That suggests a climb to just over 9, for a gain of 19%, assuming you buy in at the breakout price.

The second pattern is one that appears better on the weekly scale. Since we need to check the longer-term chart anyway, look at Figure 4.7. Trying to orient myself between Figure 4.6 and Figure 4.7 reminds me of a navigational test that I was given when applying for a scholarship as an Air Force pilot in the ROTC. I don't think that I answered any of the questions right, but I digress. For reference, AD is the measured move down and E is the top of the high, tight flag, just before the descending triangle begins.

I show a downsloping trendline from the two peaks on the far left side of the chart and join it with a horizontal trendline from another descending triangle in 2001. Price has climbed to the level of the peak at A, stalling at the intersection of the two trendlines. From the breakout near E, price peaked at 11.55. That is a 51% rise; but it assumes you buy in at the breakout price and sell at the top. Still that is a juicy return and one I decided not to take. Given the overhead resistance, I decided to pass up the trade. Just because you *think* a stock might stall at a given price doesn't mean it will. After I snapped the picture, price declined to 8 and some change and headed down. Pull up the chart on your own computer to get a clearer picture.

FIGURE 4.7 Price climbed to the old peak at A before stalling. The two trendlines indicate where overhead resistance might be a problem.

SAR Review and Checklist

For further review, see also the suggested chapter section in the list entries that follow. Look for price to stall:

- If a chart pattern appears in the price path. See *Chart Pattern SAR.*

- If a Fibonacci retracement occurs. Prices retrace 38%, 50%, and 62% of the prior move before reversing. See *Fibonacci Retracements.*

- At old peaks and valleys. SAR zones appear between 19% and 27% of the time at an old peak or valley. See *Peaks and Valleys.*

- At horizontal consolidation regions. Look for flat tops, flat bottoms, or where a block of prices share the same value. See *Horizontal Consolidation Regions.*

- At round numbers like 10, 15, and 20. Prices stop within 50 cents of a round number 20% of the time and within a buck of a round number 40% of the time. See *Round Number SAR.*

- Along trendlines. Price follows trends, so expect it to bounce off a trendline when it touches a long one. See *Trendline and Channels.*

- If high volume accompanies price. See *SAR and Volume.*

"How do I find out about a company?" Jake asked. "I want to know everything there is to know about the jerks running my health insurance company."

I had no idea that my answer would be so important to him.

Special Situations

"**T**oday I'm going to teach you about *special situations*," I told Jake. That's what I call them because they can provide trading opportunities or signs of things to come. Some situations are worth looking for and some are just informational. I discuss them in this chapter, sorted alphabetically.

Bull and Bear Markets

"What about this one?" Jake said and turned to me, smiling. He was looking for chart patterns to hone his skills paper trading.

I scooted my chair over and looked. "You're going the wrong way." If he had his glasses on, I'd take them off and clean them for him. "You'd be going long in a bear market. That's like driving the wrong way on the interstate. Try again."

One of the keys to making money trading chart patterns is to trade with the trend. If you've been in the markets for long, you will have heard the phrase, *trade with the trend.* But what does that mean? Buy in a bull market and sell short, or go into cash, in a bear market.

Once you become familiar with chart patterns, you can look at the S&P 500 index and tell which way price is likely to go in the coming weeks. You won't be right all of the time, but you will be able to make accurate predictions that help your trading. If you expect the index to climb, then go long. If you expect the index to drop, then stay out of the market or buy defensive stocks (utilities, for example, which pay dividends and are usually not as volatile as other stocks).

I'm writing this in February 2005. On January 3, I was stopped out of Vertex Pharmaceuticals for a 9% loss. Ouch! But that was only the start. The next day, another four stocks hit their stops, some for a profit, and some for a loss. By midmonth, the market had stopped me out of every stock. Sure, I was up nearly $10,000 on the trades, but I was hoping for more—much more.

My instinct was to go shopping for new trades but the market kept telling me the same thing: it was going down. And down it went. I found some footing in Exxon Mobil and Lyondell Chemical when they showed ascending triangle chart patterns. Their bull run lasted about a month and I netted $4,350 on the pair.

Let's get back to bull and bear markets. Chart patterns perform differently depending on how the market is doing. Since I mentioned ascending triangles, let's talk about them. I found 1,092 ascending triangles and measured their performance after the breakout. Table 5.1 shows the results. In a bull market, triangles with upward breakouts showed prices rising an average of 35% after the breakout. Don't think that you will make 35% trading triangles because (1) commissions aren't included; (2) you can be a lousy trader; and (3) the 35% number represents 663 *perfect trades,* exiting at the very top without any fees deducted.

Notice that the decline in a bear market (24%) is not as large as is the rise in a bull market (35%). *You can make more money in a bull market than in a bear market.*

If you want the complete set of bull/bear market numbers, grab a copy of my book, *Encyclopedia of Chart Patterns,* 2nd ed. (John Wiley & Sons, 2005). It shows the performance statistics for 63 chart and event patterns.

TABLE 5.1 Ascending Triangle Performance in Bull and Bear Markets		
Ascending Triangles	*Bull Market*	*Bear Market*
Upward breakout	35%	30%
Downward breakout	19%	24%

Trade with the trend. Trade chart patterns with upward breakouts in a rising bull market and downward breakouts in a falling bear market for the best performance. Avoid *countertrend pattern* moves such as buying an upward breakout in a falling market or shorting a downward breakout in a rising market. That's like swimming against the current. You will make it to the other side of the river, but if you don't hurry, the hot shots on the jet skis might run you over. Make as much money as you can in as little time as you can in the market.

> **countertrend pattern**
> a pattern with an upward breakout in a bear market or a downward breakout in a bull market. The breakout direction is against the prevailing market trend.

By "trade with the trend," I mean not only the market trend but the industry trend as well. If the stock market is red hot but the machine tool industry is suffering, then stay away from machine tool makers. I follow five or more stocks in the 34 industries that I track on a daily basis. When I see a buying opportunity, I check other stocks in the industry. If they are showing signs of topping out, then I stay away.

"You know they're going to go bottom fishing anyway, don't you?" Jake shook his head, having learned the hard way to trade with the trend. His most profitable trades are those he takes when chart patterns break out to new highs.

Bull and Bear Traps

Just when you see a promising situation and jump on it, the market turns, filling your portfolio with blood. Figure 5.1 shows an example. This is an ascending triangle, sporting a flat top and upsloping trendline along the bottom. Prices cross from side to side numerous times, filling the pattern not with white space but with trading action. Prices touch each trendline at least twice, and the pattern completes when price closes outside the trendline boundary (point A). An upward breakout occurs 70% of the time in an ascending triangle.

In this example, prices falter at A then tumble and bounce off the bottom trendline before plunging downward through it at B, a one-day dip of almost $3 on high volume. Those that bought at A probably sold for a loss. Those at B sell short, expecting price to continue moving down. They are right, for a time, as prices continue lower then turn and gap upward on exceedingly high volume. Prices work their way higher.

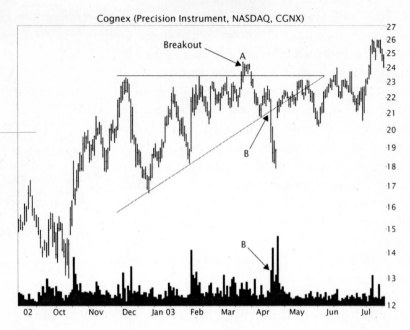

FIGURE 5.1   A bull trap snares bullish traders at the upward breakout (A) then drags them underwater until they gush blood to the right of B.

Point A is a classic bull trap. Prices rise after an upward breakout then collapse. Point B is a bear trap. Those investors expecting the stock to decline were disappointed when it gapped upward and climbed.

Jake nudged me and asked, "Did you tell them how to recognize a trap before it occurs?"

Don't listen to Jake. He doesn't know the answer either. I haven't found a way to predict when a breakout will reverse like that shown at A or B. The volume pattern doesn't vary from the actual breakout nor does the distance to the apex. Overhead resistance, underlying support, a market or industry reversal—all can trap a trader. When you trade chart patterns, these situations occur and you need to take prompt action to save your trade. That is why placing stops after you buy is so important.

Flat Base

A *flat base* (FB) is one of the setups that you want to look for periodically. I use a weekly scale because it makes FBs easy to spot. Figure 5.2 shows an example. I define a flat base as a long, essentially horizontal price movement. This one begins in March and ends at the upward breakout in October 2003. A week later, an ascending, right-angled broadening formation builds. Often, when a chart pattern forms immediately after a flat base, it means that the upward breakout is going to be a powerful one. Jump in and buy the stock; just be sure to use a stop because anything can happen.

Another tip that I've read about, but not verified, is that the longer a flat base is, the better the performance when price takes off. Some even measure the length and project it upward, but that smells fishy to me. You are taking a time measure (the flat-base length) and pretending it's a price move (projecting the length upward) . . . Go figure.

"I may have thought that one up," Jake said and puffed out his chest.

"Yeah, and Heisenberg may have slept here," I replied.

Gaps

"I hate gaps," Jake said. "Traders put too much emphasis on them." I think he's right because they don't power stocks like most think. For example, I found 120 ascending triangles with breakout day *gaps* and 543 without gaps in a bull market and with upward breakouts. Those *with* gaps showed postbreakout rises averaging 35%. Those *without* gaps rose 35%. This is exactly the same performance. Table 5.2 lists the price performance after a breakout-day gap for some common chart patterns. The results measure from the breakout to the ultimate high and represent perfect trades.

Figure 5.3 shows an example of an ascending triangle with a bullish gap on the breakout day. The gap is called an "area or common gap" because price curls around and closes the gap a few days later. Other types of gaps have moves that are more extensive.

flat base
a consolidation region in which prices touch or near the same price multiple times over several weeks or months, and identification is usually easiest on the weekly scale. The bottom of this region appears flat and sometimes forms the base of an impending up-move, hence the name, flat base. Some chart patterns (such as double and triple bottoms, or head and shoulders) form after a flat base, the bottom of the chart pattern will usually reside slightly below the flat base level.

gaps
when today's high is below yesterday's low, or today's low is above yesterday's high, a gap appears on the price chart. A gap closes when price later retraces and covers the gap.

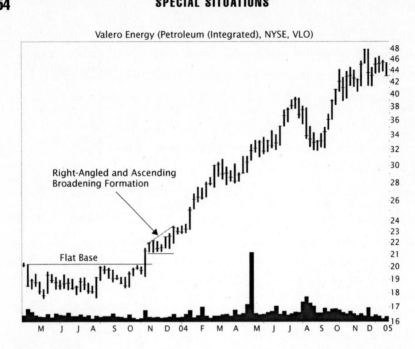

FIGURE 5.2 A chart pattern occurs after the breakout from a flat base.

**TABLE 5.2   Performance after Gap in Bull Markets
with Upward Breakouts**

Chart Pattern	Gap	No Gap	Winner
Broadening Top	26%	29%	No Gap
Cup with Handle	39%	33%	Gap
Diamond Bottoms	40%	36%	Gap
Eve & Eve Double Bottom	42%	40%	Gap
High, Tight Flag	67%	71%	No Gap
Head-and-Shoulders Bottom	43%	37%	Gap
Pipe Bottom	40%	45%	No Gap
Rectangle Top	38%	40%	No Gap
Ascending Triangles	35%	35%	Tie
Descending Triangle	44%	34%	Gap
Symmetrical Triangle	35%	31%	Gap
Triple Bottoms	34%	38%	No Gap
Falling Wedge	39%	31%	Gap

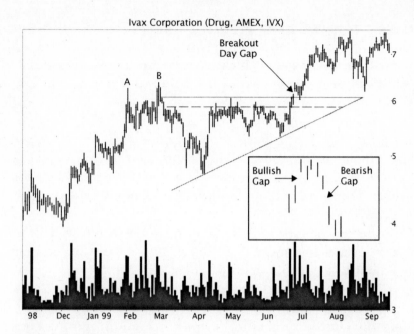

FIGURE 5.3 A breakout-day gap occurs in an ascending triangle. The inset shows the two types of gaps.

The inset shows a bullish and bearish gap. A bullish gap occurs when the intraday low price is above the prior day's high. A bearish gap happens when the intraday high is below the prior day's low. Both leave a gap of white space on the price chart.

The dashed line in the figure is an internal trendline outlining the top of the ascending triangle pattern. The trendline above the dashed one does not touch prices enough to outline a valid triangle, so I drew in the dashed one.

"I was going to complain about that," Jake said.

I smiled. Jake was an enthusiastic learner with good intentions even if Murphy's Law interfered sometimes. I guess he was serious about making enough money to afford his escalating health insurance premiums. In the months since I started helping him, he changed his initial stake into some serious money. Of course, almost anyone can make money in a bull market. The real test would come when things went wrong. Would he be able to cut his losses?

Lower Highs and Higher Lows

Want to know when the trend changes? Pay attention to peaks and valleys. A rising price trend shows higher peaks and higher valleys. A falling price trend has lower peaks and lower valleys.

Consider peaks A and B in Figure 5.4. The top of B is slightly below the top of A. Traders buying the stock lost their enthusiasm and let selling pressure halt the advance at B. With momentum swinging from up to down, additional selling pressure gathered like a snowball rolling downhill. The failure of B to rise above A *and continue higher* suggested a trend change.

B need not stop rising *below* A to signal a bearish turn. This is not an exact science, so sometimes B rises slightly above A before running into resistance. Figure 5.3 shows an example of this situation at peaks A and B. Notice that B is just above A before the trend reverses.

To the right of peak E in Figure 5.4 shows another example of a declining top. The peaks seem to slide lower over time, suggesting a bearish trend developing.

FIGURE 5.4 When a lower peak occurs (A, B), it warns of a bearish trend change. Valleys that fail to continue moving lower (C, D), also warn of a bullish trend change.

The bad news with trying to call turns like A and B is that it only works 35% of the time. That's how often a twin-peak pattern confirms as a double top. A confirmed double top means that price closes below the valley between the two peaks. Sixty-four percent of the time in a bull market, prices don't decline that far before going on to make a new high.

Do valleys also signal trend changes? Yes—see points C and D in Figure 5.4 for an example. Valley D is below C before the decline tires and prices rebound. Prices rise and stall at F, matching the old September peak at G. Prices then decline less than a point but meet support at the round number 40 before continuing up.

This scenario is an example of two peaks, F and G, *not* signaling a trend change. Valleys C and D, however, do show momentum changing from down to up. Like their peak counterparts, price can fall just short of or decline just beyond a prior valley low before recovering. A second valley correctly predicts a trend change 36% of the time. That's how often a twin valley pattern confirms as a valid double bottom in a bull market.

When your trade begins an uphill run like the straight-line rise from 37 in May to point A, your skin will begin to tingle as prices rise. Each day professionals will ask if the trend is about to change, while amateurs will count their paper profits. When a second peak occurs and stalls near the first one, you'll break out in a sweat and *feel* that the time has come to sell. Have patience—and if price closes below the valley between the two peaks, then sell. Remember, two out of three times price will resume its uphill run in a bull market, so don't be too quick on the trigger.

Partial Rises and Declines

A partial rise or decline occurs in broadening chart patterns and rectangles. Partial rises and declines are brief price moves that signal a breakout, usually an immediate one. They are early trading signals.

Let's take the partial rise first, an example of which appears in Figure 5.5. Look for a valid chart pattern. By that, I mean a pattern that has prices touching each trendline at least twice, and it meets any other identification guidelines appropriate for the individual chart pattern. Then, look for price to touch the bottom trendline, rise up, curl around, and head back down before coming close to or touching the top trendline. An immediate breakout usually follows.

Figure 5.5 shows an example of a partial rise in a broadening bottom chart pattern. The partial rise begins at A when price touches the

FIGURE 5.5 A partial rise correctly predicts a downward breakout and a partial decline predicts an upward breakout.

lower trendline and then price moves up, retraces the rise, and breaks out downward. A partial rise correctly predicts a downward breakout from a broadening bottom 67% of the time.

Statistical analysis of 649 chart patterns with partial rises shows that the height of the partial rise as a percentage of the formation height averages 60% with peaks at 36% and 62%, close or equal to the Fibonacci numbers of 38% and 62%. That means the average partial rise climbs 60% of the way up the chart pattern before curling down.

"That's good to know," Jake said. "If price climbs above a 62% retrace, then chances are price will continue moving higher."

A partial decline is nearly the same as a partial rise except it applies to upward breakouts. Price touches the top trendline, drops down but does not come close to or touch the bottom trendline before curling upward and staging an upward breakout. A partial decline applies to established patterns and it occurs before the breakout.

Figure 5.5 shows an example. Price touches the top trendline at B, drops down then reverses and stages an upward breakout. A partial decline works 72% of the time in a broadening top. Analysis of 543 partial declines shows that prices retrace an average of 59% with peaks at 36% and 75%.

The bad news is that partial rises and declines are difficult to trade. As price crosses from side to side, it often pauses midway across before continuing in the original direction. It looks as if price is going to reverse but it doesn't.

One way to combat this is to use a 62% Fibonacci retrace of the prior move. For example, in Figure 5.5 if prices retrace 62% of the drop from C to A and then appear to reverse, short the stock or sell any long holdings. This also works for 38% and 50% retrace values, so you can experiment.

Jake walked into the office sporting a new suit, silk tie, and fancy shoes. He read the page I was working on then said, "Did you tell them about that $3,000 disaster in Cisco?"

I bought a partial decline from a right-angled and descending broadening formation. The stock touched the top trendline then zipped to the wrong side and I sold as soon as it broke out downward. I lost 15%, about double the usual loss size.

"Let me tell them about my Varco trade," Jake said. "Can I, huh? Can I?" He reminded me of a kid until he grabbed his lapel as if he was Winston Churchill making a speech before parliament. Figure 5.6 shows the trade. He bought 600 shares at 9.38 in late May "as a three-year play to give oil a chance to stabilize and for them to get a good return on their oil rig investments." He predicted a target of 13 and a downside of 8.75, the low just a few days before he bought. He also saw resistance at about 11, the site of the symmetrical triangle apex. A portion of the triangle appears in April and it may look strange because price pokes out the top of the upper trendline. Additional trendline touches are off the chart.

"With summer approaching and OPEC holding firm on quotas, I expected the price of oil would hold, but I also expected the stock to underperform. I figured I would pick up more shares if the price dropped 10%."

"Averaging down." I made tsk-tsk noises. "For traders, not investors, that's a good way to lose more money."

In late July, he bought 500 more shares at 10.38. "Bollinger bands showed low volatility for the past two months," meaning that the bands were narrow, "and prior low volatility lasted three months before price shot from 8 to 13. I expected the same thing to happen this time." Downside was 8.63, the site of the May low, and upside was 13 with a move expected in the next 1.5 months.

Instead, the up move came a week later. Price shot to 14.25, forming a broadening top.

FIGURE 5.6 Jake bought the stock twice and sold it as the stock made a partial rise.

"On October 1, I sold 1,100 shares at 12 as the stock started moving back to the lower trendline in a classic partial rise." You can see the stock leave the bottom trendline at A and climb to B before heading back down. On the two trades, he netted over $2,300 or 21%. "You can see what happened to the stock after that. Sometimes you have to sell a long-term holding." The stock hit 9.19 before recovering, a decline of 23% from where he sold.

Quick Rises and Declines

Figure 5.7 shows what happens after a quick price rise from A to B. The stock rolled over and dropped, ending at C, 64% below the May high. Is this typical or unusual? The answer doesn't matter if you happen to be holding the stock. If you want to make money in the stock market, when a stock declines, sell it.

I will say that I find diamond tops an interesting play on the quick rise, quick decline scenario. The inset in Figure 5.7 shows an example

FIGURE 5.7   A slow decline from B to C follows a quick price rise from A to B.

taken from the stock charts. Prices zip up from D to the diamond top and then retrace almost all of their gains (E) after the breakout. I think this behavior is common for diamonds; but as I searched for examples, I discovered that it's less common than I thought.

As for the Fastenal example, I named an event pattern after this behavior. It's called an "inverted dead-cat bounce." Prices shoot up then drift lower. You can read about the pattern later in this book.

Does a quick rise follow a quick decline? Yes, but it happens less often than the reverse. You see this after the breakout from a diamond bottom. Imagine the inset in Figure 5.7 flipped upside down. That's what it looks like.

Let me issue this warning too: Just because you see a quick rise is no reason to expect a decline. With flags and pennants, a quick rise is what you are looking for. After the chart pattern the rise resumes, nearly equaling the rise before the chart pattern. The difference is that price breaks out upward after the chart pattern instead of downward. If you own the stock and it breaks out downward, then sell immediately. Otherwise, you might hold onto a stock that looks like the disaster in Figure 5.7.

Spikes and Tails

Some call them *spikes* and some call them *tails*. I prefer tails, but it does not matter what they're called, just so you don't panic when your stock is whipped by one. Figure 5.8 shows several examples of tails on the daily chart. Tails are long price spikes that occur in a stock and usually mark short-term turning points after a sharp price run-up or violent decline.

The inset shows a close-up of a bullish tail. The opening and closing price need not be at the same price as I show here (the left half of the horizontal bar is the opening price and the right half is the closing price). A bullish tail appears after a strong downdraft and the closing price is near the intraday high. A bearish tail is a slim antenna sticking up on a hilltop. The price rise leading to the hilltop is a sharp, robust advance and price closes near the intraday low. All of the tails shown here obey those guidelines except for the one in late September at about 41. There, the close is near the intraday high, not the low.

I remember holding a position in a declining stock that showed a downward spike. I became upset because of the paper loss. Then I smiled because I betted that the stock was forming a bullish tail. Sure enough,

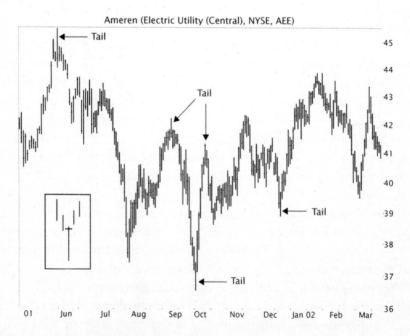

FIGURE 5.8 Several tails mark the turning point in this stock.

the stock rebounded the next day and soon posted new highs. The tail turned into a major turning point.

Tails are panic buying or selling that sends prices spiking upward or downward, respectively. They may even trigger stop running, where the execution of one stop triggers the next, forcing price to move rapidly intraday. After the run exhausts, price collapses, retracing the move as buying demand hands off to selling pressure. The close is near the low for the day, leaving a tall spike on the chart. The next day, the sellers still have the upper hand because those wanting to buy did so yesterday. The price drops and continues declining in the coming days, leaving the tail reversal as a tree standing alone on the hilltop.

One important lesson I learned about tail chasing is not to act too quickly. Let a day lapse after you think a tail appears. Why? Because the next day may also have a large trading range, covering the tail in a parallel spike, and eliminating the trading signal. In many cases, prices congest at the base of the tail for several days before resuming the move, so you have time to consider the situation before acting.

Chasing Tails

Jake used a darkened computer monitor as a mirror while he combed his hair. "I just sold a stock this morning because of a tail. Let me tell you about it."

Figure 5.9 shows the situation. Jake saw the Eve & Eve double bottom forming but failed to place a buy order at the breakout price. Doing so would have gotten him into the stock at a much better price—about 11.85. "The semiconductor stocks were weak," he said. "They were trading near the yearly low. But the Cypress situation showed promise."

His market order to buy 1,300 shares filled at a price of 12.69 as shown in Figure 5.9. "I placed a stop at 11.05, just below the pennant in February. That should support the stock in case prices turn down. I expected a climb to 15.71, according to your book." He's talking about my scoring system for chart patterns that I discuss in *Trading Classic Chart Patterns* (John Wiley & Sons, 2002).

A knot of resistance in June 2004, at 14, would be a problem to additional gains, as would the 13 to 16 range (not shown).

"The CCI said buy on Friday, and the stock is riding the top Bollinger band upward." The *CCI* is the commodity channel index, a short-term trading indicator he uses mostly to check for divergence. That's when the indicator trends one way but price moves the opposite.

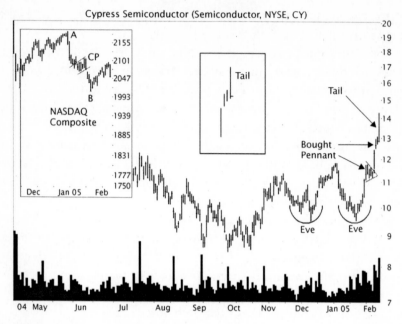

FIGURE 5.9 A tail appears on the right edge of the chart. Do you sell the stock or hang on for additional gains?

CCI

the commodity channel index, a price momentum oscillator that compares the current mean price with the average of its mean price. I use a 20-day lookback with a five-day *DCCI* signal line. I use it most for spotting divergences between the indicator and price.

The general market, as shown by the NASDAQ Composite, he expects to fall. "It trended down from the first of the year but has been rising the last two or three weeks." See the large inset in Figure 5.9. "If NASDAQ continues going up, I'll be set, but that probably won't happen." Why? "Overhead resistance. It completed a measured move down, and it's retracing to the corrective phase. It should resume the downward move soon." I show the measured move down chart pattern as the drop from A to B with the corrective phase (CP) in the middle of the larger inset in Figure 5.9.

"Yesterday, I pulled up the chart and saw the tail. I decided that the risk of a drop was much higher than the chance for addition gains. So, I placed a market order to sell the stock on the open. I expect to take a small loss."

He got lucky and the stock moved up on the open, filling his sell order at 13.28 for a profit of nearly $750, or about 4.5% in 3 days. The stock didn't turn tail and run. In fact, the price peaked near 15 as the tail evaporated into just another bar on the chart. He should have waited a day to be sure the pattern was a tail.

DCCI
dual CCI, a five-day exponentially smoothed moving average of the CCI.

Stops

A stop order is an order to buy above or sell below the current price. For example, I use a buy stop to enter a trade in ascending triangles (see Figures 5.1, 5.3, and 5.10 for examples of ascending triangles). I place the stop a penny above the horizontal trendline and automatically get filled at a good price during the breakout. I use a sell stop (stop-loss order) to protect my position. The stock sells when price drops far enough to hit the stop. Here are two other types of stops that I use.

Volatility Stops

Prices fluctuate like the illumination on a partly cloudy day. If you place a stop-loss order too close to the current price, the chances increase that price will stop you out. A *volatility stop* helps prevent that because it's based on daily price fluctuations. (I learned about a volatility stop from Perry Kaufman's *A Short Course in Technical Trading* (John Wiley & Sons, 2003). Refer to that book for detailed information.)

volatility stop
a method of stop placement such that normal price volatility will not result in the triggering of a stop-loss order. I use the average of the high-low price difference of 30 days multiplied by 1.5. A stop should not be placed closer than the result subtracted from the current low price.

To compute a volatility stop, I dump the price data into a spreadsheet and take the difference between the high and low price for each day. Then, I average the differences over the last month. Multiply the average times 1.5 and subtract the result from the current low price to get the stop price.

For example, Figure 5.10 shows an ascending triangle. Say I place a stop order to buy a penny above the breakout price (point E). How far down should I place my stop loss?

I found that the average daily high-low range a month before the breakout was 21 cents. Since the breakout was at 7.25, I should place the stop *no closer* than 32 cents ($0.32 = $0.21 × 1.5) below the breakout—6.94. Stocks below $20 tend to be especially volatile. Instead of multiplying by 1.5, try 2.

FIGURE 5.10 The stop (the horizontal lines) is raised as price makes new highs (diagonal lines).

Trailing Stops

A trailing or progressive stop is nothing more than a stop-loss order that rises along with prices. For example, Figure 5.10 shows an ascending triangle. If Jake places his volatility stop at 6.94, he's protected even as prices throw back to B. The low at B is 7.07. If the stop appears to be too close, use a 62% Fibonacci retrace of the move from F to E (E is used because that's all that was available on the breakout day). That would put the stop at 6.52, just above the 6.50 round number. A lower stop means a larger potential loss, 10% in this case, so keep that in mind.

As price climbs, Jake should move up his stop. When price makes a new high at A, for example, he should raise his stop to just below the prior valley, B. When price makes a new high at C, Jake should raise his stop to D, just below the flat support zone.

The diagonal lines show where price makes a new high and the horizontal lines show were Jake should place his stop. When price peaks at 24.25 in mid-March, there is no close plateau at which to place a stop. The one at 17 is 29% below the high—too far away. Where should Jake place his stop?

The answer is to use a volatility stop. Volatility is now 87 cents so 1.5 times this is $1.31. Jake should place the stop no closer than 21.94, or 1.31 below the intraday low (23.25) the day prices peak. A stop there would take him out the next day. The stock continued lower until finding major support at 8.50.

I have found that using stops in this manner has cut my losses dramatically and allowed me to capture tasty gains instead of riding the stock back down. The method works.

Throwbacks and Pullbacks

Throwbacks and pullbacks are names for similar price movements. Figure 5.11 shows both after breakouts from head-and-shoulders chart patterns. A pullback occurs after a downward breakout and a throwback happens after an upward one. By definition, throwbacks and pullbacks occur within 30 days of the breakout and both must have white space as price curls back to the breakout price. The white space helps differentiate a valid throwback or pullback from prices sliding along the chart pattern's trendlines.

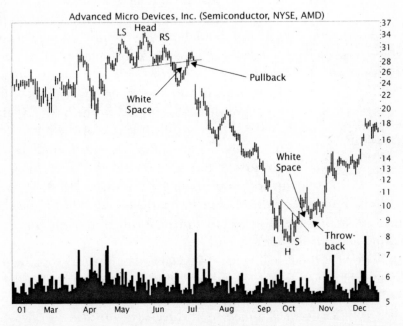

FIGURE 5.11 Prices pull back after the head-and-shoulders top breakout and throwback after an upward breakout from a head-and-shoulders bottom.

"Tell them what you found," Jake said and put his hand on my shoulder then he pointed to the screen and thumped it with his index finger. "It's all in the numbers, kid."

median

median value is the middle one in a sorted list of values such that half the values are below the median and half above. If no middle value exists, the average of the two closest values is used. For example, in the list 10, 15, 30, 41, and 52, the median is 30 because there are two values on either side of it.

swing trading

short-term trading that takes advantage of price swings from retrace low to crest high or the reverse.

Let's take throwbacks first. I looked at 12,256 chart patterns (collected over several years) and found that price throws back to the breakout or trendline break an average of 53% of the time. Prices peak a *median* of three days after the breakout, but it takes an average of 10 days total to make the return trip to the breakout. That's important for *swing traders*. They want to buy the breakout and sell a few days later as prices round over for the return trip. The average distance from the breakout to the top of the throwback is 10%—a quick and tasty return if you can time it right. A frequency distribution of the distance shows that a rise in the range of 6% to 8% happens most often.

A high-volume breakout throws back 70% of the time. By *high volume*, I mean the breakout day's volume is above the 30-day average. So, if you have a high volume breakout, expect price to throw back. It may not but it pays to play the percentages.

Once a throwback completes, price drops below the chart pattern 14% of the time. Look at Figure 5.11. If price continued down after the October throwback, closing below the head (H) then it would have qualified as one of the 14%. That failure rate doesn't sound like much until it happens to you. Still, that should give you some warm fuzzies about trading a throwback. In 86% of the cases I observed, price didn't decline below the lowest valley in the chart pattern. Thus, if you put a stop order there, it will protect you from a serious loss and usually won't be hit.

"Tell them about pullbacks," Jake said and nudged my shoulder like a German Shepherd with a wet nose begging for attention.

Pullbacks occur 56% of the time in the 10,878 chart patterns I looked at. Price declined a median of three days but took an average of 10 days (total) to return to the breakout. The average distance from the pullback valley to the breakout price is 9% but a frequency distribution shows the range from 4% to 10% occurs about evenly.

A pullback follows a high volume breakout 66% of the time—every two out of three times. When prices return to the breakout, they continue climbing 13% of the time. For example, if the June pullback kept climbing until it soared above the head in Figure 5.11, then that event would have qualified as one of the 13%.

If you review the different types of chart patterns, you will find that throwbacks and pullbacks sometimes happen as frequently as 75% (island reversals) or as little as 31% (pennants).

"Tell them about performance," Jake said, reading over my shoulder.

I turned around and said, "I heard that the CEO of JCB Enterprises died and that the stock made a big move."

Jake's eyes widened to the size of golf balls and he raced for the doorway. For a man approaching 60, he could still move fast when he wanted to. I smiled, knowing the rumor would get him off my back—for a few minutes, anyway.

When a pullback or throwback happens, performance usually suffers. Let me give you an example. Since I've been using head-and-shoulders patterns, let me continue with them. I looked at 672 head-and-shoulders bottoms and found that when a throwback occurs, the stock climbed an average of 32% before the trend changed. Without a throwback, the rise measured 43%. Both numbers are from a bull market and both use an average of *perfect trades*, so don't think that your trade will work as well.

Pullbacks show a similar trend but the numbers are closer. I looked at 815 head-and-shoulders tops with downward breakouts in a bull market. When a pullback occurs, price declines an average of 20%. Patterns without pullbacks decline an average of 24%.

Before you trade a chart pattern, look for overhead resistance or underlying support. Those two are responsible for causing most throwbacks or pullbacks.

Since throwbacks and pullbacks are so important to trading chart patterns, let's try a quiz. Figure 5.12 shows a downward breakout from a valid head-and-shoulders top. Will prices pull back?

When I consider trading a stock, I always assume a throwback or pullback will occur. The exception to this is if a stock is making a new high where there is little or no overhead resistance (a prior trendline projected upward or round number might cause overhead resistance and a throwback).

As I look at Figure 5.12, I see a low volume breakout. Pullbacks accompany most high volume breakouts as I've already said, so a low volume breakout would tend to indicate no pullback would happen.

FIGURE 5.12 A head-and-shoulders top stages a downward breakout. Will this chart pattern pull back?

However, I don't put much faith in volume. Instead, I look at the general market, industry, and especially prior support zones.

I use the S&P 500 as the proxy for the general market, and on the day of the breakout, the S&P was trending downward. A pullback happening would be like the stock swimming against the current.

Using the Dow Utility index as the proxy for the utility industry, the index was also trending downward. A spot check of the 11 central U.S. electric utility stocks I follow showed them all heading downward. That also made it unlikely a pullback would occur.

Finally, I check for underlying support. Do you see any in Figure 5.12? I do, starting in February and running through March. If I were *shorting* this stock—betting on a continued decline—that horizontal consolidation region at 38 to 39+ would cause me to change my underwear. I would expect price to enter that area and be repulsed. With the industry and market also trending down, I would not expect an immediate pullback on the approach to the area, and because strong breakouts often push through nearby support

short

when a stock is sold with the expectation that a trader can buy it back at a lower price.

zones. Thus, I would expect it to bounce off the bottom of the range, hitting, say, 38.50 or so.

What happened? Figure 7.12 of this book gives the answer. With the market and industry tide pushing the stock lower, the price shot through the horizontal consolidation region (an ascending triangle) and bounced off a second support zone shown in January 2002 at 36 to 37. Prices bounced there and pulled back to the chart pattern, as expected.

"You lied!" Jake shouted from the office doorway. He was talking about the rumored death of the CEO of JCB Enterprises and the ensuing stock move. Fists clenched, face the color of a cherry, he was breathing heavily, and I knew he had run from his office. He shouted, "I'm deleting your manuscript" and stomped to the server to which my computer was networked.

I have to go now.

The Top 10 Performing Bottoms

The good news is that I found my manuscript files intact in the recycling bin on the server. Jake knew that's where they'd go, so he was just playing with me—I think.

"I made $2,500 yesterday," he said and plopped into the guest chair beside my desk. His smile was as wide as the Grand Canyon.

"Mowing lawns? Delivering newspapers? Yesterday was Sunday."

"Trading on Friday." He slid a box of chocolates from behind his back and handed it to me as a thank you gift. I didn't have the heart to tell him that I prefer cash or checks, especially seven-figure ones. Even 10% of the profits would suffice.

The discussion reminded me of when I first started trading. About 25 years ago, I researched stocks and opened a brokerage account. Then I bought my first stock, 100 shares of Essex Chemical for $2,250, and held on. I sold it less than three years later for a profit of almost $2,000, a gain of 88% including dividends. Two months after I bought Essex, I grabbed Nuclear Pharmacy with its way-cool name. I found it in the prospectus of my mutual fund and researched the fundamentals. Everything looked good, so I bought 200 shares for $1,800. Two weeks after I bought, the stock did a dead-cat bounce. On paper, I lost a bundle. Another company swooped in and swallowed the stock on the cheap. I held it for less than three years before giving up and selling for a 25% loss.

Lesson 1: If your mutual fund owns the stock, there is no need for you to buy it—you already own it. *Lesson 2:* Don't fall in love with a stock just because it has a way-cool name.

Since those trades I have learned much about stocks and stock market behavior. In this chapter, I share some of that knowledge. Here are the top 10 buy signals—chart patterns—ranked according to their overall performance.

1. High, Tight Flag

- *Average rise* rank: 1 (best)
- Breakeven failure rate rank: 1 (best)
- Change after trend ends rank: 1 (best)

average rise or decline (ARD)

I measure the rise from the breakout price to the ultimate high, or the decline from the breakout price to the ultimate low, for each stock, and then compute the average.

I received an e-mail from a woman asking me about a symmetrical triangle after I had told her about a *high, tight flag* (HTF) I saw forming on her chart. She bought at 80 and sold at 135 for a 69% gain. Her e-mail almost shouted, "Somebody stop me before I make too much money!"

The brokerage firm she deals with protects customer accounts up to $25 million. Can you imagine her telling them, "It's not enough. Can you cover me for $50 million?" Trading the HTF just might get you there one buck at a time.

HTFs are the best performing chart pattern; they have the highest average rise (69%, based on perfect trading with no commissions), lowest breakeven failure rate (0%), and best decline after the uptrend ends (36%). None of the 253 HTFs I looked at failed to rise at least 5% (since writing this, I have found HTFs that moved less than 5%). Just five failed to rise at least 10%. However, you have to know how to hunt this animal and how to ride it, or it could be as risky as running with the bulls in Pamplona.

Identification

Here's what to look for:

- Prices should climb at least 90% in two months or less.

- After the rise, find a place where prices pause—a congestion or consolidation area.
- Volume should trend downward in the flag.

Figure 6.1 shows three examples that appear as pennants. The first one occurs in mid-August 1999 and is a tight pennant, meaning prices touch the trendlines in a small, well-shaped pattern of price crossings. Prices climb 66% until reaching the September peak and dropping at least 20%, signaling a trend change.

The middle HTF occurs in December and tops out at High 2, the top of the loose pennant, for a rise of 74%. It also is a tight pattern with prices crossing from trendline to trendline in a narrow cluster of action. The final HTF happens less than a month later and price soars 54% after the breakout (to High 3). Notice how the logarithmic scale makes the large price move appear small. On the arithmetic scale, the August HTF is a speed bump in the foothills of the Himalayas.

To find these three HTFs, I looked for a rising price trend that doubled in two months or less. The August pattern, for example, reaches its highest peak at the start of the pattern on August 16, at 7.63. On June

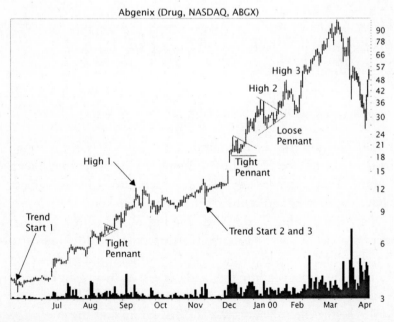

FIGURE 6.1 High, tight flags appear as flags, pennants, or random shapes after price doubles in less than two months.

16, two months before the HTF, prices reached a low of 3.78. That represents a rise of 102% in two months.

Prices pause and form a pennant shape, moving sideways then resting, gathering strength for the climb to higher ground. Volume in this example trends upward and that is unusual because it happens just 10% of the time, and performance often suffers when it does occur. The upward breakout confirms the pattern as a valid one. I found the other two HTFs using the same method—a price doubling in less than two months attended by price moving sideways.

The HTF need not appear as pretty as the ones shown in Figure 6.1. Sometimes the congestion area is irregular, looking like the loose pennant in late December. With some HTFs, you can't draw a trendline along the tops because it is as ragged as discarded clothing. Still, if HTFs breakout upward and obey the identification guidelines, then they are valid patterns. For irregularly shaped HTFs, use a close above the highest peak in the pattern as the breakout price instead of a close above the trendline.

Trading and Trading Tips

Once you have correctly identified a HTF, how do you trade it? Here are the rules for buying:

- Wait for price to close above the upper trendline or above the pattern high if the pattern has no top trendline.
- Buy the stock.
- Place a stop below the prior valley, below the pattern itself, or use a volatility stop.

With this pattern, the most important rule is to wait for an upward breakout. In a test of 78 HTFs, I found 13 patterns that broke out downward. That might not sound like much until a failure happens to you. Save your bucks and wait for the upward breakout.

The hardest thing to do when trading HTFs is to buy the stock. Chances are the stock is near the yearly high after doubling in price. How much higher can it possibly go? Buy in and find out! Remember, HTFs have the lowest failure rate and highest average gain of any chart pattern. Your selection may prove the exception and fail, so place a stop-loss order below the valley nearest the breakout. This may be below the

HTF itself. Check to make sure the stop is not too close. You don't want volatility to stop you out. Later in the book, I review two HTF trades, one where I stole two grand from someone and another in which they stole it back . . . with interest.

When identifying or trading HTFs, what should you look for or avoid? Here is a list:

- Avoid overhead resistance that may cause a throwback. HTFs with throwbacks rise just 49%, but the rise averages 100% for patterns without throwbacks.

- Avoid loose patterns. Figure 6.1 shows one loose HTF and two tight ones. Loose patterns underperform (50% average rise versus 85%). Your chance of having a losing trade increases with loose HTFs.

- Patterns with breakout volume equal to or below the 30-day average perform better than do those with heavy breakout volume, 79% average rise versus 63%.

- Keep the HTF retrace (the flag portion of the HTF) to less than 36% (the median) of the prior up move leading to the pattern. HTFs with smaller retraces show post breakout gains of 74% versus 63% for patterns with larger retraces.

- Avoid HTFs with nearly vertical rises leading to the pattern. Figure 6.2 shows an example of this. Much of the vertical move lasts just a few days. Patterns with moderate rises (typically 45 degrees) climb an average of 70% after the breakout versus 64% for the vertical moon shots.

- Wide patterns perform less well than narrow ones—65% average rise versus 71%—so keep the flag portion of the HTF width to less than the median 15 days.

- Select patterns with a top trendline that slopes downward. HTFs with downsloping top trendlines perform better (70% versus 65% average rise).

You may decide to trade a stock with an HTF that has all of the elements suggesting underperformance. Good! Just be sure to watch the stock closely and raise your stop as price makes a new high.

trend start

where the trend begins. To find the trend start, begin at the formation start and move backward in time. If prices *climb* leading away from the formation, find the highest peak before price closes 20% or more below and before the highest peak. When this occurs, the highest peak marks the trend start.

If prices drop leading away from the chart pattern (working backward in time), find the lowest valley before price closes 20% or more above and before the lowest valley. When that occurs, the lowest valley marks the trend start. In many cases, I ignored brief price overshoot or undershoot just before the chart pattern begins.

For flags and pennants, the peak (swing high) or valley (swing low) closest to the start of the trend leading to the flag or pennant is used (not a 20% trend change).

Measuring Success

How far will price rise? Find the lowest valley in the two months before the pattern and measure the rise during that time to the top of the HTF. For the stock shown in Figure 6.1, let's use the January HTF, the highest one on the chart. The lowest valley within the last two months begins at the *trend start* in November at 9.88. The top of the pattern is at 37.25. Take the difference and divide by two, leaving 13.69. Add this to the lowest valley in the flag portion of the HTF (26.19 in this example), projecting upward for a target of 39.88. The stock shown in Figure 6.1 hits the target just a few days after the breakout. This measure rule works 90% of the time.

Case Study

"Didn't you make a trade in a high, tight flag, Jake?"

"Me? No. Never."

I punched a few keys and pulled up his trading stats. "Just as I thought. Frontier Airlines. Ouch! Looks like you lost some money."

"How do you know that?"

"Lucky guess. Tell me about the trade."

Figure 6.2 shows his situation. He bought 1,300 shares at the market open two days before Christmas, filled at 11.69. After placing the trade, he put a stop at 10.33, which is slightly below the top of the November congestion region.

"I was expecting price to rise to 15, matching the left side of a failed Big W pattern in January 2004. Oil prices were dropping and that was good for airline stocks. The industry was working with me as the other airlines started moving up in October or earlier, just as this one did."

Unfortunately, the S&P 500 would change trend in six trading sessions. The airline stock

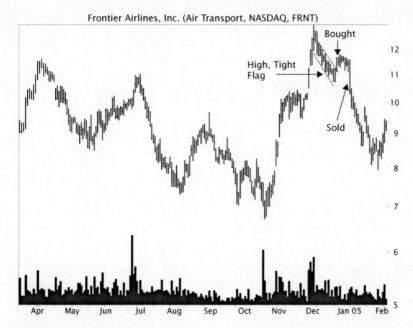

FIGURE 6.2 This high, tight flag ended in failure when price moved marginally higher before plummeting.

crashed a day later, and he was stopped out at 10.334. He lost $1,800 or almost 12%.

"The good news, Jake, is that you sold. You could have ridden it down for a loss of," I punched some keys, "$5,000 or 32%. What do you think you did wrong?"

"The stop was too far away. Volatility was 56 cents so that would call for a stop at 10.54 (that is, 1.5 times .56 subtracted from the intraday low at 11.38 on the buy date). That would have saved me $260. Other than that, it was a good trade."

Sometimes good trades go bad. That's why stops are so important. Remember this: Half of my trades go bad—*half*. But my winners are four figures or larger when my losers are three figures. So far this year (2005), for every dollar I lost I've made five.

Jake chortled and sat back in his chair. "Four figures. Ha! You're including the two digits to the right of the decimal."

I thought for a moment. "How's your debt, Jake? Better check your answering machine. I thought I heard a voice say something about a margin call, but I could be mistaken."

I heard the patter of feet pounding the pavement. I smiled. "Jake has left the building!"

2. Pipe Bottoms

- Average rise rank: 4
- Breakeven failure rate rank: 5
- Change after trend ends rank: 4

What happens when the valleys in a double bottom are close together? The answer to that question led me to discover pipe bottoms, horn bottoms, and their top counterparts. Pipe bottoms rank second for performance. They have a breakeven failure rate of 5%, meaning that 5% of the 926 patterns I looked at climbed less than 5% after the breakout. The average rise is a mouthwatering 45% (for perfect trades, remember), but if you are on vacation after prices peak and the trend changes, prices drop an average of 33%, so you may lose a major portion of what you gained.

Identification

What should you look for when searching for pipes? Here are the guidelines:

- Use the weekly chart to select pipes. Pipes on the daily chart do not perform as well.
- Find two downward, adjacent price spikes that look like parallel lines.
- The bottom of the spikes usually has a small price variation (the average is $0.24).
- Look for spikes longer than other spikes during the past year.
- The two spikes should have a large price overlap (66% is the average).
- Volume is high (above the 30-day average) 87% of the time on one or both spikes.
- The pipe should be obvious on the chart.

Most of these guidelines are self-explanatory. Pipes appear like weeds growing in a vacant lot: Some children collect and press their colorful petals between pages in a book, but the city mows down the others when they grow too high and violate ordinances. Distinguishing the collectables from the weeds is one reason for the many guidelines.

Figure 6.3 shows examples of several pipes. Look at the pipe on the right, during July 1996. The twin downward price spikes appear as parallel lines on the weekly chart and in this case, the low prices in the twin bottoms are the same. That happens infrequently as the chart shows, and performance usually suffers when it does occur.

Switch to the arithmetic price scale and look for spikes that are longer than are those over the past year. They perform better (46% average rise versus 35%). The inset in Figure 6.3 shows what I mean by long spikes. The spike length is the difference between the two horizontal lines, which is the difference between the higher of the two pipe bottoms and the lower of the two weeks adjacent to the pipes.

After the breakout—meaning that price *closes* above the higher of the two spikes, confirming the pattern as a valid one—prices climb to

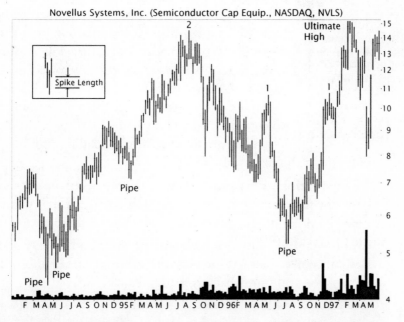

FIGURE 6.3 Look for two parallel lines well below the surrounding price action on the weekly scale.

ultimate high

I determine the ultimate high by looking after the breakout for the highest peak before prices decline by 20% or more, measured from the highest peak to the *close*. I stopped looking if price *closed* below the formation low, assuming that a stop-loss order would be placed at that location.

position trading

trading that holds a security overnight, sometimes maintaining a position for weeks, months, or longer, but not buy-and-hold forever.

point 1 and pause there. This is a common feature with pipes—prices climb to the prior high and stall or reverse. Point 2 shows another resistance location where price reversed at the *ultimate high*.

Trading and Trading Tips

Pipe bottoms are common so you can be selective. You will usually find pipes at the bottom of a price trend, many times forming a V-shaped bottom. For swing traders, they represent an excellent profit opportunity. After the right price spike, switch to the daily scale and buy when price closes above the highest peak in the two-week pattern. That will get you in sooner than trading on the weekly scale.

For *position traders* and longer-term holders, use the weekly scale for the buy signal. Wait for price to close above the higher of the two spikes before buying. In downtrends, many times pipe bottoms will not confirm (price does not close above the highest pipe high) and price will continue lower. Figure 6.4 shows an example of an unconfirmed pipe in late September 1999. Price never *closes* above the pattern's high before resuming the downtrend.

Here are some additional trading tips:

- Pipes with a long-term (over six months) downtrend leading to the pipe perform substantially better than intermediate- or short-term downtrends (79% average rise after a long-term downtrend versus 57% for intermediate-term and 21% for short-term).

- Avoid overhead resistance on both the daily and weekly scales. Resistance may cause a throwback that hurts performance (38% average rise with throwbacks versus 51% without).

- *Tall patterns* perform better than short ones (52% average rise versus 40%). Measure the height from the highest peak to the lowest valley in the pipe and then divide by the breakout price (the price of the highest peak). If the result is above 11.64%, then you have a tall pipe.

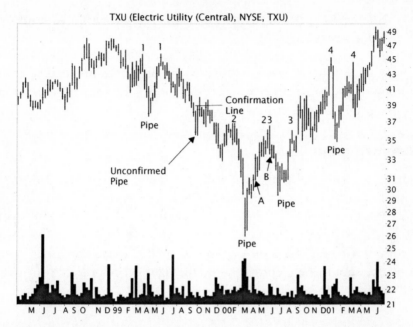

FIGURE 6.4 The peak before a pipe bottom often becomes a resistance level, halting or delaying the price advance, as the numbers show.

- Pipes with long spikes (longer than most over the prior year) perform better than do those with short ones (46% rise versus 35%). See the discussion of Figure 6.3 to determine the spike length.

- Select pipes with a large price difference between the lows (average rise 50% versus 41% for price differences smaller than the 0.83% median).

- Volume heavier on the left spike compared to the right suggests better performance (50% average rise versus as low as 42% for the other combinations).

- Pipes with a lower left spike tend to perform better than do those with a lower right spike (47% average rise versus 44%, and 42% rise for pipes with even bottoms).

- Pipes that are inside weeks (the right spike has a lower high and higher low than the

tall or short patterns

I measure the formation height by taking the difference between the highest peak and the lowest valley in the chart pattern, and then dividing the difference by the breakout price to get a percentage of height to price. I use the median value as the difference between short (values below the median) or tall (values above the median).

left spike) perform better (47% average rise versus 43% for out-side weeks).

If price closes below the lower of the pipe bottoms then exit your position. If things go right and price advances, raise your stop to just below the prior valley (a trailing stop).

Measuring Success

Notice in Figure 6.4 that price stalls or reverses at the peak before the pipe. Thus, the last peak represents the price target (called the *measure rule*). Price may continue higher as it did after the June 2000 pipe (pausing briefly at point 3), but do not stake your life on it. Consider selling if price stalls near the level of the old peak. Notice that price sometimes does not make it up that far, as the right peak opposite points 2, 3, and 4 show.

Case Study

"Margin call, bull!" Jake said.

I shrugged. "Guess I heard wrong."

"Let me show you a trade I made using a pipe bottom." He shoved me out of the chair. The only reason I let him get away with this is because I needed an example, which Figure 6.4 shows for the March 2000 pipe.

He had to wait for price to close above the highest peak in the pattern before buying. That took a month (point A).

Price moved up as it does in most trades that work. "But when it approached the old peak, I got nervous." I show that as point 2. Price was making new highs but the rate of change oscillator was showing lower peaks. "Bearish divergence—a sell signal."

He sold when price closed below the prior week (B). "If I had to do it again, I'd put a sell order just below the old high. Even if it was a buck below, that would have saved me money."

3. Inverted and Ascending Scallops

- Average rise rank: 5
- Breakeven failure rate rank: 4
- Change after trend ends rank: 5

Few people have heard of ascending scallops and even fewer have heard of the inverted variety. *Inverted* and *ascending scallops* (IASs) are patterns that I found when considering what ascending and descending scallops looked like when inverted. I went fishing and found hundreds of them swimming in the price ocean. They rank third for overall performance with an average rise of 43%, breakeven failure rate of 4%, and 32% decline after the trend ends.

Identification

What does an IAS look like? Figure 6.5 shows three scallops swimming upstream. Notice how the scallops narrow the farther up the price trend they appear. That is not always the case, but if you see that behavior, it warns that the end of the price trend may be near. This is especially true when the start and end of the scallops have nearly the same price. Here are the selection guidelines:

- On the daily chart, find an upward price trend.
- Look for an inverted and backward J-pattern. Price should start by moving up in nearly a straight line (sometimes leaning to the right), round over smoothly at the top, and then decline.

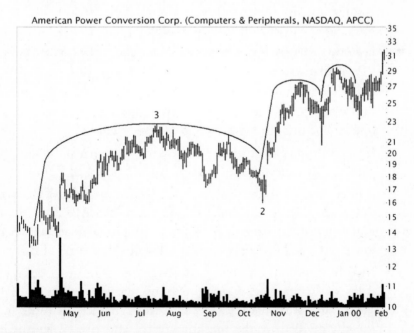

American Power Conversion Corp. (Computers & Peripherals, NASDAQ, APCC)

FIGURE 6.5 These three inverted and ascending scallops narrow as they appear in a price uptrend. Point 2 should retrace about half the distance from points 3 to 1.

- Price at the end of the pattern usually retraces 55% of the prior up move. Avoid any pattern that retraces more than 100% (drops below the start).
- The pattern becomes valid when price closes above the highest peak in the pattern.
- Volume trends downward 71% of the time from the start of the pattern to the end.

You can see what the inverted and backward J-pattern looks like from Figure 6.5. For larger patterns (points 1, 3, and 2 in the figure), the rounding turn at the top of the pattern is usually not smooth. For narrower IASs, the turn may appear squished in a vice, more of an inverted V-shape than a J. I prefer to see a gentle, rounded turn. In all cases, the start of the pattern (point 1) must be below the end (2).

Trading and Trading Tips

Here are a few tips to make trading scallops easier and more profitable:

- For swing traders, buy when price makes a higher valley after completing the inverted and backward J (a 50% or higher retrace) with a price target of the scallop high.
- For other traders, buy when price closes above the highest peak in the pattern.
- If the pattern end points follow an existing upsloping trendline, buy when price rises above the trendline after the second IAS touch. The inset in Figure 6.6 shows this scenario.
- If prices drop below the start of the pattern, then avoid trading the pattern. That means point 2 drops below point 1 in Figure 6.5
- If price forms a distinct right valley and then price drops below the valley, sell. Figure 6.6 shows this as a tiny IAS AB. Price climbs, leaving a distinct valley at B, and then doubles back and moves below B at C. Sell when price drops below the price level of B.
- IASs both tall and narrow perform better than other combinations of height and width (56% average rise versus 35% for short and wide patterns). Tall means higher than 22.51% (height divided by the breakout price) and narrow means less than 34 days.

- Patterns with a rising volume trend do better postbreakout, gaining 48% versus 40% for patterns with falling volume.
- Breakout volume above the 30-day average means a larger average gain, 44% versus 38% for light volume breakouts.

Figure 6.6 shows how to use the first tip. After price makes a higher valley on the right side of the scallop, buy. This works well if it looks like the pattern has completed, meaning that price has retraced over 50% of the prior up move on the left side of the scallop and is now heading back up. The sell target is the top of the pattern unless price is advancing in a straight-line run. Under that condition, hold on until your other indicators say sell.

> **confirmation point, price, level, or line**
>
> also known as the breakout point, price, or level—a price or location that validates a chart pattern.

The usual confirmation price is a close above the top of the pattern (see the confirmation line in Figure 6.6). Buy when price closes above the line. This works well if price is trending up at nearly the same angle as during the left side of the scallop, especially if it

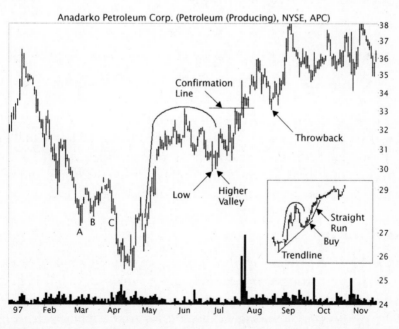

FIGURE 6.6 A close above the *confirmation line* represents the traditional buy signal. The inset shows a buy signal when the pattern follows a trendline.

is in a straight-line run. The inset in Figure 6.6 shows an example. This also shows another buying technique. When price follows a trendline, buy after the scallop touches the trendline on the right side of the scallop and bounces off, moving up.

If price drops below the valley on the right side of the scallop (point B in Figure 6.6), then the pattern is a failure and you should exit the trade. Never take a position in a scallop in which the valley on the right is below the valley on the left. A lower valley signals a trend change.

Measuring Success

Price prediction uses the height of the scallop projected upward from the top of the scallop. Using Figure 6.5 as an example, height is point 1 (13.10) subtracted from point 3 (22.75), or 9.65. Add the height to the highest peak in the pattern to get a target of 32.40 (22.75 + 9.65). This method works just 61% of the time, so be conservative in your targets and look for nearby resistance zones where price might reverse.

4. Three Rising Valleys

- Average rise rank: 6
- Breakeven failure rate rank: 5
- Change after trend ends rank: 4

The three rising valleys (3RV) pattern is one I heard of only recently. When I tested it, I was surprised at how well it performed. In a bull market, the overall performance rank is four, with an average rise of 41% after the breakout (if traded *perfectly*), 5% fail to rise at least 5%, and prices decline 33% once they reach the ultimate high and then reverse.

Identification

I show the 3RV pattern as bottoms 1, 2, and 3 in Figure 6.7. Most often, the pattern acts as a *reversal* of the downward price trend, and reversals also give the best performance. As the pattern's name implies, look for three valleys, each one higher than the last, so that the pattern begins or continues an upward price trend. Each valley should appear similar, but they need not follow a trendline. You wouldn't, for example, pair bottoms 1 and 2 with 4, the little nubbin poking downward. If you select wide bottoms, stick with wide bottoms on all three valleys. If you start with one-day spikes, then choose narrow valleys—those just a few days wide.

reversal
a price reversal occurs when price enters and exits the chart pattern from the same direction.

The pattern confirms as a valid 3RV when price closes above the confirmation line—the highest peak in the pattern. When the peak between valleys 1 and 2 is higher than the one between peaks 2 and 3, draw a downsloping trendline connecting those peaks. When price closes above the trendline, that signals a buy and it might get you in earlier than waiting for the standard breakout (a close above the confirmation line).

Try looking for 3RVs on the weekly chart, as they look like icicles and are almost as plentiful.

What selections should you avoid? Look at valleys A, B, and C in Figure 6.7. The valleys do not represent a valid 3RV pattern because

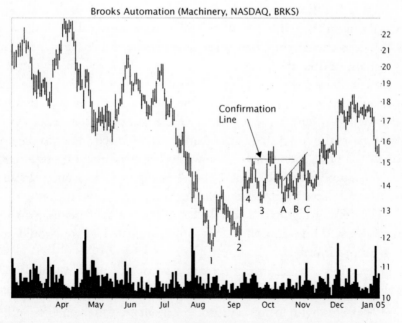

FIGURE 6.7 The three rising valleys pattern, shown here as 1-2-3, suggests a reversal of the downward price trend.

valley C is not above valley B. Instead, the pattern is a right-angled and ascending broadening formation. (Draw a horizontal line from A to C to complete the pattern.)

Here are the steps to identifying a 3RV pattern:

- Look for three valleys; each valley must be higher than the last with no ties allowed. The weekly chart might help with selection.
- Select similar shaped valleys. Pair wide ones with wide ones, narrow ones with slim valleys in both width and height.
- A buy signal occurs when price closes above the highest peak in the pattern or pierces a downsloping trendline drawn joining the peaks between the three valleys.
- Volume trends downward in two out of three cases.

Trading and Trading Tips

The 3RV pattern is a plentiful one, so you can be selective. Before trading any 3RV, switch to a higher time scale and see what the price landscape looks like. Many times, you will see overhead resistance that you will want to avoid. That usually causes me to toss a pattern and look for another one.

Figure 6.8 shows one such example, although it is on the daily scale. The 3RV appears as narrow price spikes, but each valley is above the prior one, as expected. When price closes above the confirmation line a buy signals, or does it?

If you draw a downsloping trendline joining the peaks on the chart, notice how prices rise to the trendline and then reverse. This is common behavior for 3RVs. Since 3RV reversals give the best performance, be sure the pattern passes the 1-2-3 trend change method discussed earlier in the book. Look for (1) price to close above a downsloping trendline; (2) price to retest the valley (attempt to reach a low but make a higher valley); and (3) wait for price to close above the peak between the lowest valley and the retest.

The 3RV in Figure 6.8 fails the trendline test because price does not close above it. Thus, a trend change is not indicated so you would avoid trading this pattern.

Here are some additional trading tips for this pattern. Performance numbers are averages and represent perfect trades, so your results will vary.

- Patterns with below average breakout volume tend to perform better than those with above average volume, with rises averaging 53% versus 38%, but 76% break out on high (above the 30-day average) volume.

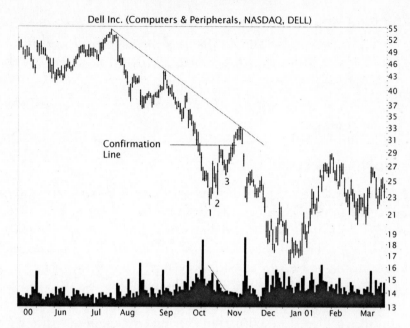

FIGURE 6.8 This 3RV fails to pierce trendline resistance, and prices reverse. To avoid similar situations, use the 1-2-3 trend change method. Notice the receding volume trend.

- When volume trends upward throughout the pattern, postbreakout performance improves: rises average 45% versus 38%, but 67% have downward sloping volume trends.

- Sixty-seven percent act as reversals, and reversals perform better than *continuations*, with rises of 46% versus 33%.

- Two out of three patterns break out within a third of the yearly high and they perform best.

- Tall patterns perform better than short ones, by 45% to 37%. Use the median height of 23.80% (the height divided by the breakout price) as the divider between short and tall.

- Narrow patterns perform better than wide ones, 44% versus 39%. A narrow pattern is one narrower than the median 43 days, measured from the first valley to the last.

> **continuation**
> for chart patterns, I use this term as a synonym for consolidation. For a continuation, prices must break out in the same direction as they entered the pattern. For example, if price enters the pattern from the bottom and exits out the top, the pattern acts as a continuation. Contrast with reversal.

- Patterns both tall and narrow show postbreakout gains of 53%.

- Throwbacks occur 60% of the time and when they occur, performance suffers (50% average rise without throwbacks versus 36% with them).

- The farther up the price trend a 3RV appears, the smaller the potential gain.

Measuring Success

The measure rule for 3RVs is the same as for most other chart patterns. Subtract the price of the lowest valley from the highest peak in the pattern to get the height. Add the height to the highest peak and the result is the target price. This method works just 58% of the time, so you might consider cutting the height in half before applying it to the highest peak. That boosts the success rate to 79% in a bull market.

Let's take the 3RV shown in Figure 6.8 as an example. Subtract the lowest valley (valley 1 at 22.06) from the highest peak in the pattern (30, at the confirmation line) to get a height of 7.94. Add the difference to the highest peak to get a target of 37.94. If you cut the height in half, 3.97, you get a closer target of 33.97.

Take the height (3.97) and divide it by the breakout price (30) to get 13%. If you traded this stock perfectly, 13% is how much you could expect to make—assuming price climbs to the target (if not higher). Of course, you won't trade it perfectly, and you need to factor in commissions, so your results might be lower. Before trading, balance the possible gain with the size of the potential loss. Is the reward substantially higher (by 2 or 3 times) than the loss?

Jake walked into my office and said, "Did you know that the government has a Department of Redundancy Department? They monitor synchronized swimming teams to make sure that the first swimmer doesn't drown because, well, you know." Then he walked back out. I'm starting to worry about him.

5. Rounding Bottoms (Tied with 6)

- Average rise rank: 5
- Breakeven failure rate rank: 5
- Change after trend ends rank: 6

I prefer to think of rounding bottoms as rounding turns because they need not be bottoms at all. Rather, many of them have prices that enter the rounding pattern from below, so they act as consolidations (pauses) of the upward price trend.

Rounding bottoms have an overall performance rank of five. The average rise, if you were to trade perfectly the bull market patterns I looked at, is 43%. The breakeven failure rate is 5%, meaning that 5% of the patterns failed to rise at least 5% after the breakout. Once the trend changes after reaching the ultimate high, prices tumbled 31%, on average, so it pays to sell as close to the top as possible. No surprise there, right?

Identification

Figure 6.9 shows a rounding turn on the daily scale. In this example, prices climb into the pattern, curve downward, and soar out the right side without pausing. A rising approach happens 62% of the time and when it does, it predicts better performance after the breakout—an average rise of 57% versus 36% for rounding bottoms with downtrends leading to the chart pattern. Thus, select patterns in a rising price trend.

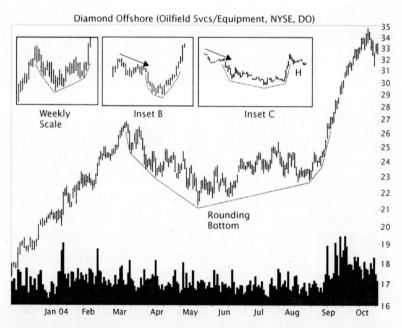

FIGURE 6.9 This rounding bottom is on the daily scale. Even so, the rounding turn is clear.

I show the same rounding bottom on the weekly scale in the inset on the far left. You still have to use your imagination; the turn doesn't appear as smooth as it could, but few chart patterns are perfect. That's part of the identification challenge.

Insets B and C have prices trending down into the pattern. Inset B is on the weekly scale and the rounding turn looks smooth. The exit does not pause at the price level of the left cup rim. Inset C is on the daily scale, and I picked this rounding bottom to show you what a handle looks like. The handle is on the right (H).

Here are the identification tips for rounding bottoms:

- Use the weekly scale. Rounding bottoms are large enough to appear there and the graceful turn becomes apparent easily.

- Price enters the pattern trending upward 62% of the time (best) or downward (38%).

- Look for a peak that occurs before the rounding turn. This forms the left cup lip.

- Price should round downward in a bowl shape, usually smooth but allow variations.

- Midway through the turn, prices *may* shoot up and then ease down to just above where they started.

- Volume trends upward 51% of the time.

- Volume shape splits between dome (51%), U (43%), and everything else (6%).

Trading and Trading Tips

Unless I am making a trade, I rarely look at the weekly scale, but I make the effort monthly. Each month, price adds four or five additional bars to the chart, and sometimes that's enough. I found a rounding turn about halfway through its development in Lam Research and decided to trade it. Because I knew (*hoped*, really) that prices would rise to the height of the left cup lip, I decided that the trade would be a long-term one. Nevertheless, I used a trailing stop that I raised as prices climbed. The general market downturn at the start of the new year cashed me out, but not before I made some money. (I detail the trade later in the book.)

The point of mentioning it now is to convince you to look at the weekly scale (or a higher period than the one you usually use) to find this pattern. If you can spot a gentle turn in development, then buy the stock and ride it upward. However, be aware of the midway bump that sometimes happens. Figure 6.10 shows an example.

Prices start the rounding turn at B and slide downward to the September low in an almost straight-line decline. Then prices retrace a good portion of the decline. When the retrace completes, prices drop to point A, slightly above where they started the rise. Then, the rise resumes, ending at C before forming a handle and moving higher.

If you buy a rounding turn and prices shoot up midway through the bottom, you can exit at the top of the retrace if you are a swing trader. Those traders with a longer-term perspective might do well holding onto the stock. You can add to your position or buy back in once price returns to just above the launch point. Don't expect it to meet the launch point low because it usually makes a higher valley like that shown in Figure 6.10.

Most times a handle forms when price reaches the high of the left cup lip (resistance at a prior peak). I measured the time from the right cup lip to the breakout and found that 90% of the patterns took longer than

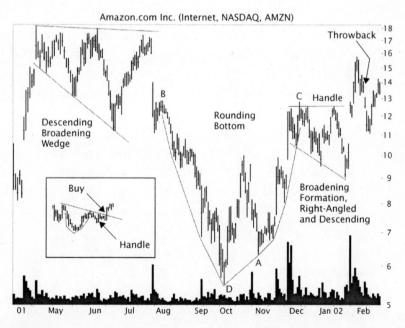

FIGURE 6.10 This rounding turn has prices rising upward midway through the turn. When the rise completes, prices return to near where they began.

seven days to climb to the breakout. That gives plenty of time for a handle to form.

Here are some additional trading tips:

- Use the weekly scale to find a rounding turn that is at the midway part of its development. Buy if you expect the industry and general market to trend upward.

- Swing traders can sell if prices bump up after the midway point—retracing a portion of the downward move that forms the left side of the cup. For all others, don't get too disappointed when prices return to just above the launch point. When prices resume the uptrend, consider adding to your position.

- Count on price pausing near the level of the left cup lip. If the general market or industry is weak, then sell. You can always buy back in when price bounces off the handle low.

- If the rounding bottom has a handle, try drawing a downsloping trendline connecting the two cup lips and extending the line down beyond the handle. When price closes above the trendline in the handle, buy the stock or add to your position. The inset in Figure 6.10 shows this scenario.

- The standard buy location is when price closes above the right cup lip—if it has a right lip. If not, buy when price closes above the price of the left cup lip.

- If prices are predominantly flat leading to the rounding bottom— a flat base of several months duration—that often leads to a powerful rise after the breakout.

- Throwbacks only occur 40% of the time and when they do occur, performance suffers (33% average rise versus 50% without a throwback). Avoid nearby overhead resistance to avoid a throwback. Figure 6.10 shows a throwback to the handle on the far right.

- Patterns taller than the median 31.58% (height divided by the breakout price) perform better than short ones, 52% versus 38% average rise.

- Wide patterns—wider than the 196-day median—perform better, 48% average rise versus 38% for narrow patterns.

- Patterns with breakouts near the yearly high perform best.

- The median time from the right cup lip to the breakout is 33 days.

Measuring Success

The measure rule for rounding bottoms uses the height of the cup from the bottom to the right cup lip if it has one (otherwise use the left cup lip). Add the height to the breakout price—usually the right cup lip or trendline break if a handle is used (otherwise use the left cup lip)—to get the target. Unfortunately, this works only 57% of the time.

For a more conservative measure, use half the cup height and add it to the breakout price. Using this method boosts the success rate to 78%.

For example, the height of the rounding bottom pictured in Figure 6.10 is C (at 12.80) minus D (the lowest valley in the pattern at 5.51) or 7.29. The target price is the height added to the breakout price, or 20.09 (12.80 + 7.29). A more conservative target uses half the height, or 3.65, for a target of 16.45.

6. Descending Triangles (Tied with 5)

- Average rise rank: 2
- Breakeven failure rate rank: 7
- Change after trend ends rank: 7

Descending triangles are tied for fifth place with rounding bottoms. This chapter assumes an upward breakout from a descending triangle, although a downward breakout occurs 64% of the time.

The 47% average rise ranks second, and the number assumes perfectly traded patterns, so your results will vary. The breakeven failure rare is 7%, meaning that 7% of the patterns have prices that fail to rise at least 5% after the breakout. Once price reaches the ultimate high, it tumbles 30%, placing the pattern in seventh place.

Identification

Figure 6.11 shows an example of a descending triangle. Prices along the bottom of the pattern touch a horizontal or near horizontal trendline. Along the top, the trend slopes downward, ending when the two trendlines touch at the triangle apex. This one shows a throwback to the top trendline that occurs just 37% of the time, so you should not depend on it happening to enter a position.

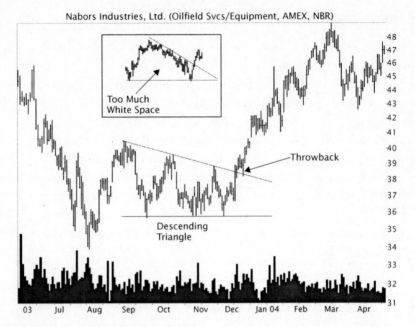

FIGURE 6.11 A descending triangle is flat along the bottom and the top slopes downward. Prices throwback to the top trendline in this example. The inset is not a descending triangle because prices do not cross the pattern enough times to fill the white space.

What should you look for when trying to find descending triangles? Fortunately, triangles are easy to spot, but here are a few guidelines to make the job easier:

- Look for two price trends, the valleys align horizontally or nearly so, and the peaks slope downward. Both trends should follow trendlines connecting them.

- Prices must touch each trendline at least twice.

- Prices must cross the pattern from side to side, filling the pattern with price movement, not white space. *Do not cut off a rounding turn and call it a descending triangle.* The inset to Figure 6.11 shows this situation. It's not a descending triangle because of too much white space.

- Prices usually break out downward, but we want to stay on the bullish side, so trade only upward breakouts. A breakout occurs when price closes above the downsloping trendline.

- Volume slopes downward 83% of the time and can become quite low days before the breakout.

Trading and Trading Tips

Because descending triangles break out downward 64% of the time, always wait for the upward breakout. If you are lucky, prices *will* break out downward, spin around, and then soar out the top. I show that scenario in Figure 6.12.

The busted triangle, where prices break out downward and drop less than 10% before rebounding, often leads to large gains. Trading busted chart patterns is an easy way to make money, so I devote an entire chapter to them later in this book. For now, if you see a situation like that shown in Figure 6.12, buy it. Also, watch for the throwback to occur, as you don't want to be stopped out prematurely.

busted pattern performance
a chart pattern that reaches the ultimate high or low less than 10% away from the breakout and then reverses direction. The performance measures how far prices move in the new direction (the direction opposite the breakout) before reaching a new ultimate high or low.

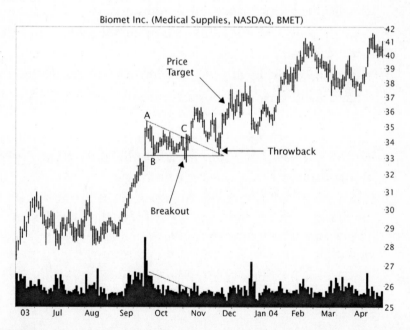

FIGURE 6.12 This descending triangle breaks out downward then shoots out the top. *Busted pattern*s, such as this one, suggest a powerful upward move.

Figure 6.12 shows what I used to call a premature breakout. That's when prices break out in one direction and return to the triangle within a day or two before staging the real breakout later. Preemies are rare, however. Just 6% break out upward and 20% break out downward. As I mentioned, the downward preemies are a blessing as they sometimes lead to a busted pattern.

The average distance to the breakout is 64% of the way to the triangle apex. However, my research says that the most powerful breakouts happen 80% to 85% of the way. The sample size (31) is small, so do not depend too much on the numbers.

Descending triangles that appear far up a rising price trend tend to flame out quicker, meaning that the rise after the breakout is less. My study showed that those near the beginning of a trend rise an average of 39%. Those closer to the trend's end rise 34%. The median rise to the triangle is 72 days, so rises shorter than that are, well, short.

Here are some interesting tidbits I found on descending triangles. They may help you select better performing triangles to trade.

- Nimble swing traders can buy near the horizontal trendline and sell when prices turn at the top trendline.

- Extend the two trendlines into the future for support and resistance zones.

- The triangle apex acts as a future region of support and resistance.

- A buy signals when price closes outside the top trendline (an upward breakout).

- Narrow patterns perform better than wide ones with rises averaging 38% versus 32%. The median width is 47 days. Patterns shorter than the median are the narrow ones.

- Patterns both tall (above the 10.72% median height divided by the breakout price) and narrow (narrower than the median 47 days) perform better than the other combinations of height and width.

- If prices rise into the triangle, expect an upward breakout (which occurs 73% of the time), but always wait for the breakout before trading.

- Patterns with breakout day gaps do well, with prices rising an average of 44% after the breakout versus 34% for those without gaps.

- Above average breakout day volume tends to push prices higher: 36% versus 33% for those patterns with breakout volume below the 30-day average.

- Postbreakout performance improves when volume slopes upward in the formation—40% average rise versus 34% for those with a receding volume trend.

- Triangles with U-shaped volume tend to outperform with prices rising 44% after the breakout versus 29% for those with dome-shaped volume.

- Seventy-three percent acted as continuations of the prior price trend, 27% were reversals.

Measuring Success

The measure rule for descending triangles is simply the height added to the breakout price. The height is the difference between the price of the horizontal trendline (the lowest valley) and highest peak in the pattern. Add this difference to the breakout price—the point where price crosses the trendline. This method works 71% of the time. It's fallible, but it does provide a price target you can work with. After you compute the target, look for nearby support and resistance zones. Price may stop there.

As an example of how to apply the measure rule, Figure 6.12 shows the highest peak in the pattern at point A and the lowest valley at B (ignore the downward breakout). The price difference is 35.34 − 33.17, or 2.17. The breakout price is 34.31—the value where price *pierces* the downsloping trendline (since we are looking for an upward breakout target). Thus, the target is the breakout price plus the height, 34.31 + 2.17, or 36.48. I show the price target on the figure.

I walked into my office and there was Jake, yawning. "A yawn is a silent shout," I said.

He lightly slapped his cheeks as if to wake up and then pointed at the computer screen. "I'm reading your manuscript. It's boring. It needs something. Like jokes. Lots of jokes."

"It's not supposed to be funny, Jake. It's nonfiction finance, not a novel."

"But it's boring!"

"If I fill it with jokes, readers will post nasty notes on Amazon saying it's trite."

He shrugged, but hair stood up on the back of my neck. He was up to something. I just couldn't figure out what it was.

7. Ascending Broadening Wedges (Tied with 8)

- Average rise rank: 9
- Breakeven failure rate rank: 2
- Change after trend ends rank: 6

Ascending broadening wedges (ABWs) rank seventh for performance, tied with Eve & Eve double bottoms. ABWs show an average rise of 38% if you trade this one perfectly. The breakeven failure rate is 2%, meaning that 2% of the patterns failed to rise at least 5% after the breakout. That performance places the chart pattern in second place. Finally, once price reaches the ultimate high, it tumbles 31%, ranking sixth.

Before I get too far, I studied 255 ABWs, but only 58 broke out upward in a bull market, and those are the ones I discuss in this chapter.

Identification

Figure 6.13 shows what an ABW looks like. Two trendlines follow the price action. Both slope upward but the top one is steeper than the bottom one, so they diverge. The pattern reminds me of a cheerleader's megaphone tilted upward. To make sure you identify an ABW correctly, look for *three touches* of each trendline. That helps select patterns that have the broadening characteristic and improves performance.

Here are the guidelines for selecting ABWs:

- Three peaks and three valleys should near or touch upsloping trendlines.
- Neither trendline should be horizontal.
- The top trendline should slope upward more steeply than the bottom one.
- The pattern should look like a megaphone tilted upward.
- Volume trends upward 64% of the time.

If you draw a trendline across peaks A, B, and C in Figure 6.13, it would make a larger ABW. The bottom at D marks a partial decline that accurately predicts an upward breakout 35% of the time. That's not very good, so you shouldn't put much faith in it.

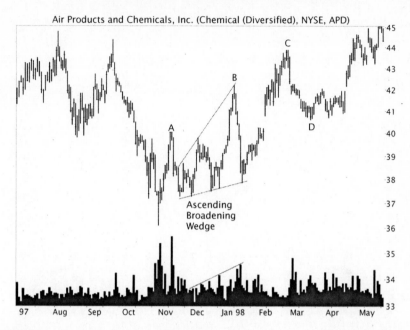

FIGURE 6.13 An ascending broadening wedge appears as shown, but a larger one connects ABC on the top. D marks the bottom of a large partial decline correctly predicting an upward breakout from the ABC pattern.

A partial decline occurs when price leaves the top trendline and heads down but swings upward before coming close to or touching the bottom trendline. An immediate upward breakout follows if the partial decline works as expected.

When searching for a partial decline, work with an established chart pattern, meaning the peaks and valleys touch the each trendline at least three times. Only then should you look for a partial decline, and it must begin before the breakout.

For the larger ABW (points A, B, and C), a breakout occurs when price closes above point C in Figure 6.13. For the smaller ABW (between points A and B), the breakout occurs when price closes above B, the highest peak in the pattern.

Trading and Trading Tips

For experienced traders, 73% of ABWs breakout downward, and a partial rise can get you in before the breakout. In Figure 6.14, a partial rise is at point A, and it predicts a downward breakout. (That does not happen in this example, but pretend that it does.)

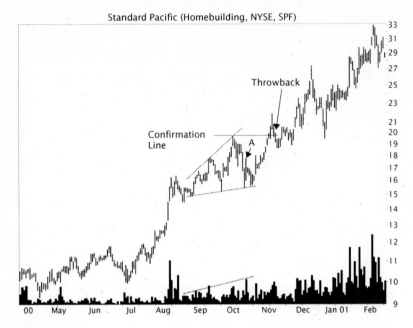

FIGURE 6.14 The partial rise shown at point A usually predicts a downward breakout from the pattern. Here, the breakout is upward.

How do you identify a partial rise? Once the price pattern is established (meaning price touches each trendline at least three times), look for prices that rise off the bottom trendline but don't come close to or touch the top trendline. When prices return to the lower trendline, an immediate downward breakout occurs 74% of the time. Trading a partial rise is not easy because it can look like the pause that often occurs midway through a rise heading to the top trendline. Short the stock once it's clear prices are heading back to the lower trendline. If prices bounce upward off the trendline, cover your short immediately. Price may still breakout downward, but the odds shift against that happening.

If you don't have a partial rise or decline to trade, here are additional trading tricks. Warning: Performance numbers are based on 58 perfect trades, too few in many cases to be reliable.

- For swing traders, buy when price touches the lower trendline and sell as it approaches the top trendline, and then reverse the trade.
- Place an order to buy just above the third peak. If prices rise and make a fourth trendline touch then begin heading down, sell immediately to avoid a return to the bottom trendline.

- For aggressive traders, place a buy order when price touches the bottom trendline for a third time and begins moving up. Watch for a partial rise to occur, and if one does, sell your position when price closes below the bottom trendline, as prices are likely to continue falling like a rock down a steep hill. If price bounces off the top trendline instead of pushing through it, sell when price retraces 62% of the prior up move.

- For experienced traders, if the ABW is the corrective phase of a large measured move down, then expect a downward breakout. I discuss measured move chart patterns in Chapter 7.

- Tall patterns do better than short ones, with prices climbing 50% versus 30% after the breakout, respectively. Tall or short means the pattern height divided by the breakout price compared to the 18.60% median.

- Wide patterns, those wider than the median 66 days, perform better than narrow ones, with prices rising an average of 39% versus 35%, postbreakout.

- Seventy-six percent acted as continuations of the prior price trend. Reversals made up the remainder.

The traditional breakout price is a close above the confirmation line, the highest peak in the pattern, as shown in Figure 6.14. Unfortunately, it can be difficult to tell when the stock has quit following the top trendline and is breaking out. Many times, a close above the third peak will correctly signal an upward breakout, so use that.

For example, Figure 6.15 shows another ABW with price touching each trendline three times. The multiple trendline touches at 2 are close enough together to be considered one touch. The same goes for point A. The traditional buy point is a close above C, which I show as the horizontal line, Buy 1. If you place a buy order at or above the third top trendline touch, you will be on the correct side of the trade the majority of the time. Price may retrace once it encounters the top of the pattern (as it does by dropping to B), so factor that into your stop price.

If you spot the ABW soon enough, you can trade it as prices swing from side to side. Again, place a buy order when price begins rising after the third trendline touch (Buy 2). You can ride the stock upward to the price level of C, or the stock may curl back into a partial rise and break out downward. Be sure to sell if it closes below the lower trendline because the downward breakout means prices will tumble.

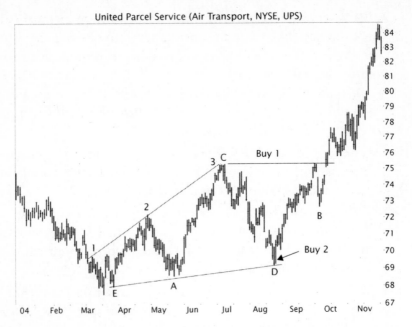

FIGURE 6.15 Place a buy order at C for the traditional breakout, or at D, the third bottom touch, once price begins heading back up.

If price rises to the top trendline and bounces downward, swing traders should take their profits. For others, sell if price drops below a 62% retrace of the prior up move. By that, I mean measure the price difference between where the stock stops moving upward and the prior valley. Take 62% of that and subtract it from where the stock stopped moving up. In this example, the decline to B is less than 62% of the D to Buy 1 move, so a sale is not needed. Hold onto the stock and hope price recovers as in this example.

Measuring Success

The measure rule for ABWs helps predict a target price. Compute the ABW height and add it to the breakout price to get the target. For example, the pattern in Figure 6.15 has a height of C – E, or 7.35. Add the height to C (the breakout price) to get a target of 82.64. If support or resistance is nearby, then expect price to stall there and adjust your target accordingly.

The measure rule for upward breakouts works 69% of the time. That is well short of the 80% I like to see, so you might want to use half the height in the computation. For the example shown in Figure 6.15, the height becomes 3.68. When added to the price of C, the new target becomes 78.97. Prices hit the nearer target 93% of the time.

8. Eve & Eve Double Bottoms (Tied with 7)

- Average rise rank: 7
- Breakeven failure rate rank: 4
- Change after trend ends rank: 6

The Eve & Eve double bottom (EEDB) is what most chartists call the classic double bottom. It has an overall performance rank that ties with ascending broadening wedges. The average rise from perfectly traded stocks is 40%, placing it seventh. The breakeven failure rate is 4%, for a fourth place finish. Finally, the 31% decline after the trend changes places it sixth among bullish chart patterns.

Identification

The Adam and Eve combinations of double bottoms are a somewhat recent addition to the chart pattern landscape. The names describe the appearance of each bottom in the twin valley formation. Adam bottoms are narrow, usually one-day downward price spikes while Eve is more rounded looking and considerably wider than Adam.

Figure 6.16 shows what an EEDB looks like. The two valleys are wide, rounded appearing turns, spaced several weeks apart. The rise between the bottoms is rather extensive. The double bottom confirms as a valid EEDB when price closes above the peak between the two valleys (shown as the confirmation line).

What should you look for when trying to spot EEDBs?

- Prices should trend downward before the left valley, but should not drop below the valley. In other words, you don't want to see a lower valley adjacent to the first valley.
- Each valley should appear similar: wide, rounding turns.
- The rise between the two valleys should be at least 10%.
- The two bottoms should appear near the same price—less than 6% apart.

FIGURE 6.16　An Eve & Eve double bottom has two wide rounding valleys, not narrow price spikes as does its Adam counterpart.

- Several weeks (two to seven for the best performance) should separate the two valleys.
- Volume is usually higher on the left bottom (volume trends downward 65% of the time).
- Price must close above the confirmation line (the highest peak in the pattern) before the twin bottom becomes a true EEDB.
- If a double bottom forms a third bottom before the double bottom confirms, treat it as a triple bottom.

For example, the EEDB shown in Figure 6.16 has a downward price trend that leads to the first valley without dropping below it on the way down. Both valleys are wide, rounding turns (compare with the Adam & Adam double bottom in March). The rise between the two valleys measures 20% from the lowest valley (the left one) to the peak. The two valleys are less than 2% apart in price (22 cents) and are 11 weeks apart, as measured from the lowest valley in each bottom. That's a little wide, yet close enough for government work, as they say. Volume is higher surrounding the left valley, as expected. Price closes above the confirmation line in early September, confirming the pattern as a valid EEDB.

Figure 6.17 shows what the various combinations of Adam and Eve bottoms look like. Eve is wide and rounded appearing. Adam is often a single spike or just a few days wide, long, and needle sharp. Eve sometimes has spikes but they are shorter and more clustered, like shallow roots of a tree.

Trading and Trading Tips

I have noticed that EEDBs, and all double bottoms for that matter, are riskier than many other chart patterns. Why? Because you find them at the bottom of a price trend. The problem occurs after price confirms the pattern. That's when traders come along and swat price back down. The stock drops below the lowest valley, emptying your wallet.

How can you prevent investing in busted patterns? Before taking a position in any stock showing a chart pattern, look at the general market. I use the Standard & Poor's 500 index as the proxy.

I look for any chart patterns in the S&P and find it surprisingly easy to determine whether prices will trend up or down in the coming weeks.

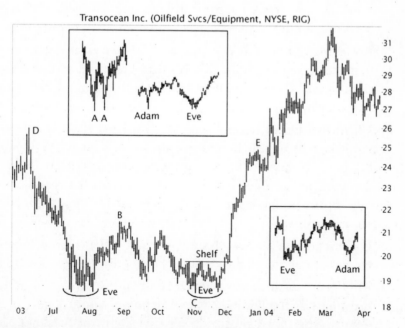

FIGURE 6.17 Shown are the different combinations of Adam and Eve bottoms. Pattern AA is an Adam & Adam double bottom.

I also look at the NASDAQ composite, Dow Jones Industrials, Utility, and Transportation averages to round out the picture, depending on the type of stock that I'm considering.

Then I check the industry in which the stock belongs. Because I follow five or more stocks in the same industry, it's easy to pull up each stock and look at the chart. Is price trending upward? Are there any chart patterns that signal a trend reversal (bearish patterns)? Are they trading near the yearly high?

Often, either the general market (which I consider *very* important) or the industry will be weak enough to keep me on the sidelines. However, when the clay pigeons line up, I grab my rifle and start shooting. Here are additional tips for trading EEDBs:

- Look for a shelf on the right bottom, a flat top that can act as a support zone. I show it on the November Eve bottom in Figure 6.17. For swing traders, buy when price closes above this threshold and sell at confirmation if price stalls there. Be aware that the double bottom may become a triple bottom.

- For position traders and investors, buy when price closes above the confirmation price—the highest peak between the two bottoms. Trading before confirmation means a loss 64% of the time. That rate is how often price never makes it up to confirmation.

- Sometimes, price will confirm the EEDB and then waffle up and down, forming a handle. When prices break out of this congestion region, they often (but not always) move up in a strong trend. Figure 6.16 shows the EEDB with handle scenario.

- When the double bottom forms after a long, flat price trend (a flat base), the double bottom usually sports a large gain after the breakout. Switch to the weekly scale and look for a flat base. Think of the double bottom as a pothole in a flat road before a hill. If price bounces out of the hole, it can drive uphill for an extended move.

- If a pipe bottom (or any other bullish chart pattern) forms as part of the right Eve bottom, then buy the stock when the pipe confirms.

- EEDBs both short and narrow tend to outperform (49% average rise) the other combinations of height and width. Short means less than the 16.4% median height divided by the breakout price. Narrow means less than the median 50 days wide.

- Patterns with breakouts within a third of the yearly low outperform the other two ranges (middle and high thirds).

- EEDBs without throwbacks perform significantly better than do those with throwbacks. Prices rise 48% versus 33% after the breakout, respectively. Look for trades without nearby overhead resistance.

- Double bottoms with volume heavier on the right bottom than the left do better after the breakout with price gains averaging 43% versus 39%.

- Look for a big W pattern—an EEDB with unusually tall sides. The decline leading to the EEDB is a straight-line run of several points. Expect the breakout to return prices to where they started the decline. Figure 6.17 shows a big W between points D and E.

Measuring Success

The measure rule for double bottoms is the height added to the breakout price. The height is the difference between the highest peak and the lowest valley in the pattern. Add the difference to the breakout price—the highest peak in the pattern—to get a target price. Prices meet the target 67% of the time after an EEDB breakout. That percentage is a little low, so be conservative with your targets—as in archery, the closer the target, the better the accuracy.

The measure rule applied to the EEDB shown in Figure 6.17 is the difference between B and C added to B. B is at 21.39, and C is at 18.49. The difference between the two, 2.90, is the height. Add the height to the breakout (B) to get a target of 24.29. In this example price reaches the target in mid-December.

Case Study

"There you are." Jake said. He found me in the barn, cleaning out the horse stalls. "I had a great vacation! Let me tell you about . . ."

"You were stopped out of Guess."

The corners of his mouth turned down. Fists clenched, his fingers combing his hair backward, showing a receding hairline, he stomped back to the house to survey the damage. Figure 6.18 shows his trade.

He bought 1,000 shares at 16.13 the day after the pattern confirmed (when price closed above the peak at point A, 16). Immediately

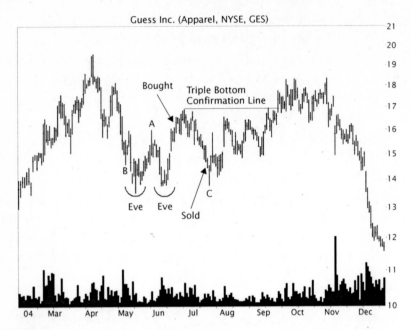

FIGURE 6.18   An Eve & Eve double bottom confirmed but price backtracked and changed into a triple bottom. Price didn't rise very far before tumbling.

he placed a stop at 14.57, three cents below the valley at B, for a potential loss of about 10%.

"I expected price to stall near the April high at 18.50," Jake said and pointed to his notes on the computer screen. He read, "I don't expect this to work out well. I think the market is about to tumble. Guess I was right on Guess."

"Why did you buy it?"

He searched through his notes then read, "I bought the Eve & Eve double bottom. The apparel market seems to be doing well. In the last few days, the stocks have moved higher, strongly. Many are like this one: They've reached a yearly high then backtracked and are struggling to recover. The bad new is that Guess has a PE (price to earnings ratio) of 50. Ouch. I have my doubts about this one working, but if the market continues to climb, this might do well, too."

On July 16, he was stopped out at 14.55, two cents below his stop price and just a day before the stock made a bullish tail at C. The market continued down into early August before staging a nice up move leading into October.

"I lost $1,600 on the trade." He slumped in the chair.

I stood up and picked a piece of straw off the chair, ready to return to the horses. "Don't you remember that you made a bundle two weeks ago?"

"Yeah. Fifteen grand. I had a good week." He smiled and his dimple mixed with the sun's rays sprinkled from the nearby window.

"Exercise is good for you. Come help me in the barn."

His dimple disappeared and so did he. Good help is hard to find these days.

9. Triple Bottoms (Tied with 10)

- Average rise rank: 10
- Breakeven failure rate rank: 4
- Change after trend ends rank: 4

If you know what a double bottom looks like, you can imagine what a triple bottom (TB) looks like. Triple bottoms tie with head-and-shoulders in terms of overall performance. The average rise measures 37%, ranking the triple bottom tenth out of 23 contenders. The breakeven failure rate is 4%, meaning that just 4% of the triple bottoms failed to rise at least 5%, placing triple bottoms in fourth place. Finally, once price reaches the ultimate high, it tumbles 33%, also placing the pattern fourth.

Identification

Identification of triple bottoms shares many of the guidelines of double bottoms. Look for three valleys, all bottoming at about the same price, widely spaced so that they are not part of the same valley, and with a distinct peak between them. I set no minimum price rise between the valleys as I did with double bottoms because these patterns are rare enough without such qualifiers. Here are the guidelines:

- Prices should trend downward to the first valley, but should not drop below it. In other words, you don't want to see a sinkhole before the first valley.
- The three bottoms should appear near the same price, but allow variations.
- Several weeks usually separate each valley.

- Volume trends downward 67% of the time from the first bottom to the last, but may be high beneath the individual valleys.
- Price must close above the confirmation price (above the highest peak in the pattern) before the pattern becomes a true triple bottom.
- If a double bottom forms a third bottom before the double bottom confirms, treat it as a triple bottom.

Figure 6.19 shows an example of a triple bottom. Price trends downward to the bottom. The three bottoms, 1, 2, and 3, are near the same price level. Each bottom is a valley in its own right with a rise between them. Volume trends downward but is high beneath the base of each valley in this example. When the stock closes above the price of point A, that confirms the chart pattern as a true triple bottom and signals a buy.

Trading and Trading Tips

If the rise between the first two bottoms is higher than is the rise between bottoms 2 and 3, draw a downsloping trendline connecting the tops.

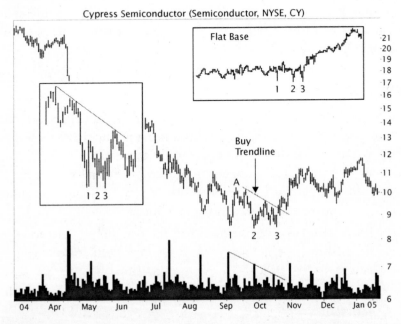

FIGURE 6.19   A triple bottom (valleys 1, 2, and 3) appears at the end of an extensive decline. A breakout occurs when price closes above the price of point A or above the downsloping buy trendline.

When price crosses this trendline, that's a buy signal. Figure 6.19 shows an example of this scenario.

Figure 6.20 shows another example of a triple bottom. In this example, bottom 3 is above the price level of bottom 2. When that situation happens, price after the breakout tends to move farther than when bottom 3 is at or below bottom 2. Every situation is different, but keep this one in mind.

The dashed line extending downward from point A shows an early buy trendline. The horizontal trendline from point A is the traditional buy signal. In this case, prices throw back to the breakout price before resuming their uphill run.

I also highlight a small flag. Flags often appear in strong, straight-line runs like the one shown in Figure 6.20, and they sometimes mark the midpoint of the rise. Thus, they have the nickname half-staff formations. The rise from the *bottom* of the flag to the trend end at B is nearly as long as the rise from point 3 to the *top* of the flag.

Here are additional trading tips:

- Triple bottoms that appear after a flat base tend to outperform. Look for a long (months) horizontal (or nearly so) price trend leading to the triple bottom. Use the weekly scale because the

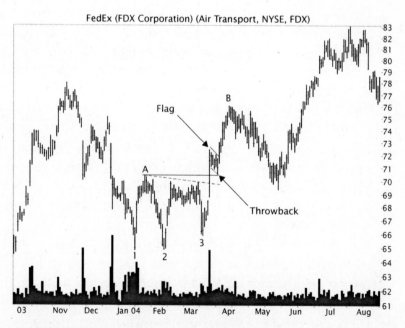

FIGURE 6.20 A triple bottom (1, 2, and 3) has a third bottom above the other two. This suggests a better performing triple bottom.

trend becomes clearer there. The pattern does well because price pushes its way through overhead resistance to find clear skies above, and ample room to rise. The flat base–triple bottom combination is the best setup for triple bottoms. The inset of Figure 6.19 shows the flat base, triple bottom setup.

- Triple bottoms often appear as the corrective phase of a measured move up (picture a flat step in a rising staircase). The rise after the breakout may not be as high as you expect. Avoid trading triple bottoms that occur after an extensive (months) price uptrend. The trend may be ending.

- When a triple bottom appears after a decline, draw a downsloping trendline along the peaks before the triple bottom. Expect price to stall once it reaches the trendline. It may push through the overhead resistance, but play it safe. The left inset in Figure 6.19 shows this situation on the weekly scale. Price reaches the trendline then collapses.

- Triple bottoms with short-term declines leading to the pattern have postbreakout rises averaging 39%. Intermediate-term declines yield rises of 35% and long-term declines, 37%. Trade triple bottoms with short-term declines.

- Here's another variation on the small decline scenario: Triple bottoms with a price decline less than the 21% median decline leading to the chart pattern have postbreakout rises averaging 44% versus 29% for those with a larger decline. A triple bottom that forms after an extensive decline suggests serious problems that will take time to fix. The rise after the breakout is often just a retrace in a downtrend, not a trend change.

- If a triple bottom appears after a decline from a peak, assume that prices will stall when they return to the peak. The triple bottom becomes the valley between two mountain ranges. This is a variation of a big W chart pattern (ends D and E) (see Figure 6.17 and accompanying text).

- If the third bottom has a flat top, then swing traders should buy when price closes above the flat threshold and sell at the confirmation price if price stalls there. Place a stop just below the bottom. This is similar to the shelf shown in Figure 6.17.

- For position traders and investors, buy when price closes above the confirmation price—the highest peak between the three bottoms (or above a downsloping trendline connecting the peaks between the bottoms. See the earlier discussion).

- Throwbacks happen 64% of the time and when they do occur, performance suffers: 41% rise postbreakout without throwbacks versus 34% with throwbacks.
- If the last valley bottom is above the price of the second valley bottom, then expect better performance: 43% average rise versus 32%.

Measuring Success

The measure rule for triple bottoms is the pattern's height added to the breakout price. This works 64% of the time, so be conservative when picking a price target (that means select a closer target). If the target is near overhead resistance, then expect price to stall there.

For example, point A in Figure 6.20 shows the highest peak in the pattern and the lowest valley at point 1. The height is the difference between those two, 70.40 − 64.84, or 5.56. Add the height to the highest peak to get a target of 75.96.

Case Study

Jake looked over my shoulder and groaned. "Not another one. Why don't you show them one of my winning trades?"

"Because the reader learns from your mistakes. Like this one." I pointed at the screen and Figure 6.21 shows the image. "You should have known the trade wouldn't work out."

"Your hindsight works perfectly."

I swung my chair around and faced him. That's when I noticed his gold cuff links. Exquisite. "Tell me about the trade." He went to the keyboard 8 feet away and started typing, pulling up his notes.

"First, let me say that it was a long time ago, when I didn't know what I was doing. Anyway, I put a *limit order* to buy 400 at 28 on the triple bottom confirmation of 27.88. The limit order should have been a stop order to buy. So, I picked up the 400 at 27.64 instead of 28."

> **limit order**
> an order to buy for no more or to sell for no less than a specified price.

He predicted overhead resistance would hit at 30 and then again at 32, corresponding to knots of price action at those levels in June.

FIGURE 6.21 Resistance highlighted by a downsloping trendline warned of this failed triple bottom trade.

"Upside was 36, near the old high where I thought I'd sell."

On the downside, he was looking at a 14% loss to 24.50, the price at valley 2.

"This trade might have worked out except for one thing," he said. "I bought two days before 9/11, when the terrorists struck."

Trading resumed on 9/17 and the price touched the downsloping trendline on that day then drilled down.

"I used a mental stop at 24.50, but price shot through that and I sold at 23.64, a day before price bottomed. I expected the price to continue moving down."

"This is an example of market risk," I said. "Something comes along and just pulls the rug out from under you. That's why you want to be out of the market as much as possible. Unlike you, I was lucky. I sold Alaska Air three trading days before 9/11 for a loss of less than $250. Had I waited until 9/27, I would have lost over $4,000. The stock was down 44% from where I sold."

10. Head-and-Shoulders Bottoms (Tied with 9)

- Average rise rank: 9
- Breakeven failure rate rank: 3
- Change after trend ends rank: 6

The head-and-shoulders formation is arguably the most famous of the chart patterns, but that distinction is reserved for tops, not bottoms. Still, the head-and-shoulders bottom (HSB) ranks tenth for overall performance. The average rise is 38% in a bull market, placing it ninth. The breakeven failure rate is quite low, 3%, ranking third. Finally, once the trend changes after price reaches the ultimate high, prices tumble an average of 31% for sixth place.

Identification

Figure 6.22 shows a near perfect example of a HSB. The head protrudes well below the bottoms of the shoulders. The two shoulders look similar—needles in this case—and are nearly an equal distance from the head. They look symmetrical, which I consider important. The volume pattern, however, is backward. Most often, you'll find volume heaviest beneath the left shoulder or head, and diminished below the right shoulder. A neckline joins the armpits and slopes downward in this case and in most HSBs. When price closes above the neckline, that's the buy signal and it confirms the pattern as a valid HSB. Without confirmation, you don't have an HSB.

To identify HSBs, look for the following:

- Find three valleys with the center valley below the other two.
- The shoulders should appear similar in shape.
- The shoulders should be almost equidistant from the head.
- The shoulders should have valleys that stop near the same price.
- Volume is highest on the head 48% of the time, the left shoulder 37% of the time and the right shoulder 15% of the time.
- Volume trends downward 66% of the time (between the left and right shoulder valleys).

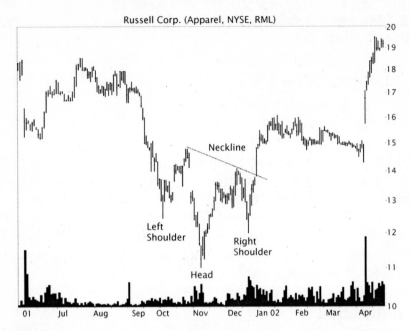

FIGURE 6.22 Shown is a head-and-shoulders bottom with pronounced shoulder symmetry and a downsloping neckline. Only the volume pattern is backward in this otherwise perfect example.

Trading and Trading Tips

Figure 6.23 shows another example of an HSB. In this example, the bottom of the right shoulder is above the price of the left, but they are close enough. The shoulders look similar and are almost the same distance from the head. Volume is highest on the head.

A neckline joins the armpits and signals a buy when price closes above it. This works well when the neckline slopes downward as in Figure 6.22, but you can see what a disaster it is in Figure 6.23. You give up profit by waiting (price closes above the neckline at point A). In fact, sometimes the neckline slopes so steeply that price never closes above it. That's like walking to school uphill, both ways.

A solution to the steep neckline problem is to use the highest peak in the pattern as the buy signal. When price closes above the value of the highest peak, buy. I show this scenario in Figure 6.23 as the dashed line.

Here are additional trading tips. Many are the same as for triple bottoms.

- For downsloping necklines, a close above the trendline signals a buy.

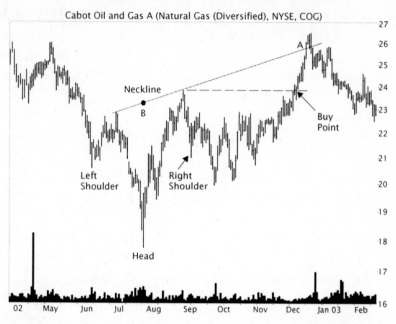

FIGURE 6.23 A head-and-shoulders bottom appears with an upsloping neckline. Buying using the traditional method of price closing above the neckline can lead to reduced profits. Instead, when the neckline slopes upward, draw a horizontal line from the highest peak in the pattern and buy when price closes above it.

- For upsloping necklines, use a close above the highest peak in the HSB as the buy signal.

- HSBs that appear after a flat base tend to outperform. Look for an extended horizontal price move of several months duration before the HSB forms.

- When price declines in a straight line run leading to the HSB, expect price to recover to the top of the pattern. Figure 6.17 shows a big W pattern (ends D and E). The HSB replaces the double bottom. Expect price to stall or reverse at E.

- HSBs with short-term declines leading to the pattern have post-breakout rises averaging 42%. Intermediate-term declines yield rises of 37%, and long-term declines give rises of 32%.

- Throwbacks happen 45% of the time and when they do occur, performance suffers: 43% rise postbreakout without throwbacks versus 32% with throwbacks. Avoid selecting patterns with overhead resistance that may cause a throwback.

- When volume is higher on the right shoulder, the HSB tends to outperform: 40% average rise versus 37%.
- Postbreakout performance improves for those HSBs with downsloping necklines: 42% average rise versus 34% rise for those with upsloping necklines.
- HSBs with a falling volume trend from shoulder to shoulder outperform: 39% average rise versus 36% for those with a rising volume trend.
- Patterns taller than the 18.81% median height divided by the breakout price rise an average of 41% postbreakout versus 36% for short HSBs.
- Breakout day gaps occur 18% of the time. HSBs with a breakout day gap rise 43%. Those without a gap rise 37%.
- HSBs with breakouts near the yearly high perform best, 42% average rise versus 37% for those in the middle and lower thirds of the yearly price range.
- Ninety percent acted as reversals of the prior price trend.
- From the right shoulder valley, it takes an average of 16 days for the stock to climb to the breakout price.

Measuring Success

The measure rule for HSBs is slightly different than for other chart patterns. First, compute the pattern height from the head vertically to the neckline. In Figure 6.23, the black dot at B shows the neckline intersection at about 23.25. Directly below, the head low is at 17.75 for a height of 5.50. Add the height to the breakout price to get a target. Using the highest peak in the pattern as the breakout point (23.83) would mean a target of 29.33. Using a trendline pierce as the breakout (25.59) would give a target of 31.09.

For the statistics, I used the average price of the neckline start and end points (the two armpits) instead of projecting it upward from the head to the neckline. Prices meet this measure rule 74% of the time.

"What's next?" Jake asked.

"I'm thinking of buying American Power Conversion Corp. It's showing a rectangle top, and it just completed a throwback."

He smiled. "I meant, what's next in the book?"

"Common chart patterns. They act as wrenches when your teeth won't do. Let me show you."

7

Common Patterns for the Toolbox

J ake held up a pile of papers an inch thick. He slammed it down on my desk as if to make a point. "They have a fleet of private jets, all manned with flight crews. They own three choppers. Their executive suite has 35 vice presidents, each earning over $300,000. Plus, they all get stock options worth seven figures, cars, massive expense accounts—"

"What are you talking about?"

"My health insurance company! I finished researching them. They own real estate, a co-op in Manhattan, box suites at the track, sports arena, and opera, bodyguards for the big boys. . . . No wonder my premiums go up each quarter by double digits!"

"Why don't you just change companies and be done with it?"

"I can't. If the health insurance company denies your application, your name goes on a computerized black list that other companies check before issuing coverage. I can't take the chance. I have to wait five years for my medical history to clear before I apply to a new company. What good is universal coverage if you can't afford it?"

"Take a deep breath, Jake. Every problem has a solution. Your trading has improved enough that you're making money on a consistent basis. That income is high enough to pay those premiums with plenty left over. If you make your stock selections carefully, use stops on each trade, and have some luck, you'll be able to self-insure. Imagine telling the insurance company to get lost because you have ten million bucks in the bank protecting you."

He unclenched his fists, sat back in the chair, and smiled. "What are your favorite patterns to trade?"

I will trade almost any chart pattern provided the setup looks good. This chapter looks at more chart patterns. Some will help you get out near the top. Others tell you how far price is likely to move. They help you avoid buying too soon or they suggest staying longer in a trade. They are specialized tools you will need to diversify your toolbox and help make money easier.

I'm going to mention a lot of boring performance numbers in the trading tips section of each chart pattern. For a pattern you're interested in trading, piece together the tips you find valuable. If tall patterns outperform short ones by a huge margin, then put that on your selection checklist. If a decreasing volume trend is important, put it on your list. Consider the tips as menu items from which to choose and then apply them to your chart pattern selections. The results can help you select better performing patterns.

Broadening Patterns

Broadening patterns come in six varieties and we've seen one already, the ascending broadening wedge. I cover the others here. The first two are broadening tops and bottoms. The difference between the two is how price enters the pattern. Tops have price entering from the bottom. Bottoms have price dropping into the pattern.

My study of this pattern confirms the breakout direction is random, so wait for the breakout instead of guessing. Just because price is trending downward doesn't mean the breakout will be downward. Remember that.

Broadening Tops and Bottoms

Figure 7.1 shows an example of a broadening bottom. Price enters the pattern from the top and eases out the bottom before reversing in late February and embarking on a sustained up move.

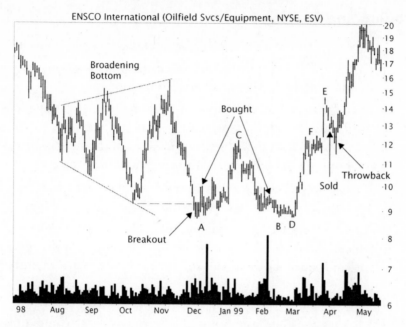

FIGURE 7.1 A broadening bottom led to two profitable trades.

Identification

When trying to identify broadening tops (BT) or bottoms (BB), look for the following:

- Bottoms have prices trending downward into the chart pattern; tops have prices trending upward.

- Find a megaphone price trend—higher peaks and lower valleys. Price broadens out over time, giving the pattern its name.

- Prices follow two trendlines. The top trendline slopes upward and the bottom one slopes downward.

- Price should touch each trendline at least twice.

- Price should cross the pattern from side to side and not leave much white space. Too much white space and you risk trading a pattern that does not exist. The trendline touches need not alternate but usually do.

- Volume trends upward between 57% and 60% of the time. That is not much above a random 50%, so don't depend on it.

Trading and Trading Tips

Here are some general trading tips for broadening tops and bottoms:

- For skilled swing traders, buy when price bounces off the lower trendline and sell when it reverses at the top one.
- For all traders, buy after price touches the lower trendline for the third time. Watch for a partial rise to occur, but hope for an upward breakout. A partial rise occurs 25% of the time in broadening bottoms and 49% of the time in broadening tops.
- If price drops below the lower trendline, then sell a long holding because the breakout is downward.
- Trade in the direction of the breakout. That means buying after an upward breakout. But where is the breakout? If price punches through one of the trendlines and closes outside it, that's a breakout.

For broadening tops (price trends upward into the pattern):

- The best postbreakout gains (38% average rise) come after an intermediate-term rise leading to the pattern, followed by short-term (32% rise) and long term (21% rise). Downward breakouts follow the same trend with intermediate, short, and long terms doing well, in that order.
- Those with breakouts near the yearly low perform best, regardless of the breakout direction.
- Upward breakouts on light volume have better performance.
- BTs with downward volume trends perform better after the breakout, regardless of the breakout direction.
- A partial decline correctly predicts an upward breakout 72% of the time.
- A partial rise works 61% of the time.
- The breakout is upward 50% of the time.
- Prices throw back (upward breakouts) 54% of the time and pull back (downward breakouts) 48% of the time. Throwbacks hurt postbreakout performance (24% average rise postbreakout versus 34% without throwbacks), but pullbacks have no influence on performance.
- The median height divided by the breakout price is 14.66% for upward breakouts and 15.95% for downward breakouts. Tall BTs

perform substantially better than short ones for both breakout directions.

For broadening bottoms (price trends downward into the pattern):

- The best postbreakout gains (30% average rise) come after a short-term decline leading to the pattern, followed by the long-term (24%) and intermediate-term (23%) rises. Downward breakouts show the intermediate-term trend doing best but samples are few.

- Those with upward breakouts near the yearly high perform best (30% average rise, postbreakout), the lowest third comes in second at 28%, and the middle third is last at 24%. Downward breakouts have too few samples to be meaningful.

- Upward breakouts with downward volume trends throughout the pattern show the largest rise postbreakout. Downward breakouts with rising volume trends perform best (prices decline farthest).

- A partial decline correctly predicts an upward breakout 80% of the time.

- A partial rise works 67% of the time.

- The breakout is upward 53% of the time.

- Prices throw back (upward breakouts) 41% of the time and pull back (downward breakouts) 42% of the time. Throwbacks hurt postbreakout performance (25% versus 28% without throwbacks). Pullbacks are similar with postbreakout declines averaging 12% for those with pullbacks versus 17% for those without.

- The median height divided by the breakout price is 15.13% for upward breakouts and 17.50% for downward breakouts. Tall BBs perform marginally better than short ones for both breakout directions.

Measuring Success

Use the measure rule to help predict a price target. Find the height of the pattern from the highest peak to the lowest valley in the pattern. For upward breakouts, add the height to the breakout price (where price crosses the trendline boundary). Price reaches the measure rule target between 59% and 62% of the time.

For downward breakouts, subtract the height from the breakout price. The result is the target but this works only 37% to 44% of the time. For both breakout directions, it might be best to use half the formation height, instead of the full height, to find a price target.

Case Study

Here is my notebook entry for the first trade (point A in Figure 7.1):

> 12/8/98. I bought 500 shares at market and received a fill at 9.75. *RSI* says it's oversold and the stock has hit the bottom of a broadening formation. Oil service stocks were strong yesterday on a small rebound in oil price. MACD just turned green yesterday, but is in negative territory. CCI said buy 3 days ago. Looks like resistance at 14 and again at 17. Stop should be at the bottom of the formation, about 8, call it 7⅞. The way the markets are acting, I would say this will traverse to the other side of the formation, but you never know. Somehow, that sounds just too optimistic especially with oil predicting to go into single digits. Pessimism abounds. I trimmed my 1,000 share buy to 500 on the uncertainty.

For those versed in technical indicators, the relative strength index (RSI) was oversold, meaning price was unusually low and represented a bargain. But the stock could go on sale tomorrow at an even lower price. The moving average convergence/divergence histogram (MACD) suggested that momentum was turning upward (green). As a swing-trading indicator, the commodity channel index (CCI) issued a buy three days before I bought, suggesting a short-term trade. (Please note: I use indicators like CCI, RSI, MACD, and Bollinger bands on a sporadic basis with default settings. Since this is a book about chart patterns and not indicators, I don't detail how the indicators work in this text.)

RSI
the Welles Wilder relative strength index, a price momentum indicator.

Unfortunately, I did not log the entry for the second buy; but I grabbed 1,000 shares at 9.56 on February 8. Together, the two trades represented an investment of about $14,500.

Bottoms A and B are an Eve & Eve double bottom, with a confirmation point at C. If I had seen the EEDB at the time, I am sure I would have stayed in the trade instead of selling on April 1. Price threw back to the double bottom breakout price and then rebounded, as is usually the case.

A measured move up, with the stair step-rise from D, a pause at F, and completing the pattern at E, pointed the way higher. Price often falls back to the corrective phase (F) as it did in this case, before rebounding. I may have been worried about the quick rise leading to E. Quick declines often follow quick rises, and you can see how price slid like a car on ice, giving back all of the gains from the two-day rise.

Expecting a short-term trend change, I sold the stock at 13, pocketing $19,500 for a net gain of over $5,000 or about 35%, including dividends.

Descending Broadening Wedge

Figure 7.2 shows the next type of broadening pattern, a descending broadening wedge (DBW). It's similar to the ascending variety that I discussed in Chapter 6, but this one has trendlines pointing downward.

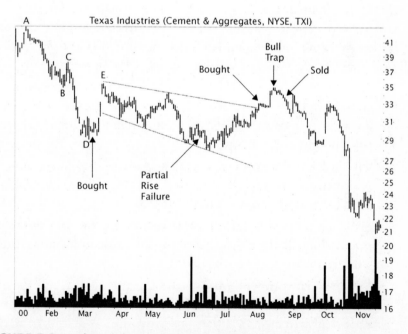

FIGURE 7.2 A descending broadening wedge led the way to riches but only for a few weeks before a bull trap became clear.

Identification

The following tips identify a descending broadening wedge:

- Look for two downsloping trendlines that broaden out—a megaphone tilted down.
- Price should touch each trendline at least twice.
- Price should cross the pattern from trendline to trendline.
- Volume trends upward 66% of the time.

Trading and Trading Tips

I found 47 DBWs with downward breakouts and 270 with upward breakouts in a bull market. Since downward breakouts are so rare, I only discuss those with upward breakouts.

Research from the second edition of my *Encyclopedia of Chart Patterns* (John Wiley & Sons, 2005) reveals that you should avoid trading DBWs that are both short and wide. By *short*, I mean the measure from the highest peak to the lowest valley in the chart pattern divided by the breakout price. Patterns both shorter than the median 21.77% in a bull market and wider than the median 52 days perform substantially worse than the other combinations of height and width. The average rise for short and wide patterns is 22%, but tall and narrow patterns showed prices climbing an average of 49% postbreakout. Keep that in mind the next time you are salivating over a descending broadening wedge. Choose wisely.

- For swing traders, trade between the trendlines. The best profit comes from the short side with this pattern because both trendlines slope downward. Short at the top trendline and cover when price bounces off the lower one.
- The best postbreakout gains (39% average rise) come after an intermediate-term rise leading to the DBW, followed by the long term (35% rise) and short term (33% rise).
- Sixty percent have breakouts above the 30-day average volume and prices climb 38% postbreakout. Light breakout volume shows worse performance with rises averaging 28%.
- Volume trends downward 34% of the time and those patterns show postbreakout rises averaging 35%. DBWs with upward volume trends average 33% rises postbreakout.

- A partial decline correctly predicts an upward breakout 87% of the time.

- Prices throw back 53% of the time. Throwbacks hurt postbreakout performance (37% average rise postbreakout versus 30% without throwbacks).

- The median height divided by the breakout price is 21.77%. Tall DBWs perform much better than short ones, with rises of 43% versus 26% respectively.

Measuring Success

Use the measure rule to set a price target. For DBWs, the target is the top of the pattern (point E in Figure 7.2). Price reaches the measure rule target 79% of the time, so be conservative in your estimates, especially for tall patterns.

Case Study

In a study I unearthed 464 DBWs and found that 79% broke out upward. So I decided to trade on that. Here's my notebook entry for the trade shown in Figure 7.2, during March:

> 3/8/00. I bought 400 shares at market this morning after the stock inched up from its low of 29.88. Filled at 30.06. In 10 days or so, the company will announce earnings. I think this will be stronger than expected because steel sales in the fourth quarter of 1999 improved, and I expect cement trends to be heavy as well. Looking forward, the economy may slow and this will hurt the company, as the Federal Reserve is intent on raising interest rates. Still, I expect this stock to recover somewhat, maybe completing a head-and-shoulders complex top. That's the time to get out. The target price for the MMD is 29.50.

The measured move down (MMD) is a stair-step pattern from A to D with the corrective phase B to C. In well-behaved patterns, the decline from C to D matches the drop from A to B. After reaching D, prices often return to the corrective phase as they did at E.

An earnings announcement sent prices gapping upward at E. Because I called this perfectly, it would have made a good swing trade: Buy where I did and sell on the earnings news. Did I sell? No. I held on expecting price to climb back to 39 or 40, forming another shoulder of a complex head-and-shoulders top (not shown). Picture a head-and-shoulders chart pattern in your mind and add additional shoulders for the complex variety. Complex patterns are rare, and I should not have bet on one happening.

In August, I bought more. Here's my notebook entry for that purchase:

> 8/3/00. I bought 300 shares at 33.0625 this morning. Reasons for purchase: It has made an upward breakout, on weak volume, from a descending broadening formation. The Federal Reserve is going to impose antidumping penalties as high as 95.29% on imports of certain types of coated-steel sheet. This may help the company. After reviewing statistics in my book, *Encyclopedia of Chart Patterns,* for descending broadening wedges, it looks like a good trade. Upside is 36, downside is 30, evenly split from 33. I think this will continue moving higher, maybe to the old high at 43.38.

The dreaming almost turned into a disaster as prices rounded over in a bull trap. That is when price breaks out upward and bullish traders jump into the stock. Everyone that wanted to buy the stock already has, so there is little buying demand to send the stock higher. Price drops, trapping bullish traders into a losing position. You see this on the charts as a curling action after a trendline break. If this happens to you, sell immediately and if you are an experienced trader, short the stock.

Here's how I handled it according to my notebook: "8/23/00. I sold 700 at 33.56. I think the stock is heading down as it is following the other stocks moving down. All are off their peaks by 1.50 to 2.50 points, and I don't see a turnaround."

On the two trades, I made 7% or over $1,500, including a dividend. That is not bad considering the massive loss I could have suffered had I not chewed off my leg and freed myself from the bull trap. The stock bottomed at 20.88 for a decline of 38% from where I sold.

Before we move onto the next pattern, look at the failed partial rise. A partial rise signals an impending downward breakout. The signal fails when price bounces off the bottom trendline instead of punching through. In a study of 270 patterns, a partial rise failure occurs 10% of the time. Just remember, the probability is not zero.

Right-Angled Broadening Formations, Ascending and Descending

Figure 7.3 shows two right-angled broadening formations, one is ascending (RABFA) and the other is descending (RABFD). Notice that one of the trendlines is horizontal and the other slopes away, forming a broadening pattern.

A partial rise or decline at the end of the pattern predicts an immediate breakout when price returns to the trendline. Partial rises and declines are early trading signals that I'll discuss in a moment.

Identification

Look for the following in the ascending variety of broadening patterns:

- The top trendline slopes upward (ascends).
- The bottom trendline is horizontal.

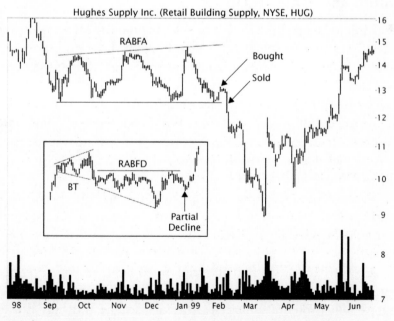

FIGURE 7.3 The figure shows a right-angled broadening formation ascending (RABFA) and descending (RABFD) along with a broadening top (BT).

- Prices broaden out over time.
- Prices should near or touch each trendline at least twice to assure a properly selected broadening pattern.
- Patterns with upward breakouts have volume that trends upward 51% of the time. Downward breakouts have upward volume trends 55% of the time.

The following are identification guidelines for the descending broadening pattern. Many are the same as in the ascending variety.

- The bottom trendline declines (descends).
- The top trendline is horizontal.
- Prices broaden out over time.
- Prices should near or touch each trendline at least twice to assure a properly selected broadening pattern.
- Patterns with upward breakouts have volume that trends upward 54% of the time. Downward breakouts have upward volume trends 59% of the time.

Trading and Trading Tips

In the inset to Figure 7.3, I show a broadening top (BT) with a downward breakout. Price enters the chart pattern from the bottom, hence the *top* characterization. The broadening top precedes a descending right-angled broadening formation in this example.

The RABFD pattern is typical except for the partial decline. Prices leave the top trendline and head lower but do not touch or come close to the bottom trendline before curling upward and soaring out the pattern top. A partial decline correctly predicts an upward breakout from an RABFD 87% of the time in a bull market.

When looking for a partial rise or decline, be sure the RABFA or RABFD pattern is established—the pattern must meet all of the identification guidelines. Also, the partial rise or decline never occurs *after* the breakout.

One way to verify a partial decline is to use a Fibonacci retrace of the prior up move. If price turns about 62% of the way down to the lower trendline, then assume it is a partial decline and buy. Pauses at 38% and 50% are also effective, but more risky, as price could continue lower instead.

The RABFA pattern shows a partial *rise,* and Bought points to it in Figure 7.3. A partial rise is when price touches the bottom trendline and begins moving up before curling over and heading down. In well-behaved patterns, a downward breakout follows 74% of the time, like that shown here.

For both RABFAs and RABFDs, try buying into the stock when price touches the bottom trendline for the third time and begins climbing. If a partial rise occurs or if price closes below the lower trendline, then sell immediately.

Watch for price to stall at the top trendline, but you might get lucky and have an upward breakout.

Consider these additional trading tips for RABFAs:

- Sixty-six percent breakout downward, so this is a bearish pattern.

- The best postbreakout gains (30% average rise) come after a short-term rise leading to the pattern, followed by the intermediate-term (29%) and the long-term (26%) rises.

- The samples are few for intermediate and long term, so do not rely on the numbers being solid. Downward breakouts show declines averaging 20%, 11%, and 12%, respectively, for the three terms.

- Those with upward breakouts near the yearly high perform best (31% average rise, postbreakout), and the other two-thirds tie at 18% each, but the sample size is small. For downward breakouts, the declines are 10%, 15%, and 21% for patterns with breakouts within a third of the yearly high, middle, and low, respectively.

- Patterns with upward breakouts on heavy volume perform best: 30% average rise postbreakout. Light breakout volume has rises averaging 22%. Downward breakouts have declines averaging 17%. Light breakout volume shows postbreakout declines averaging 11%.

- Patterns with downward volume trends from pattern start to end perform better than do those with upward volume trends, on average.

- A partial decline correctly predicts an upward breakout 81% of the time.

- A partial rise works 74% of the time.

- Prices throw back (upward breakouts) 47% of the time and pull back (downward breakouts) 65% of the time. Throwbacks hurt postbreakout performance (23% average rise versus 35% without throwbacks). Pullbacks are similar, with postbreakout declines averaging 15% for those with pullbacks versus 16% for those without.

- The median height divided by the breakout price is 13.24% for upward breakouts and 14.70% for downward breakouts. Tall patterns perform better than short ones for both breakout directions. Upward breakouts from tall patterns have rises that average 36% postbreakout versus 23% for short ones. Downward breakouts drop an average of 16% for tall patterns and 15% for short ones.

Also consider these additional trading tips for RABFDs:

- Fifty-one percent break out upward.
- The best postbreakout gains (31% average rise) come after intermediate- and long-term rises leading to the pattern. Prices after a short-term rise climb 28% postbreakout. The samples are few for intermediate- and long-term rises, so don't rely on the numbers being solid. Downward breakouts show declines averaging 13% (short term), 23% (intermediate term) and 16% (long term). Again, the intermediate- and long-term declines have few samples.

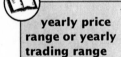

yearly price range or yearly trading range
the price range that the security traded over the prior 12 months. To determine the yearly trading range, start from the day before the breakout and find the highest peak and lowest valley over the prior 12 months. I divided the yearly price range into thirds and compared the breakout price with each third.

- Those with upward breakouts in the middle of the *yearly trading range* perform best (37% average rise, postbreakout), the highest third comes in second with a 27% rise, and the lowest third is last with an 11% rise, but the low and middle ranges have few samples. For downward breakouts, the declines are 16% (for middle and high thirds), and 14% (lowest third). The middle and high ranges have few samples.

- Upward breakouts perform better after a light volume breakout (37% average rise versus 26% for breakout volume above the 30-day average). Downward breakouts show heavy breakout volume leading to larger declines postbreakout, but the performance difference is minimal and the samples few.

- A partial decline correctly predicts an upward breakout 63% of the time.

- A partial rise works 54% of the time.
- Prices throw back (upward breakouts) 52% of the time and pull back (downward breakouts) 51% of the time. Throwbacks hurt postbreakout performance (21% average rise versus 36% without throwbacks). Pullbacks are similar with postbreakout declines averaging 15% for those with pullbacks versus 16% for those without.
- The median height divided by the breakout price is 13.13% for upward breakouts and 14.20% for downward breakouts. Tall patterns perform better than short ones for both breakout directions. Upward breakouts from tall patterns have rises that average 35% postbreakout versus 23% for short ones. Downward breakouts drop an average of 18% for tall patterns and 13% for short ones.

Measuring Success

Use the measure rule to predict a target price. The rule is the same as for broadening tops—the height added to or subtracted from the breakout price. For upward breakouts from RABFAs, price reaches the measure rule target 68% of the time. For downward breakouts, the success rate is just 32%. For RABFDs, upward breakouts hit the target 63% of the time and downward breakouts meet or exceed the target 44% of the time.

I consider the performance poor, so be conservative in your projections. Look for overhead resistance and underlying support to better gauge where price is likely to reverse. As with many other chart patterns, you can try using half the pattern height in the computation to find a target price.

Case Study

Figure 7.3 shows the sample trade in a RABFA. Here are my recollections:

> On the expectation of price zipping across the pattern to the top trendline, I bought 800 shares at 13 once it was clear that price was moving up. At that time, I purchased stock in a minimum of $10,000 lots, so this buy was for $10,400. When price curled around and dropped below the horizontal trendline, that was the sell signal. I was stopped out of 600 shares at 12.38 and the other 200 at 12.34. I lost just over $500 on the trade, or 5%, but a massive $34 dividend boosted the return. Okay, so it wasn't *massive*, but it was an unexpected gift.

"I love free money," Jake said, "especially when it's a qualified dividend that's subject to a lower tax rate." This dividend didn't qualify because the hold time was too brief.

The stock tumbled to a low of 8.94, for a decline of 28% below my sell price.

If a chart pattern doesn't work as expected, then close out the trade and do it quickly! If you were trading this stock, would you have sold or ridden the stock lower?

Diamond Tops and Bottoms

Some years ago, I wrote a romance novel in which the main character walks into a jewelry store with his girlfriend and picks out a diamond ring priced at $25,000. Later, he returns to the store alone and tells the owner to substitute the diamond rock for cubic zirconium. She finds out about the switch, learns how much he makes—a quarter million—and calls him cheap, starting a fight that propels the story forward.

His feelings about diamonds echo my own. Both the rock and the ones on the computer screen are pretty, sure, but both can be difficult to trade.

Figure 7.4 shows two diamond patterns. In early November, price plunges after point A then consolidates and forms a diamond bottom pattern before shooting upward to B. Notice how the price at A and B are about equal. A quick rise/decline often follows a quick decline/rise.

The diamond top pictured in the inset shows the same situation flipped upside down, although the rise and decline take longer to form. Price begins the rise at D and ends at E. Point C is a pullback, where price returns to the breakout price briefly before continuing down. Notice the premature (false) breakout on the top. Because price turned around and broke out downward, the chart pattern is a busted diamond, suggesting lower prices ahead.

As an end-of-day trader, I would have missed the diamond bottom by buying into the situation a day after the breakout—the day before prices peaked at B. If you are a nimble swing trader, diamonds might be trading candidates, but for everyone else, I'd steer clear. Use them as guideposts lining the way along the price path.

One last comment about diamonds. They have a high performance rank (downward breakouts are ranked 1, best, tied with head-and-shoulders tops), but I discarded them because of few samples.

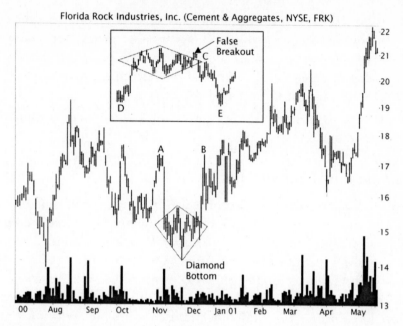

Florida Rock Industries, Inc. (Cement & Aggregates, NYSE, FRK)

FIGURE 7.4 A diamond bottom appears after a quick decline. A quick rise often follows, returning prices back to the launch point.

Identification

What should you look for when prospecting for diamonds? Glue a broadening top or bottom with a symmetrical triangle and you'll have forged a diamond. At the start of the pattern, prices broaden out, forming higher peaks and lower valleys (a broadening top or bottom). Then the price action reverses, forming lower peaks and higher valleys (a symmetrical triangle). If you draw trendlines along the peaks and valleys, you should get something like that shown in Figure 7.4. Your diamond is apt to be lopsided as perfect ones are rare.

The identification guidelines for diamonds include the following:

- Look for a quick price rise or decline. Diamond tops have prices entering the diamond from the bottom and bottoms have prices entering from the top. The quick rise or decline, a straight-line run, is key. Yes, you will find other diamonds forming as a normal congestion pattern, but the ones when prices race forward are easiest to spot.

- Look for prices to broaden out (higher peaks and lower valleys) then narrow forming a diamond shape. The diamond usually tilts to one side.

- Price should touch each trendline one or twice, but it depends on how you draw the diamond and whether prices cooperate with you. Don't be alarmed about cutting off price tails when you draw the trendlines. Sometimes you have to use your imagination to see the actual diamond shape.

- Sixty-six percent have a downward volume trend within the diamond.

Trading and Trading Tips

Here are some trading tips. One of these I want to pass on applies to all chart patterns that act as reversals of the prevailing price trend, but especially diamonds. *Price must have something to reverse.* If price is moving sideways for a month or two and bumps up two bucks and then a diamond reversal appears (meaning it has a downward breakout, reversing the rise leading to the diamond), expect price to return to the base two bucks below. Don't expect a larger decline because there is little price rise to reverse. A larger decline does happen on occasion, but that's not how to finesse the probabilities.

When the diamond acts as a continuation or congestion pattern, meaning that price exits the diamond traveling in the same direction that it entered, the diamond can act as a half-staff pattern. That means the rise (decline) after the diamond mirrors the rise (decline) after the breakout in price change, elapsed time, and slope. Look for overhead resistance or underlying support as locations where price is likely to stall as the target price approaches. The postbreakout move will not be as long as the move leading to the diamond, so keep that in mind, too. For example, my study of 69 diamond bottoms had a decline before the diamond of 24% and a postbreakout drop averaging 21%.

Another idea I tested concerned *velocity.* A high velocity move leading to the pattern resulted in better postbreakout performance than did a slow velocity move. For example, prices climbed 26% after the breakout from a diamond top with velocity below the median 7 cents per day. Those with higher velocity leading to the diamond climbed 29% postbreakout. Diamond bottoms were similar. Low velocity trends saw postbreakout drops of 17%, but high velocity trends suffered declines of 23%. *High velocity moves leading to a chart pattern result in high velocity moves after the breakout.* This assumes that the chart pattern is a continuation pattern (not a reversal).

Here are additional trading tips:

- Diamonds with short-term price trends leading to the pattern perform better than intermediate- or long-term trends. Diamond tops with downward breakouts show the best results: Short-term declines leading to the pattern yielded 24% declines postbreakout; intermediate-term trends averaged a 22% decline, and long-term declines had postbreakout declines of 15%.

- Avoid overhead resistance or underlying support. Diamonds with throwbacks or pullbacks have postbreakout performance that suffers. For example, diamond bottoms with upward breakouts and throwbacks show rises averaging 30%. Those without throwbacks climb 43%.

- Select tall patterns for the best performance. Compute the height from highest peak to lowest valley in the pattern and then divide the height by the breakout price. For diamonds bottoms, patterns above the 13% median are tall. For tops, use an 11% median.

- Diamonds with upward volume trends do better postbreakout than do those with falling volume trends. For example, diamond bottoms with upward breakouts and rising volume trends within the diamond soared 41% after the breakout but climbed 35% when volume receded.

- Diamond bottoms perform best when the breakout is near the yearly low (42% rise) and worst is near the yearly high (26% rise), regardless of breakout direction.

Measuring Success

As Figure 7.4 shows, price after the breakout often retraces the move leading to the diamond, but not always. When a quick, near vertical price move precedes the diamond, look for price to return to the launch point (assuming the diamond is a reversal like those shown in the figure).

The measure rule for diamonds is no different than for other chart patterns. Measure the height (highest peak to lowest valley) and add it to the price of an upward breakout or subtract it from the breakout price of a downward breakout. A breakout occurs when price closes outside the diamond trendline boundary. The following list shows how often the measure rule works:

- Diamond tops, upward breakout: 69%
- Diamond tops, downward breakout: 76%
- Diamond bottoms, upward breakout: 81%
- Diamond bottoms, downward breakout: 63%

Because the numbers fall well short of 100%, be conservative in selecting your price target. Look for nearby support or resistance and expect price to reverse there. It may not, but it pays to be prepared. Try using half the pattern's height as it applies to the measure rule to get a closer target.

Case Study

I searched through my notebook of trades and found an example of a diamond trade I made (Figure 7.5). Here is my notebook entry:

> 8/18/03. I bought 450 shares at market, post split, filled at 25.17. This is an earnings flag trade, but I'm a few days late to the game. I hope for a 29.11 target with a downside of 24+ where it should meet support. Must sell is the bowl low of about 23.33 or so, but try to estimate an exit at 24. Upside is based on a 19% average rise of an earnings flag (EF) from the formation high.
>
> Although this has risen only 10% from the day before the earnings announcement to the formation high, about half the average, I'm still hoping for a continued rise. However, this one makes me nervous, and I did not want to trade it because I feel it will throw back as most EFs do. With the economy turning around and this making new yearly highs, it is a risky trade that I am willing to take. I have to monitor it, however, and if it starts to slip, then I will consider selling.

A three-for-two split occurred since I made my notebook entry, so I show the split-adjusted prices. That is why the amounts seem unusual. I illustrate the earnings announcement during July in Figure 7.5. Price climbed in a straight-line run up and then formed a pennant (which I call an "earnings flag" as the generic name for it). A buy signals when price closes above the highest peak in the chart pattern, point B in this case.

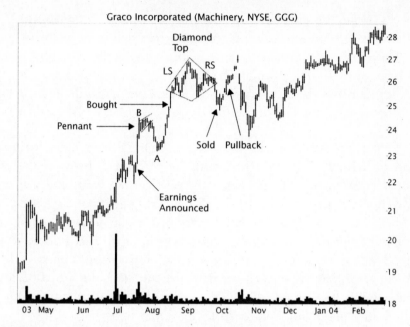

FIGURE 7.5 This diamond top scared me out of the stock because I thought price would decline back to the launch point at A.

The mention of a few days late in my notebook entry is because I bought two days after I should have. A better entry would be to have an existing order to buy the stock at the price of B so that when price reaches it, the order executes automatically.

The target price is point B multiplied by 19% to get a target of 29.11. Downside support at 24 was a good call as that's where price stalled in late October. The bowl low I refer to is the rounded turn at point A.

Here is my next notebook entry:

9/29/03. The market has tumbled for almost a week straight and this stock is down to my breakeven point. A head-and-shoulders top has confirmed, suggesting a sale. September is almost over, the worst month of the year, historically. October isn't much better though. Support from the July top at 24–24.67 should stop the downturn. I expect a decline to that level. My hope is that the market will turn around today and push the stock up—probably as a pullback to the head-and-shoulders top.

When the diamond top appeared, I suspected a downward breakout and retrace of its gains, but decided to go with the hope of a continued uptrend. Oops. The stock is up by a penny at 10 this morning (EST). I expect a continued decline to 23.33 where the stock will stall and move in a trading range between 23.33 and 24.67. If it drops below 23.10, then sell.

I show on the chart the left (LS) and right (RS) shoulders with the head of a head-and-shoulders top at the price peak between the two shoulders. When price closed below the valley low, between the head and right shoulder, that was the sell signal. I guessed right about a pullback to the head-and-shoulders, too. As I mentioned in the notebook entry, the breakout from the diamond top was a bearish omen that I chose to ignore. Hope will not make a stock rise. Here's my notebook entry: "I sold the stock anyway. Why wait for it to decline and take a $1,000 loss? Since I know it's going down, sell now near breakeven and buy in later if I think it's a good deal. Sold at 25.13."

I lost $45 on the trade. That's excellent. Imagine the stock tumbling to 23 (the price near point A), or lower.

Double Tops

Many investors recognize the name double top, but only the lucky ones can accurately pick it out of a lineup. What they miss is that price must confirm the pattern. That means price must close below the valley between the two peaks before any twin-peak pattern becomes a true double top. More about that later—first, let's talk about identification.

Identification

Figure 7.6 shows two double tops (DTs), Eve & Eve and Eve & Adam. DTs split into four combinations of Adam and Eve peaks, just as they did for double bottoms. Eve peaks are wide and rounded appearing. Adam peaks are narrow, usually composed of a long, one-day price spike. The inset shows an Adam top, and you can see how tall and narrow it is. Eve appears more rounded and wider. Here are the identification guidelines for DTs:

- Price trends upward to the double top. As I mentioned before, price must have something to reverse, and double tops act as reversal patterns.

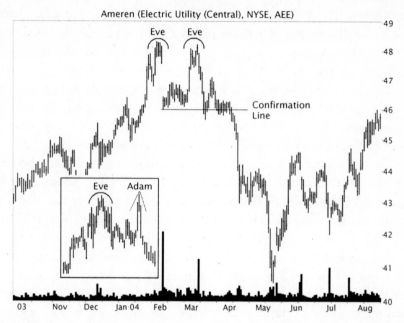

FIGURE 7.6 An Eve & Eve double top acts as a reversal of the upward price trend. Price confirms the pattern as a true double top when it *closes* below the confirmation line.

- Adam peaks are narrow, usually composed of one or two long price spikes.

- Eve peaks are wide and more rounded looking. They may have spikes, but the spikes are numerous and shorter.

- The valley between the two tops usually drops 10% to 20% or more.

- Peak to peak price variation is minor, usually 0% to 3%. The two peaks should appear near the same price.

- Most peaks are two to six weeks apart, but allow variation, especially on the top end. Performance deteriorates for tops spaced more than about two months apart.

- Price *must* close below the lowest valley between the two peaks; otherwise, it is not a double top. This is called *confirmation,* and I show the price as a line in Figure 7.6.

- Volume is usually heavier on the left peak than the right. Only Eve & Adam DTs have volume consistently heavier on the right peak.

Technically, the Eve & Eve double top in Figure 7.6 does not qualify as a true double top. Why? Because the decline between the two peaks measures just 5%, half what it should be, but you get the idea of what an Eve & Eve double top should look like.

Figure 7.7 shows the other two combinations of Adam and Eve tops. The Adam top has a tall, one-day price spike, and Eve is more rounded and wider. When trying to determine whether you have an Adam or Eve peak, ask yourself if the two peaks look similar. If so, then you have an Adam & Adam or Eve & Eve double top. If not, then you have the other two varieties: Adam & Eve or Eve & Adam. The left Adam top of the Adam & Adam pattern, if you ignore the one-day price spike, could be called an Eve top when you broaden the view a few weeks to the left.

Sometimes, looking at the base of the top will help differentiate between and Adam and Eve peak. It is not easy but Adam will usually remain narrow over much of its height. Eve will grow wider as you scan down the top toward the base. The inset shows this. Adam remains comparatively narrow but Eve broadens out. Figure 7.6 shows this clearly in the Adam peak.

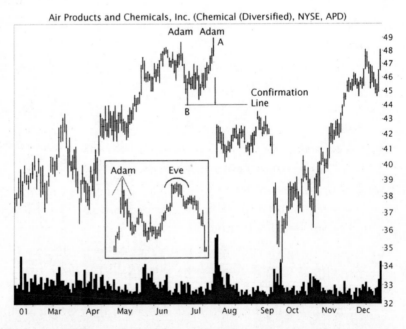

FIGURE 7.7 Shown are the other two combinations of Adam and Eve tops.

Why the emphasis on peak shape? Because performance varies depending on the type of pattern you are dealing with. Eve & Eve double tops are the classic chart pattern, the one people think of when they visualize a double top. Adam & Adam has the highest average decline after the breakout and the lowest failure rate of the four combinations, but stumbles when the trend changes, meaning that price does not recover as far. For that reason, Eve & Eve has a better overall performance rank, placing second. Adam & Adam places fourth. The other two are down the list at 13 (E & A) and 15 (A & E). *Encyclopedia of Chart Patterns,* 2nd ed. discusses the full range of performance statistics on the patterns.

Trading and Trading Tips

One quick statistic about double tops. I did research and found that if you sell your holdings before the double top confirms, you will be making a mistake 65% of the time. That's how often price resumes the uptrend before confirming the twin peak pattern as a true double top. For beginning traders, wait for confirmation before selling an existing position unless you have a compelling reason for selling immediately.

For tall patterns, compute the decline from the current price to the confirmation price. If the potential decline is a large one, then consider selling immediately, especially if the market or stocks in the industry are moving downward. If the stock drops to the confirmation price before reversing, you may save a bundle. Look for support areas between where the stock is trading and the confirmation price. Price may reverse at those support areas.

The *worst* (smallest) decline, postbreakout, comes from an Eve & Adam double top. Prices drop an average of 15% below the confirmation price (the best is an 18% decline, so the other combinations are similar). Can you tolerate a loss of that size? If not, then sell once the DT confirms. Since this is an average of 212 perfectly traded DTs in a bull market, your results will vary. Again, look for support zones where price might reverse and recognize that you can always sell now and buy back later at a lower price.

If you have a DT appear after a long-term *decline*, confirmation of the pattern may mean that the end of the trend is near (10% to 20% above the turning point and perhaps less than a month away). However, *don't* use that as an excuse to avoid selling. Just be aware that the trend may reverse soon.

Switch to a higher time scale than what you trade. For me, that means switching to the weekly scale. If you see a double top standing like two redwoods on a flat plane, expect price to return to ground level. In technical terms, price will often return to the flat base from which it grew, especially if the rise to the DT is a steep one.

The following are additional tips pulled from my spreadsheet of Eve & Eve double tops (EEDTs), the most plentiful of the four combinations. Much of what you learn here is applicable to the other combinations.

- Short-term trends leading to the pattern suggest better postbreakout performance than intermediate- or long-term trends. Short-term rises leading to the pattern yielded 20% declines postbreakout; intermediate-term trends averaged a 15% decline, and long-term trends had postbreakout declines of 16%.

- Avoid underlying support because it can cause a pullback. EEDTs with pullbacks have postbreakout performance that suffers; 16% decline for those with pullbacks versus 22% for those without.

- Select EEDTs narrower than the median 43 days. Narrow patterns outperform wide ones with losses of 20% versus 16%, respectively, after the breakout. In fact, all four combinations of double tops perform better when the pattern is tall or narrow. For EEDTs, tall means the height from the tallest peak to the lowest valley between the two peaks divided by the breakout price (the lowest valley). If the result is above the 17.13% median, then you have a tall pattern.

Measuring Success

Since measure rule performance for double tops is so poor, I changed it to be half the height subtracted from the breakout price. For EEDTs, prices reach the predicted target 73% of the time.

For example, the EEDT shown in Figure 7.8 has a higher right peak at 9.06. The valley low between the peaks is at 7.63. Take half of the difference to get the height (0.72). Subtract the result from the breakout price (7.63) to get a target of 6.91. The stock does not hit even this meager target as prices stop declining at 7.20.

Case Study

I use double top chart patterns in my trading as sell signals for long positions. When a double top confirms, I know that price is going down, but

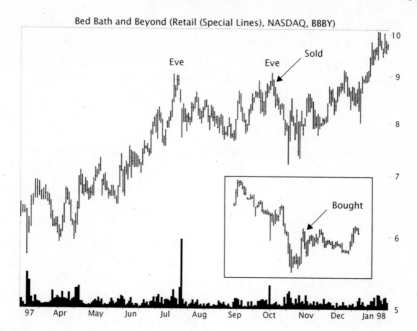

Bed Bath and Beyond (Retail (Special Lines), NASDAQ, BBBY)

FIGURE 7.8 I bought after a short-term downtrend and just after price reversed.

how far depends on underlying support. If the market is weak, I'll sell immediately. Rarely will I hang onto a stock, knowing that additional losses are coming. Here's an example from my notebook about how I used a double top:

> *7/22/96.* I purchased 800 shares at 5.81 today, at the market. Yesterday, I was reviewing my trend channel trades notebook and noticed that MACD forewarned me not to purchase Varco the first time and to wait on Health Management Systems. This indicator parallels the on-balance volume (OBV) & Bollinger band indicators. So, I compared its signal with Bed Bath and it said buy. OBV & Bollinger bands said the purchase was okay, too. Price just bounced off the trend channel bottom three days ago after hovering there for a while. Although I am late off the channel bottom in buying the stock, I trust it will continue rising. I did not buy earlier because general market conditions were horrible (general downturn), and I believed that the stock would continue down.

When it turned around, I bought. With its 30% annual growth rate in new stores and other fundamental factors, this stock could be a good holding for the long haul. If they can continue store growth with internally generated cash flow, this will be a good stock to own. If they get ahead of themselves, then the stock will suffer.

Nearly a decade ago, I fell in love with trend channels and did much research on them. Now, I rarely look at them. Your trading style will evolve over time, and you'll find that you toss off indicators and methods like spare change into a Salvation Army bucket. OBV and MACD are examples. I don't use them anymore because I found that they don't add value to *my* trading style. I recently added Bollinger bands back into my toolbox. These indicators are beyond the scope of this book, but I examined prior trades to see what worked and applied the lessons to this trade. That's important. If you can't learn from your mistakes, you won't be able to recognize them when they happen again—that's a joke.

linear regression

a mathematical method to fit a straight line to a series of numbers; the slope of the resulting line gives the trend.

The trend channel I write about in my entry is a channel of two parallel lines, each two standard deviations away from a centerline which I found using *linear regression* on prices. The problem with trend channels is locating proper starting and ending points. By selecting different points, you can make the channel look much different (both channel slope and width).

When price touches or nears the bottom channel line, it means that the stock is oversold, so it's a buy signal. I bought soon after prices bounced off the bottom, upsloping channel line.

I also mentioned checking the general market. I think a weak market is the major reason trades do not work out. Always check the market and industry trends before trading and learn to predict the future price direction of them.

I show the buy side (July 22, 1996) in the inset of Figure 7.8 on the daily scale. But on the weekly scale, the buy is at the bottom of the corrective phase of a measured move up chart pattern, suggesting further gains. I bought an additional 800 shares at 6.22 on October 31, 1996.

I held the stock for over a year. During that time, it moved up just after I bought then planed out like a speedboat and went horizontal. In early 1997, the stock started to make its move, but I did not get nervous until I saw a double top. From my notebook:

> Sunday, 10/4/97. I placed an order to sell half my holdings at the market tomorrow (800 shares). Why? A budding double top formation. I know that you should wait for confirmation, but the decline to 7.63 from the current 9.06 is just too far to wait (16% drop). If the stock continues to rise (fundamentally speaking, the prospects are bright), then I still have half my holdings. If it declines to the formation base, at 7.63, or continues down for another 18% (average for a double top reversal), then I'll have the opportunity to buy more.

Figure 7.8 shows where I sold the stock (filled at 8.88), the day after prices peaked at the second Eve top. For a swing trade, that was a good call, but this was a long-term holding. The stock did drop as I predicted and even confirmed the double top (which I consider lucky because the odds of it happening are slim, one in three), but prices soon recovered and vaulted to new highs—doubling in price.

I made $2,400 on the double top trade, or 52%. For the 800 shares I held onto, I sold them at 15.84 on February 1, 1999, for a profit of $7,650, or 153%. By selling before the double top confirmed, I was saving money in the short term but sacrificing it in the long term. In 2003, the stock reached a high of 45, almost 8 times my 5.81 purchase price. Along the way, the stock did have two spectacular dips of 45% that make potholes look like dental cavities by comparison, the first just three months after I sold.

Jake shook his head. "You're book is still boring. You need a joke right here." He jabbed his finger at my computer screen. "If a train station is where a train stops, then what's a work station?"

"There are three types of people in this world, Jake. Those who can count and those who can't. I have to get back to work."

Flags and Pennants

Flags and pennants are the workhorses of the swing trader. They appear as black little knots where price movement hangs in the balance, trying to decide whether to explode upward or plummet to earth. Often, they are called half-staff formations because they appear midway in the price trend—in theory. Unfortunately, price sometimes reverses just to keep traders guessing, and when the chart patterns do break out in the anticipated direction, they only hit their targets two out of three times at best.

Identification

How do you identify a flag or pennant and what's the difference between the two? Figure 7.9 shows the six varieties. Pennants occupy the top three figures and flags the bottom three. Pennants have two trendlines that converge but flag trendlines are essentially parallel. Both flags and pennants form after fast price moves, either upward or downward, when momentum pauses to catch its breath. The slope of the flag or pennant can be in any direction, but is usually against the prevailing price trend. That means if price is falling, the flag or pennant is likely to slope upward.

Here is what to look for when trying to identify flags or pennants:

- Look for price action bounded by two trendlines. If the trendlines converge, then it's a pennant. If the trendlines are essentially parallel, then it's a flag.

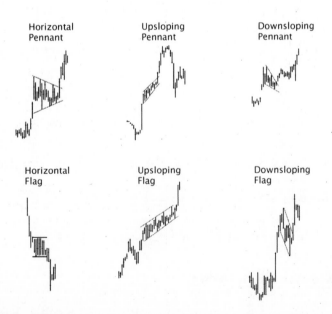

FIGURE 7.9 Pennant price action follows two converging trendlines while flags have parallel trendlines. Flags and pennants can slope in any direction but usually form against the prevailing price trend.

- Pennants and flags are shorter than three weeks. Patterns longer than that are channels, rectangles, symmetrical triangles, or wedges (rising or falling).

- The flagpole, the price run-up or -down leading to the flag or pennant, should be unusually steep and quick.

- Eighty-eight percent have a downward volume trend measured from the flagpole end to the day before the breakout (that is, the flag or pennant portion of the pattern, excluding the flagpole).

Trading and Trading Tips

As I was researching flags for this book, I read that a prominent author recommends buying before the flag or pennant breakout. A breakout occurs when price moves above (upward breakout) or below (downward breakout) the flagpole or trendline boundary on the flag or pennant. The case study in this section shows what happens when you follow that advice and buy before the breakout: You increase your risk of a loss. For that reason, I recommend you wait for a breakout before placing a trade. My numerous trades in an earnings flag reinforces the wait-for-breakout trading style.

Do flags and pennants that slope with the price trend predict improved performance? I researched this and found that the answer is no. Figure 7.9 shows examples of this scenario in the middle picture for each pattern ("Upsloping" flag or pennant). Contrast the upsloping pattern with the more prevalent downsloping ones (on the right of the figure). Remember, the price trend can also be down—imagine each picture flipped upside down.

I looked at 526 flags and 470 pennants and found that when the flag or pennant slopes in the direction of the prevailing price trend, performance suffers. For example, the postbreakout rise to the trend end in a downsloping pennant in a price uptrend is 24%. Those pennants with upsloping patterns climbed 17%. Flags were closer (20% versus 17%). Thus, *select flags or pennants that slope opposite the prevailing price trend for the best performance.*

If the flag or pennant appears near the top (upward breakout) or bottom (downward breakout) of a flat base, then expect the move to be a large one. This also applies to any chart pattern near the breakout from a flat base. A flat base, as you will recall, is when price trades in a horizontal (or near horizontal) range for months, bouncing from the high of the range to the low. When the breakout from this range occurs, prices often take off. A chart pattern forming just before or just after the breakout are areas where price seems to rest, gathering strength before resuming the trend.

Some additional trading tips include the following:

- This bears repeating: Trade flags and pennants only after price has made a sharp, quick move. Figure 7.10 shows an example in the January flag. Prices shoot up four points in four days.

- Pennants are more reliable than flags. In other words, the average rise after an upward breakout from a pennant is longer than one from a flag. That gives you more opportunity to profit from the trade, even if you are late to the game.

- Tight flags and pennants perform better than loose ones. By *loose*, I mean prices in the flag or pennant that poke outside the trend-line boundaries or contain white space and look jagged. Tight flags or pennants are solid blocks of black. Figure 7.10 shows an example of a loose and tight flag in the inset. Think of loose and tight as the difference between baggy pants and hip huggers. Embrace the huggers and lose the baggies.

- Avoid overhead resistance or underlying support. Patterns with throwbacks or pullbacks have postbreakout performance that suffers. For example, when a flag with an upward breakout has a throwback, prices rise 14% after the breakout. Those without throwbacks climb 26%, on average.

- Prices move up more than twice as far after tall patterns than short ones. Compute the height from highest peak to lowest valley in the flag or pennant (exclude the flagpole that is the move from A to B in Figure 7.10) and then divide the height by the breakout price. For both flags and pennants, patterns above the 6.68% median are tall. That is the difference between B and C in the figure, divided by C.

- Pennants with heavy breakout volume perform substantially better (30% versus 20% average rise postbreakout) than do those with breakout volume below the 30-day average. Flags show marginally better performance, 18% versus 16%.

- Flags and pennants act as half-staff patterns (the measure rule). Statistics show that the move from the trend start to the top of the flag averages 22% in 15 days, but the move from the flag low to the trend end measures 23% and takes 19 days. Pennants are similar but the rise is 27% in 14 days before the pennant and 25% in 23 days after. Because these numbers are averages, do not expect the flag or pennant to hit the target. Be conservative and choose a closer target. The next section describes this in detail.

- Pennants throw back 47% of the time and pull back 31% of the time.
- Flags throw back 43% and pull back 46% of the time.

Measuring Success

Flags and pennants have a measure rule and you already know what it is. Since flags and pennants often appear midway in a price trend, project price in the direction of the trend to get a target. For example, the flag in Figure 7.10 has a peak high (B) of 26.50, a low price where the trend starts of 22.50 (A) for a height of 4. For upward breakouts, the target would be the height added to the flag low (C at 25) for a target of 29.

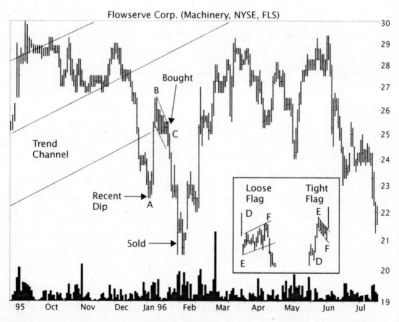

FIGURE 7.10 This flag unexpectedly broke out downward, creating a losing trade.

Since the breakout is downward, subtract the height from the high price at the end of the flag (just above C at 25.50) for a target of 21.50.

The inset to Figure 7.10 gives the following measure rule equations that might help you understand the measure rule. For downtrending flags or pennants, use F − (D − E). For uptrending patterns, use F + (E − D). D is the start of the flagpole; E is the end of it; and F is the end opposite the breakout direction.

The measure rules work 64% of the time for flags with price trending up, and 60% for pennants, so be conservative in your estimates. If price stalls as it nears the target, assume the move is over and consider taking profits. Using half the height in the target computation will improve your chances of a profitable trade.

Case Study

I don't consider myself a swing trader, so I don't actively trade flags. I do use them to project price movement (using the measure rule). Here's an example of the trouble you can get into when trying to trade a flag. Figure 7.10 shows the trade.

> 1/14/96. The stock is forming a flag formation. The measure of this is $4. The flag also happens to be on the bottom of the trend channel. I am going to buy 400 shares and pray. If the flag succeeds, that should net me about a $1,500 profit. If I hold for the duration of the channel swing, the profit could be $3,000. The stop-loss level, at $22.25, is just below the low of the recent dip [point A]. I think this might be a better channel play than a flag play.

I show the three trend channel lines, the middle of which is the linear regression line of prices. The outer two lines are two standard deviations away from the middle one. Because price was at the bottom of the channel, it was a good bet that price would rebound to the middle of the channel (where it often pauses) before continuing on to the top of the channel. Here's what my notebook says:

> 1/17/96. I expect to be stopped out of this stock tomorrow as it closed at 22.75 and my stop is for 22.25. There is a lesson here, and that is, if the formation and your expectations of its performance go wrong, sell it. In this case, the flag broke down

on high volume when the stock dropped 75 cents after purchase. I should have sold. Selling would have saved me about $900 (for a $300 loss including commissions). Instead, I will take a $1,200 loss.

1/23/96. I was stopped out of the stock today at $22. I lowered the stop by 1/8 point to 22.13. The decline seems to have caught me. As I watched the stock each day, it rose in the morning and fell in the last hour (except today: it sank from the beginning). It looked to me like manipulation as some mutual fund sold shares in the afternoon forcing the price down for whatever reason. Well, I should have sold the stock after the flag broke down. Instead, I now have a loss of $1,361. Live and learn.

The exit on this trade was bad for so many reasons. If a chart pattern doesn't do as you expect, then sell it and look for another more promising situation. I even refer to this on January 17, but I did nothing about it. If you feel that a stop is going to trigger, why not sell now and save yourself some money? Instead, I lowered the stop—something traders should never do—and lost even more money. I threw away 9% on the trade.

Head-and-Shoulders Top

When I used to work for Tandy Corporation, I followed its stock daily and discovered a head-and-shoulders top (HST) standing by itself. It reminded me of a tall English castle surrounded by a moat. The run-up to the chart pattern was swift and steep and so was the return to the swamp. I liked the pattern so much that I printed it out and pasted it up on my office wall. At the time, I had no idea what to look for in a HST, but the pattern intrigued me.

Identification

Figure 7.11 shows an excellent example of an HST. Three peaks appear like the spires of a cathedral, the middle one soars above the other two. The HST confirms when price closes below the neckline. That's a problem

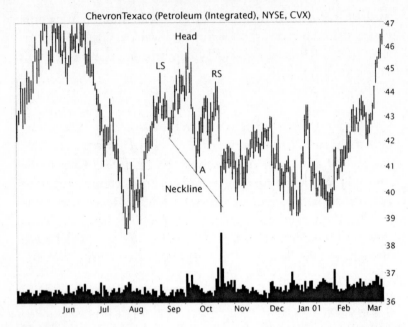

FIGURE 7.11 A head-and-shoulders top is a three-peak pattern with the middle peak towering above the others. The pattern confirms when price closes below the neckline.

with steep-sloping necklines like the one shown. Price never closes below the neckline and a breakout never occurs. For HSTs with downsloping necklines, use a close below point A—the lowest armpit—to signal a breakout and confirm the pattern as a valid HST.

Here's a list of characteristics that you should look for when searching for HSTs:

- Look for two shoulders flanking a head. The head must tower above the shoulders.

- The shoulders should top out near the same price, but allow variations. Imagine that the HST were your newborn child. Would you want one with lopsided shoulders?

- The shoulders should appear similar in shape.

- The shoulders should be near the same distance from the head. Symmetry is key.

- Volume is higher on the five days (two days before the peak to two days after) surrounding the left shoulder 43% of the time, on the head 40% of the time, and 18% on the right shoulder.

- Sixty-three percent have a downward volume trend measured between the shoulder peaks.

- The pattern confirms when price closes below an upsloping trendline or below the lowest valley in the HST for downsloping trendlines.

Trading and Trading Tips

As I was looking at HSTs, I came up with the idea that a high velocity move leading to the HST seemed to propel prices downward after the breakout. Diamonds often show this behavior—quick declines follow quick rises. I researched velocity and found that when it rose above the median six cents per day, the postbreakout declines averaged 25%. Low velocity rises showed postbreakout declines of 18%. The test involved 605 HSTs, so the numbers should be rock solid. However, after a high velocity rise, a pullback is more likely to occur. It happens 54% of the time in a bull market.

I measure the velocity from the trend start to the chart pattern. Usually, you can look at the chart pattern and find where the trend starts, but sometimes not. I use a more rigorous definition (a 20% price change), so see the Glossary for details on finding where the price trend starts.

A short-term rise leading to the HST gives better performance after the breakout than intermediate- or long-term ones. I found that HSTs with a short-term rise declined 26% postbreakout; intermediate- and long-term rises both dropped 19%.

Additional trading tips include:

- Pullbacks occur 50% of the time.

- Patterns with pullbacks have postbreakout performance that suffers—an average decline of 20% postbreakout with pullbacks versus 24% for those without pullbacks. If you want to short a stock showing an HST, avoid those with underlying support.

- Patterns taller than the 17.27% median height divided by the breakout price perform better than short ones (24% decline versus 20%). I measure height from the tallest peak to the lowest valley in the HST. Avoid trading HSTs that are both short and wide (wider than the 49-day median). Prices decline just 17% after the breakout.

- HSTs with upsloping volume (as measured between the two shoulder peaks) tend to perform better postbreakout than do those with downsloping trends, 24% decline versus 21%.

- The neckline slopes upward 51% of the time, is flat 4%, and slopes downward 45% of the time. Patterns with upsloping necklines perform better than do those with downsloping ones (23% postbreakout decline versus 21%, respectively).

- HSTs with a higher left shoulder peak when compared to the right shoulder peak perform better, 25% postbreakout decline versus 20%, respectively.

Measuring Success

The measure rule for HSTs is different from other chart patterns. Measure the height from the highest peak in the head vertically to the neckline as Figure 7.12 shows in the inset. Subtract the result from the breakout price, the point where price closes below the neckline. The result is the target price.

For example, say the head peaked at 12, the neckline was at 9, and the breakout was at 10 in the inset. The height would be 3 (12 − 9), and the price target would be 7 (10 − 3). Since 7 represents a 30% decline from 10, that's an unlikely plunge so look for a closer target. In my tests, the measure rule worked just 55% of the time. That's slightly better than a coin toss, so look for underlying support where price may rebound.

If you own a stock showing an HST, compute the target price. Is the decline large enough so that you should sell now? Most times, the answer will be yes, as you can't be sure how far price will decline.

Case Study

Like all bearish chart patterns, HSTs shout a sell signal that you can hear if you cock your head just so and listen. Here is one trade where I caught their message and escaped before a dramatic downturn, as my notebook suggests:

> 12/20/01. Filled 300 at 35.10, up from 35.05 asked when I logged in. This is an upward breakout from a symmetrical triangle with a book score of +1. A long-term holding yielding 6%, the downside is limited because of massive support zone in the 32–34 range. Upside is the old high.

I show where I bought the stock in Figure 7.12. The symmetrical triangle is one of the tools with which every trader should be familiar.

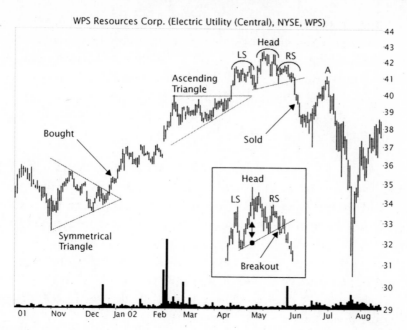

FIGURE 7.12 An upward breakout from a symmetrical triangle signaled a buy and the head-and-shoulders said sell.

Prices cross the pattern from side to side before breaking out. The book score I refer to is a method for predicting how well a chart pattern will do after the breakout. For more information, read my book *Trading Classic Chart Patterns* (John Wiley & Sons, 2002). Scores above zero mean the chart pattern is likely to beat the median rise. The stock missed the 44.55 price target by $1.43 when you include the two dividend payments.

The location where I bought in Figure 7.12 points to a small, tight flag. This knot of congestion just after the breakout confirms the up-move. Swing traders should look for the combination of breakout and nearby tight pennant or flag. It can lead to a sharp, vertical move.

Because I wanted to collect the dividend for the long term, holding on was not a problem. An ascending triangle came and went with the good fortune of having an upward breakout. A downward breakout would have been a sell signal, regardless of the buy-and-hold mentality. Then the head-and-shoulders top appeared and I was concerned. My notebook again:

6/5/02. I sold 300 shares, my holdings in the company, at market this afternoon. The stock dropped below round number support at 40, confirming an HST. I think interest rates are headed up and the stock has been climbing for so long, it's worth taking the 13% gain, 6% dividend rate, and running with the cash. The market has been struggling recently and utilities along with them. I can always buy back in at a lower price. Still, support is at 38–39 and that might be as far down as she goes. Filled at 39.52.

You can see the drop that resulted after my sale. As an end-of-day trader, I am usually a day or two late in my trades. Swing traders would have sold sooner, when it was clear that price had pierced the neckline. Price pulled back to the breakout price (point A) before tumbling from over 41 to just above 30, a decline of 26% in about a month.

Prices paused at 38 to 39, as predicted, before pulling back to A. As price dropped from A, it also paused near the same region (37–38) before continuing the decline. On the trade, I made over $1,600 or 15%, including dividends.

Measured Moves and the Simple ABC Correction

Measured moves are unlike other chart patterns because they don't have breakouts, so performance is difficult to gauge. Nevertheless, they are as useful as a frying pan is to bacon.

Measured moves come in three flavors: measured move up (MMU), down (MMD), and the simple ABC correction. The simple ABC correction is a special case of an MMD. Measured moves point the direction and extent of future price moves, and that helps you determine when to sell.

Identification

Figure 7.13 shows several examples of measured moves, two up, and two down. Downward measured moves are represented by the zigzag pattern EFGA and the larger one EADH. Measured moves up are ABCD and HIJK.

Let's take the first one, EFGA. The length of the first leg, EF is supposed to equal the length of the second leg, GA. The move FG is called the corrective phase. It retraces the prevailing downward trend. Similarly, AB is the first leg, CD is the second leg, and BC is the corrective phase.

FIGURE 7.13 Shown are a variety of measured moves, such as EFGA, ABCD, EADH, and HIJK.

What should you look for when searching for measured moves? Here's a list:

- Measured moves act as reversals of the prevailing price trend. For MMUs, look for a downtrend before the chart pattern begins. For MMDs, look for an uptrend preceding the pattern.
- The first leg should be a straight-line run with little curve to it.
- The corrective phase should be proportional to the first leg. Prices usually retrace 40% to 60% of the first leg move. Be suspect of larger retraces. Pair large first legs with large retraces; small first legs with small retraces. Avoid patterns that look like horizontal saw teeth—the retrace has gone too far.
- The second leg should approximate the slope of the first leg, but allow variation.
- Volume trends downward throughout the pattern.

The Simple ABC Correction

Figure 7.14 shows a simple ABC correction. I think of it as a nested measured move. The first measured move is an MMU spanning the run

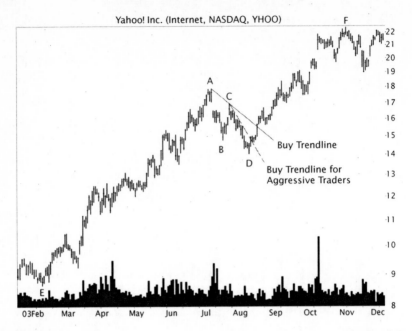

FIGURE 7.14   This chart shows a nested measured move, a simple ABC correction.

EADF. It's a large move, and that's the excitement behind this pattern. If you buy in after the measured move down, you can make a chunk of change.

The smaller pattern is an MMD, located at ABCD. That's the simple ABC correction. The pattern corrects (retraces) a portion of the larger move. Here is how to identify the simple ABC correction:

- Point E must be below point D, meaning that the MMD must not correct too far. MMDs that correct to or below the start of the MMU (point E) tend to fail more often.

- The corrective phase of the large MMU is an MMD, like the ABCD pattern shown. Only one MMD should be present with two *straight-line* runs, AB and CD. Discard patterns with pronounced turning points within those two down legs.

- Within the MMD, points B, C, and D are below A. Be especially careful that C not be above A. You don't want the measured move down to correct too far.

- Point D starts a major price up swing.

That's all there is to it, but it sounds more complicated than it really is. If you can identify an MMD and an MMU, then look for the first nested inside the second. A buy signals when price makes the turn at D.

Simple ABC Correction Trading Tips

Here are tips to trading the simple ABC correction (refer to Figure 7.14):

- Draw a trendline from A to C and extend it downward. When price closes above the trendline, buy.
- For more aggressive traders, draw a trendline down from C and buy when price closes above it (see the dashed line in the figure). Also, a close above the intraday *high* at valley B works.
- For more conservative investors, a close above C or even A is the buy signal.
- Buy only if the market and industry are both trending upward, so the stock can make the most of upward momentum.
- Be prepared for price to reverse at A—36% do, and prices drop, confirming a double top.

MMD and MMU Trading Tips

Trading an MMD or MMU is difficult because they often flame out sooner than you hope or expect. I recommend buying in once the corrective phase completes. If a flag, pennant, or any price patterns that follows a trend appears from B to C (see Figure 7.15), then draw a trendline along the peaks. Once price pierces or closes above the trendline, then buy the stock. For MMDs, once price pierces the bottom trendline, then short the stock.

In either case, watch for price to reverse. The run may be a sharp one like that pictured in Figure 7.15, or it may die as price climbs to B and then reverses. If price does not follow a trend from B to C, then wait for price to rise (fall) above the corrective phase high (low) for MMUs and MMDs, respectively. Even waiting for such a breakout is no guarantee of success. Measured moves are not easy to trade. I use them mostly to help predict the eventual price move. They behave themselves better when my money is not in the trade.

If the projected top of the MMU (point D in Figure 7.15) intersects a downsloping trendline set up by prior price action, then expect

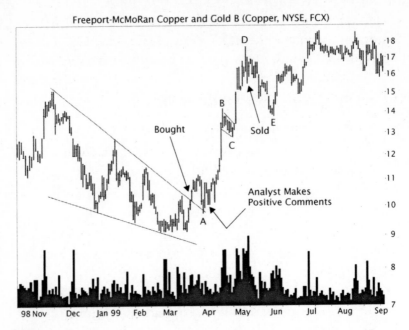

Freeport-McMoRan Copper and Gold B (Copper, NYSE, FCX)

FIGURE 7.15 I bought after a falling wedge and sold at the top of a measured move up.

price to reverse there. For example, in Figure 7.13 a downsloping trendline drawn along peaks E and G comes close to the top of ABCD, where price reverses. Notice that the measured move down EADH stops at point H, meeting a downsloping trendline joining valleys F and A. Then the price trend reverses.

Like most chart patterns, measured moves perform best when there is no overhead resistance (to stop an MMU) or underlying support (to stop an MMD). Always check for resistance and support before trading. Trendlines drawn on the weekly scale highlight where price is likely to reverse. This is the single best indicator of how profitable your measured move will be.

If I am in a stock that forms a measured move, I want to know what happens to price after the measured move completes. I studied the pattern and found that for MMUs, price remained above the corrective phase 19% of the time. Price stopped somewhere within the corrective phase 35% of the time, another 31% continued lower but stopped before the start of the pattern, and the remaining 15% dropped below the start of the MMU. What you should remember is that *81% of the time, price returns to the corrective phase* and perhaps goes much lower.

For MMDs, 16% remain below the corrective phase, 35% stop rising within the corrective phase, 31% rise above the corrective phase but below the MMD's start, and 18% continue rising above the MMD's start. The numbers are similar to MMUs, with *84% rising to at least the corrective phase* and sometimes much higher.

Here are additional tips that I dug up for measured moves:

- The larger the corrective phase retrace, the better the chance of meeting the price target.

- Patterns with U-shaped volume reach their price targets more often than do those with dome-shaped volume.

- A longer corrective phase means a more powerful move. For MMUs, corrective phases longer than the median 26 days mean second leg rises averaging 36%. Corrective phases shorter than the median show second leg rises of 29%. For MMDs, the median corrective phase length is 21 days and the second leg decline averages 28% versus 22% for long/short corrective phase lengths, respectively. Because the corrective phase should be proportional to the first leg move, I think this means that wide patterns perform better than narrow ones.

MMU and MMD Performance Profiles

Here is the performance profile for 577 MMU patterns in a bull market:

- The first leg rise averages 46% in 87 days.
- The corrective phase retraces an average of 47% in 32 days.
- The second leg rise averages 32% in 60 days.
- Volume trends downward 61% of the time.
- Volume is dome shaped 62% of the time.

Here is the profile for 647 MMD patterns in a bull market:

- The first leg decline averages 27% in 61 days.
- The corrective phase retraces an average of 48% in 30 days.
- The second leg decline averages 25% in 62 days.
- Volume trends downward 74% of the time.
- Volume is dome shaped 61% of the time.

Measuring Success

The beauty of the measured move is its predictive power. The measure rule for MMUs and MMDs is that you take half the first leg move and add it to the lowest valley in the corrective phase. For the MMU shown in Figure 7.15, that means taking the difference between points A (9.75) and B (14.19), for a height of 4.44. Divide the result in half (2.22) and add it to the low at C (12.81) to get a target of 15.03. This works 85% of the time.

For MMDs, the measure rule is similar. For measured move EFGA in Figure 7.13, measure the decline from E to F, take half of it, and subtract it from the peak at G. To put numbers to the letters, E is at 27.13, and F is at 21.13 for a height of 6. Half of the height is 3. Subtract 3 from the high at G (24.50) to get a target of 21.50. Prices reach the target 83% of the time.

In my test of over 1,200 measured moves, I found that 45% of the second legs were as long as the first ones in MMUs, and 35% of MMDs had second legs that were as long as the first legs. Thus, don't depend on the second leg being as long as the first. Use half the first leg move instead.

The most frequent corrective phase retrace of the first leg move is 40% to 60%, close to the Fibonacci numbers of 38% and 62%.

Case Study

Figure 7.15 shows a near perfect trade as far as timing goes. I followed the construction of the falling wedge and bought 500 shares, filled at 10.50. A falling wedge has price action that follows two downsloping and converging trendlines. The measure rule says the top of the pattern is the price target. Price hits the target 70% of the time. So, I had a 70% chance that price would rise to the round number 15.

After I bought, you can see that price struggled to move higher. It threw back to the upper wedge trendline at A before beginning its climb. A few days later, a mining analyst said that the company would be the only U.S. copper producer to be in the black for the quarter because of its Indonesian mine. Price started moving up then shot skyward like a model rocket, pausing in its flight at B.

Two days after B, the company reported a 33% drop in earnings but the company remained profitable. The stock seemed to ignore the news as the corrective phase of the MMU continued building the tight flag BC.

After refueling the second stage, the model rocket took off again, shooting higher for two days before waffling upward. The parachute popped out at D, completing the MMD, and I bailed out a day later, selling the stock at 16 for a gain of $2,700 or a massive 51%.

Notice how prices slipped back to E, the top of the corrective phase. Expect that type of decline, or worse, after a measured move completes.

Pipe Tops

Pipe tops are a pattern that I found several years ago. At the time, I wondered what a double top would look like and how it would perform if the tops were just a week apart. I explored pipe performance on the daily and weekly charts and found that those on the weeklies performed better than did those on the dailies. If you know what a pipe bottom looks like, then flip that image upside down and you'll have a pipe top.

Identification

Figure 7.16 shows several pipe tops and a few pipe bottoms sprinkled in for variety. The pipe bottoms call the turning points quite well as do many of the tops. Look at point A. This pipe acts as a continuation pattern because prices are already trending downward. Unfortunately, this pipe top appears near the end of the trend. The pipes shown in this figure work much better as reversals, such as the one at the peak in September 1999. It calls the turn exactly.

Clustered together like neighbors with small lots are pipes B, C, and D, and they act as continuation patterns. Pipe C doesn't confirm until after D completes. The inset shows confirmation, which occurs when price closes below the lower of the two pipe spikes; a lower close confirms the pipe as a valid chart pattern. Without confirmation, you don't have a pipe top.

What should you look for when trying to find pipe tops?

- Use the weekly scale. It gives better performance than those found on the daily scale.
- Look for two adjacent, upward price spikes. The spikes should be longer than most over the prior year and should tower above the surrounding landscape.
- The two spikes should have a large price overlap.

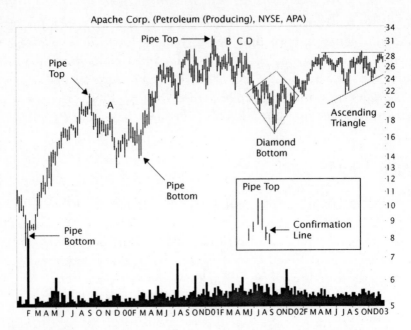

FIGURE 7.16 Pipe tops and bottoms appear on the weekly chart, along with a diamond bottom and ascending triangle. The pipe top confirms when price closes below the lowest low in the pattern.

- The price variation between the tops of the spike is usually small, but can vary up to $1 or more for high-priced stocks. The median difference is 13 cents, average: 21 cents.
- The right spike has lower volume than the left one 62% of the time.
- The pattern confirms when price closes below the lower of the two spikes.

That's all there is to it. The most important feature of pipes is that they look unique—twin birch trees towering above a forest of dwarf pines. Pipes should look unusually long and obvious.

Trading and Trading Tips

Shorting a stock is fine for an experienced trader, but most investors should not attempt it. Thus, pipes serve as warnings of a coming price decline. Here are some numbers to help you decide whether to sell a long holding after a pipe top confirms:

- Pullbacks occur 41% of the time.

- Patterns with pullbacks have postbreakout performance that suffers an average decline of 16% versus 22% for those without pullbacks. If you see underlying support, the stock may reverse there. If price declines to the support zone, can you tolerate such a loss? What if price drops lower?

- Patterns taller than the 10.23% median height divided by the breakout price perform better than short ones (23% average decline versus 17%). I measure height from the tallest spike to the lowest one in the two-week pattern.

- Pipes within a third of the yearly low decline most, 22% versus 19% for the middle and high thirds of the yearly trading range.

- Pipes with long spikes perform better (prices decline more postbreakout) than do those with short ones. This is the reason for selecting pipes with unusually long spikes.

- Pipes with a lower left spike tend to perform better than do those with a lower right spike (declines averaging 21% versus 18%, and 20% for pipes with even spikes).

Measuring Success

The measure rule for pipe tops is the chart pattern high minus the low subtracted from the low. By high and low, I mean the higher and lower of the two spikes. That difference finds the height. Subtract the height from the lowest spike to get the target price. This method works 70% of the time in a bull market.

For example, the pipe top shown in the inset at the top of Figure 7.17 has a high price of 10 and a low of 9. The difference, 1, is the height. Subtract it from 9 to get the target of 8.

Case Study

Jake smokes cigars. In February 2000, he was so engrossed in a pipe top on his monitor that he forgot about the cigar wedged between his teeth. The ash dropped off and burned a hole in his office chair. Figure 7.17 shows what he saw (on the screen, not on his chair).

The pipe top was a church steeple, but Jake knew it did not point the way to heaven. When price made a lower low a week later, he sold short, getting an average price of 14.61. He leaned back in his chair and

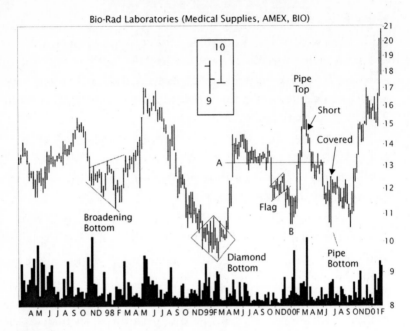

FIGURE 7.17   A pipe top leads to a profitable trade.

puffed on his cigar, chugging away like a locomotive climbing a steep grade.

He estimated that the stock could decline to the support area shown by the horizontal consolidation region (represented by the line at A), but more likely would retrace the entire decline back to B. Why? "Price climbed too fast and was unsustainable. Look at the rise from the diamond bottom back in April 1999. Price climbed from 10 to 14 in five weeks and then gave back most of it. I expect price to do the same."

That was his wish, but things rarely work out that well. When price paused at A, he was not worried. He rechecked the company fundamentals and the current news, and was satisfied with what he found. Nevertheless, he tightened his stop—meaning he moved it closer to where the stock was then trading.

Prices worked their way lower and when they neared the price at B, he started covering his short, closing out half of his position at an average price of 10.75.

With the remainder, he decided to hold on. The following week, the stock made a lower low, but he became distracted. By the time he returned to the trade, the stock had risen a point, or almost 10%. He closed out the remainder of his position at an average price of 12.40.

Ascending and Symmetrical Triangles

I checked my spreadsheet of trades and found that I win most often trading symmetrical triangles, followed by descending triangles. I get my butt kicked trading ascending triangles. Your luck may be different, and I am sure the results will change over time. I have two ascending triangle trades on now, and both became profitable the day after I bought, so I am hopeful. (Both led to big, quick gains).

Identification

Figure 7.18 shows two symmetrical triangles and one ascending triangle. The symmetrical triangles have two converging trendlines that bound price action. The breakout direction is unknown until it happens. The ascending triangle has a flat top and upsloping price trend on the bottom. An upward breakout is assumed, but it can be downward as the figure shows. Since the breakout direction is unknown, it is critical that you wait for the breakout.

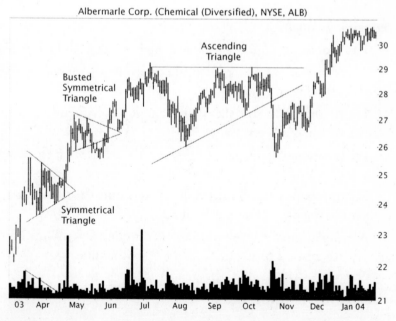

FIGURE 7.18 Two symmetrical triangles lead the way to a large ascending triangle.

The key to identifying chart patterns is to look for straight lines along peaks or valleys. Those are the lines your brain wants to construct on the price chart. Then look for curves. Between straight lines and curves, you've got the gamut covered. Triangles are like cumulus clouds near the great lakes: They appear often, but here's what to look for.

Ascending Triangles

- Look for peaks that top out near the same price (a horizontal top).
- Find prices that make higher valleys. Prices should touch an up-sloping trendline drawn beneath the valleys.
- Prices must touch each trendline at least twice.
- Prices must cross the chart pattern from side to side, leaving little white space within the body of the pattern.
- The two trendlines converge at the triangle apex.
- Volume trends downward 77% of the time from pattern start to the day before the breakout.
- A breakout occurs when price closes outside the trendline boundary. An upward breakout occurs 70% of the time.

Symmetrical Triangles

- Look for a converging price trend: higher valleys and lower peaks.
- Trendlines drawn along the peaks and valleys form two converging trendlines that join at the triangle apex.
- Prices (the peaks or valleys) must touch each trendline at least twice (four trend reversals).
- Prices must cross the pattern from side to side, leaving little white space.
- Volume trends downward 86% of the time from the pattern's start to the day before the breakout.
- A breakout occurs when price closes outside the trendline boundary. An upward breakout occurs 54% of the time.

Trading and Trading Tips

I learned the first tip from two independent sources and examined the charts to be sure it held promise. That is, when a symmetrical triangle forms at the start of an uptrend, expect a large move. You can see this on the weekly scale. Symmetricals well along in the trend tend to fail more often than those at the start. By *trend*, I don't mean the *trend start* or *ultimate high* because those terms have specific definitions. I mean the long-term price trend on the weekly scale.

Additional tips for ascending triangles include:

- Throwbacks occur 57% of the time. Pullbacks occur 49% of the time.

- Always check for support or resistance before trading because they can cause pullbacks or throwbacks. Patterns with pullbacks have postbreakout performance that suffers an average decline of 17% versus 20% for those without pullbacks. Throwbacks have results even farther apart: 31% for those with throwbacks and 41% postbreakout rise for those without throwbacks. If you see underlying support or overhead resistance, the stock may reverse there and you may end with a loss.

- Tall patterns perform better than short ones. Tall means taller than the 10.13% median height divided by the breakout price (upward breakouts) or 12.02% median for downward breakouts. Tall patterns, for example, have price that rises 44% postbreakout versus 30% for short patterns.

- Those with a long-term *rise* leading to the chart pattern climb an average of 37% after the upward breakout. Those with a short-term *decline* leading to the pattern show a 41% rise after an upward breakout.

Tips for symmetrical triangles follow:

- Throwbacks occur 54% of the time. Pullbacks occur 59% of the time.

- Patterns with pullbacks have postbreakout performance that suffers an average decline of 15% versus 21% for those without pullbacks. For upward breakouts, the rise is 25% for those with throwbacks and 38% postbreakout rise for those without throwbacks.

- Tall patterns perform better than short ones. Tall means taller than the 14.48% median height divided by the breakout price (upward breakouts) or 14.50% median for downward breakouts. Tall patterns, for example, have price that rises 38% postbreakout versus 26% for short patterns.

- Patterns with heavy (above the 30-day average) breakout volume do better. For example, symmetricals with heavy volume show postbreakout rises averaging 35%. Those with weak breakout volume rise 24%.

- Patterns both tall and narrow outperform. Tall uses the median height already described. Narrow means narrower than the 42-day median (upward breakouts) or 39-day median (downward breakouts). Tall and narrow symmetricals with upward breakouts rise an average of 41%. Short and narrow triangles, by contrast, show price rising just 25% after the breakout.

- Symmetricals with breakouts within a third of the yearly low perform better than do those with breakouts in the other ranges. Those near the yearly high perform worst. This reinforces what others have found about symmetricals doing well at the start of trends.

Measuring Success

The measure rule is the same as what we've seen before, but we can add a twist. First, let's discuss the standard model. Consider the inset in Figure 7.19. It shows another version of the August symmetrical triangle. The measure rule gauges the height from F to G and adds/subtracts the result to the breakout price at H (where price closes above/below the trendline).

For ascending triangles, the height is the difference between the lowest valley in the chart pattern and the price of the horizontal trendline. Add or subtract the result from the breakout price for upward and downward breakouts, respectively.

Another method to predict a price target is to draw a line parallel to the upsloping (for upward breakouts) or downsloping (for downward breakouts) trendline, beginning from the start of the pattern. I show this in the inset as line D which is parallel to line E, starting at F. *Where price breaks out of the triangle, the value of line D directly above is the target price.*

For downward breakouts, draw a line parallel to the downsloping trendline (starting from G), and where price breaks out of the symmetrical triangle, the value of the parallel trendline on that day is the target price.

This method works for ascending and descending triangles as well. If prices break out in the direction of the sloping trendline, just draw a parallel line beginning from the start of the pattern until the day of the breakout.

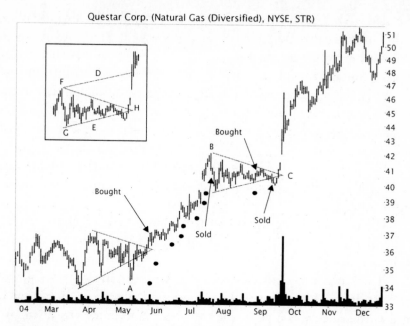

FIGURE 7.19 Two symmetrical triangles presented trading opportunities. The black circles are the locations and prices of stop-loss orders.

If you use both methods to determine a target price, choose the one that is closest to support or resistance (where price is likely to reverse), or one that is closest to the chart pattern. It doesn't hurt to be conservative in your target.

For ascending triangles, the standard measure rule works 75% of the time for upward breakouts and 68% for downward breakouts. For symmetricals, upward breakouts hit the target 66% of the time and downward breakouts score 48% of the time. The numbers are below the 80% hit rate that I like to see, so be conservative in your target selection.

Case Study

Jake's grin was a large as a watermelon slice. He seemed positively buoyant. "I see you're looking at Questar. Let me tell you about two triangle trades I made in that."

Figure 7.19 shows two symmetrical triangles, both with downward breakouts, and both are busted patterns.

"A busted pattern provides an excellent trading opportunity because everyone is so upset with losing money, it gives traders an easy entry,"

Jake said. "Two days after the breakout, I bought the first time." He bought 400 shares at 36.85. Then he put a stop at 34.19, just below the breakout low where prices stopped declining in early May. The triangle apex is a support zone, but he wanted the stop farther away, just in case.

As prices rose, he raised the stop as the black circles on the chart shows. Each circle represents the price and day at which he raised his stop. The circles generally correspond to price peaks—new highs that signal it's time to raise the stop.

"When price started going exponential [climbing steeply], I tightened the stop to 40.75. Those steep rises never last. In fact, I was stopped out the next day."

The price target he was shooting for was 39.26, which is the height of the triangle added to the breakout price, so he did better than that. "I made just over $1,500 or 10%."

"I was taken to the cleaners on the second trade." He bought 400 shares at 40.91. He expected the symmetrical triangle to break out upward as the stock was higher when the S&P 500 index was down as he placed the trade. That showed strength, but natural gas prices were trending lower—"not good for a company with gas," he said and smiled, then sniffed the air and crinkled his nose as if smelling something unpleasant.

He anticipated the stock completing a measured move up pattern to 48 (34.26 at point A to 42.06, point B, projected upward from 40.50 point C, the apex of the triangle then rounded down to 48).

For support, the round number 40 would help, he reasoned, keeping any loss to a minimum. On the weekly scale, a downward breakout could take the stock back to the consolidation region at 36—the site of the prior symmetrical triangle.

"A symmetrical triangle in an uptrend usually breaks out upward, so that's the bet I made. Later I found out that the uptrend-upbreakout scenario happens only 55% of the time. That's about random."

Just after he bought the stock, he placed a stop at 39.43, for a potential loss of 3.6%. He selected 39.43 because it was below the triangle and below the 39.50 round number (everyone else would place their orders at the even 50 cents).

"When price closed outside the lower boundary of the symmetrical triangle, I decided to sell. Other stocks in the industry were soaring gangbusters while this one moved horizontally. Yes, a region of consolidation is expected after a run-up, but this stock didn't do what I expected." He sold the stock at 40.20, for a loss of 2% or $300.

A chart pattern not acting as expected is always a good reason for selling. Imagine the stock backtracking to 36 or even lower. You can see what happened to the stock. It bottomed a day later, and then shot out the top of the triangle and continued higher. Nevertheless, Jake cut his loss short as soon as the trade went against him.

Triple Tops

Many know triple tops yet few have actually caught one in the bush. Why? Because they are a rare breed, coming out most often in a bear market. While it's common for prices to make a second top at the same price, adding a third one is unusual. A third top shows formidable overhead resistance and a chance to make money or get out of an existing trade before the smart money catches you trespassing.

Identification

Figure 7.20 shows a triple top at peaks 1, 2, and 3, with a horizontal confirmation line joining the lowest valley in the pattern. When price closes below the line, it confirms the three-peak pattern as a valid triple top and predicts the price raft is about to tumble over the falls. If unconfirmed, then you don't have a triple top, just more squiggles on the price chart.

Triple tops are rare, so don't expect them to appear often. In your trading, if you think a triple top is going to form because you have two peaks at the same price and price is climbing to the third, don't bet on it. Chances are that price will continue moving up, invalidating the triple top, or prices may reverse before coming close to the other two peaks. I've been burned trying to predict a triple top.

What should you look for when hunting for triples? Here are the guidelines:

- Find three peaks, each a distinct, well-separated peak. The peaks are often sharp, inverted V-shaped, or one-day price spikes.
- The three peaks should top out near the same price. Often the middle peak is slightly below the other two.
- Volume trends downward 59% of the time but is usually high beneath each peak. The first peak usually has the highest volume.
- The pattern confirms as a valid triple top when price closes below the lowest valley in the pattern.
- More triple tops occur in a bear market than in a bull market.

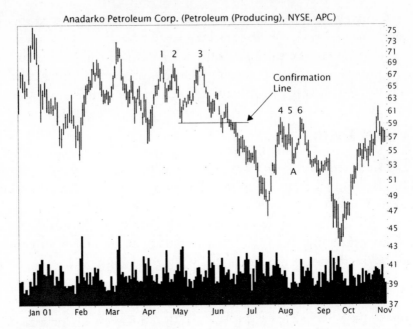

FIGURE 7.20   A triple top (peaks 1, 2, 3) appears just before prices tumble. The three-peak pattern becomes a true triple top when price closes below the confirmation line.

Are peaks 4, 5, and 6 a triple top in Figure 7.20? Yes. The three peaks are unique tops, not ones that are part of the same consolidation pattern (although peak 5 does look suspicious). The peaks don't top out at the same price but they are close, with the middle peak 1.7% below the other two. Volume trends downward and is highest on the first peak. Finally, the pattern confirms when price closes below the lowest valley in the pattern (point A).

Sometimes, the triple top is actually a right-angled and descending broadening pattern. Look at the valleys, especially to the left of the chart pattern. If you can draw a downsloping trendline connecting the valleys, then you may have a broadening pattern. Look for a partial rise or decline to trade the pattern.

Trading and Trading Tips

If you can draw an upsloping trendline along the two valleys between the three tops, use that as the sell signal (a close below the trendline). That will get you out much sooner than waiting for confirmation—a close below point B in Figure 7.21.

Another tip deals with peaks 2 and 3. When peak 3 is below the middle peak (peak 2 in Figure 7.21), then expect a stronger decline. A lower top suggests weakness because price attempts to make a new high and fails.

Triple tops have a high failure rate: 10% fail to decline at least 5% after the breakout. Look for underlying support to gauge how far price will drop. If price drops to the support zone and then rebounds, can you tolerate the loss? What happens if price pushes on through and tumbles to the next support zone?

Measure the rise leading to the triple top and check for a Fibonacci retrace of 38% to 62%. Price will often sink that far before recovering and moving to new highs. It may pay to hold on, especially if the market and industry are moving up and you have a long-term position in the stock (or want to hold it long term for tax reasons). Otherwise, sell when price closes below the confirmation point, whether using an upsloping trendline or below the lowest valley.

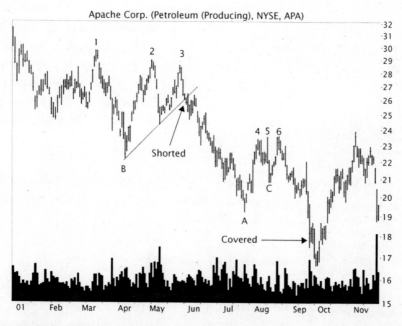

FIGURE 7.21 Two triple tops appear like the prior figure: different stocks but the same industry.

Finally, a high velocity rise (above the median 10 cents per day) leading to the triple top gives a larger decline after the breakout than does a low velocity rise. I used the trend start to the highest high in the triple top as the measure, so check the Glossary to find out how to find the trend start. You can see this behavior most easily on the weekly scale. Triple tops with prices sliding into them almost horizontally tend to break out downward then reverse quickly.

Here are additional tips:

- Pullbacks occur 61% of the time.

- Patterns with pullbacks have postbreakout performance that suffers an average decline of 18% versus 21% for those without pullbacks. Before trading, check for underlying support.

- Patterns within a third of the yearly high decline most, 21% versus 19% for the middle third and 18% for the lowest third of the yearly trading range.

- Volume trending upward between the three peaks means a larger decline postbreakout, averaging 21% versus 18% for those with upsloping volume.

- Patterns both tall and narrow perform better than the other combinations of height and width by declining an average of 23%. For height, use the difference from the highest peak to the lowest valley divided by the price of the lowest valley. If the result is above the 19.44% median in a bull market, then you have a tall pattern. Patterns narrower than the median 75 days are, well, narrow. Avoid those that are both short and wide. They have declines averaging 17% postbreakout.

- A quarter of the triple tops reach the *ultimate low* in the first week after a breakout; a third bottom in less than two weeks.

ultimate low

I determine the ultimate low by looking after the breakout for the lowest valley before a minimum 20% price rise, measured from the lowest valley to the *close*. I stopped looking if price closed above the formation high, assuming that an investor would have placed a stop-loss order at that price.

Measuring Success

Use the measure rule to predict a target price. The rule is the height of the pattern subtracted from the breakout price. The height is the lowest valley subtracted from the highest peak. The breakout price is traditionally the price of the lowest valley but you can use a trendline pierce like that shown in Figure 7.21.

For example, the measure rule for the triple top 456 in Figure 7.21 is the price at peak 6 minus C subtracted from C. That gives a target of 18. In a bull market, price hits the target a paltry 40% of the time, so select a target closer than the predicted one. If you see underlying support between the breakout and the target, then expect price to stall when it nears support. It may not, but that's the way to play it.

As a check, change the dollar decline into a percentage. In Figure 7.21, the stock was expected to drop 2.79, or 13.5% below the breakout price. That seems possible, as the loss is comparatively small. An unlikely decline would be something like 30% or 40%.

Case Study

The chart in Figure 7.21 looks suspiciously like Figure 7.20. Both occur during the same periods in the same industry, but in different stocks. "Instead of waiting for the usual confirmation," Jake gestured at point B, the lowest valley in the pattern, "I was able to jump the gun by shorting at the trendline break."

Why did he short the stock? "I checked the S&P 500 Index and it started declining in September 2000. In fact, if you draw trendlines starting from the November highs and lows, you get a descending broadening wedge." Think of a megaphone tilted downward. "The pattern wasn't perfect, but when price bumped up against the top trendline in May and headed down, I knew the rise was at an end. That decline coincided with peak 3 in the triple top."

Both the stock and the index declined in step, bottoming in late September. Jake measured the drop from peak 3 to A and projected half the decline downward from point 6, in a measured move down–type decline. That gave him a price target just below 19.

Why didn't he cover the short at point A, when price started moving up?

"Straight-line runs like the drop from point 3 to A often retrace. I allowed up to a 62% retrace of that down move, but prices only climbed halfway before reversing at the triple top. Then I used the measure rule for triples to project a new target price. It coincided with the MMD target," the measured move down.

When price started moving sideways in mid-September after hitting his target, he covered his short. "I was worried the quick decline from 22 to 18 would reverse and zip back up to 22, so I got out."

Chapter 8

Event Patterns

What They Are and How to Trade Them

I found nearly a dozen events that happen often, some every few months. Many you can trade, but they are a risky bunch (the failure rates are much higher than chart patterns) and require nimble trading skills to make a profit. I describe most of them in this chapter.

The Dead-Cat Bounce

Jake stumbled into the office as if he were on drugs, with eyes glazed and a blank stare. "Is your arthritis acting up again?" I asked, not knowing if he was in pain.

"Is that a joke?"

I returned to working on my manuscript until he was ready to talk.

"Merck just pulled their drug Vioxx (an arthritis painkiller) off the shelves. The stock plunged from yesterday's close of 45.07 to 32 and change. I own almost a thousand shares."

"A dead-cat bounce."

"Yeah. What should I do?" He looked at me, his body white, wringing his hands as if he was trying to squeeze the last drop of water out of a dishtowel. Worry lines etched his face. Not a pretty sight, but I had an answer.

"Wait for it to bounce and when it peaks, sell what you've got, and then short it."

His face regained its color. The corners of his mouth turned up and he bounded out of the chair, heading for the door.

Figure 8.1 shows what happened to the stock. The event decline took the stock lower 28% then prices bounced. That lasted just two days before the stock resumed tumbling again. Eventually, the stock bottomed at 25.60, for a total decline of 43%.

If you trade stocks long enough, a dead-cat bounce (DCB) will likely snare one of your stocks. I've been caught three times and have lost a total of $15,000.

A typical dead-cat bounce pattern takes the shape of the inset in Figure 8.1. The smart money knows something is wrong and they start dumping the stock at point A. In the Merck example, the stock peaked in June and the event occurred in September. The smart money got out early.

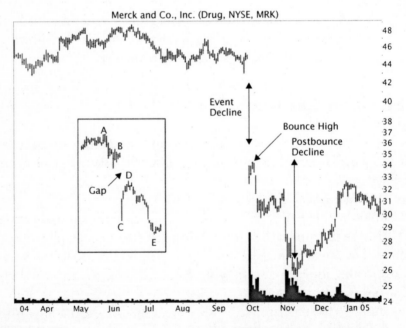

FIGURE 8.1 The stock dropped 28% in one day when the company pulled Vioxx from distribution. After a bounce of just a few days, the downtrend resumed.

When the event decline begins, it takes price down from B to C, a massive drop. Then the brokerage firms start touting the stock. "If you loved it at 50, it's a steal at 25." "It's a fire sale! You can pick up a share of stock for 30 cents on the dollar. Buy aggressively." The hype pushes the stock up and it bounces to D. That's when the smart money begins shorting the stock.

If the company announces a stock buyback and insiders say that the price represents value and that they are buying like crazy, the stock may continue recovering but that's rare. Most likely, the stock eases over and continues down to E, below the event low at C. If the event is earnings related, chances are that another DCB will occur in three months time.

DCB by the Numbers

I've studied the dead-cat bounce extensively—almost 700 events—so let me tell you what I found. The event begins in the middle third of the yearly price range 44% of the time. Just 25% of the time does the event begin within a third of the yearly high. Clearly, the smart money is selling the stock, forcing it lower.

The event decline averages 31% but can range from 15% to over 75%. By *event decline*, I mean the price decline as measured from the close the day before the event announcement (B) to the trend low (C) posted before prices begin the bounce. The median decline lasts two days. Forty-six percent make a lower low the day after the massive decline, 17% make another low the next day, then 9% and then 3%. A price gap occurs 74% of the time.

Once price hits bottom after the event, it begins to bounce (C to D). This phase sees price rise an average of 28% and it takes 23 days. Twenty-two percent of the time, the bounce will be high enough to close the gap made during the event.

Then the fun resumes. Prices ease lower, declining an average of 30% from the high at the bounce (D) to the new postbounce low (E). On average, it takes 49 days before price hits bottom. When everything is completed, in 67% of the DCBs I looked at the stock will bottom 18% below the event low (C).

Another massive decline (at least 15%) follows the first one 26% of the time within three months and 38% suffer a decline of at least 15% within the next six months. For those stocks recovering, 38% close the event day gap in three months, and 58% close it in six months.

Trading and Trading Tips

If you are caught in a DCB, the best thing to do is wait for the bounce and sell a long holding then. An upsloping trendline works well to time the exit. Draw it beneath the valleys as price rises. When price closes below the trendline, then sell. The odds suggest that the price will continue to go down, plus another DCB could happen in three or six months.

For aggressive traders, short the stock once it crests during the bounce phase (point D in Figure 8.1). On the way to E, the stock may stall at the event low price (C), so watch for that.

If you see a stock with a wonderful chart pattern in which you would like to invest but a DCB happened within the last six months, *avoid the stock*. Higher failure rates from chart patterns come from stocks with DCBs.

Case Study

"Here's how I traded a DCB," Jake said and pushed me off the chair where I was working. He pulled up a chart of Airgas, shown in Figure 8.2. "I bought 500 shares at 15.94 after the breakout from a head-and-shoulders bottom." The measure rule for the pattern said price would rise to 15.63, just a little above where he bought.

"If the profit potential was so low, why did you take the trade?"

At first he shrugged his shoulders then said, "I thought it would climb to resistance at 18 easily, and it might even go up to meet the June high at 21. With a little luck the old high at 27 would fall by the wayside, and then only the stars could stop it."

"Wishful thinking."

"No kidding, but I was right. The stock made it up to 18."

"What happened here?" I pointed to A on the monitor.

"Earnings announcement. The stock tumbled 15% (A to B). I waited for the stock to bounce and when it did, I sold. It turns out, I sold too soon as the stock *really* bounced, almost closing the gap (C)."

"Did you make any money?"

"Yeah. $220. That may not sound like much but it could have been worse." The chart doesn't show it, but the stock made a near straight-line run down to 7.88, recovered to 14 then sank to 4.63 in June 2000."

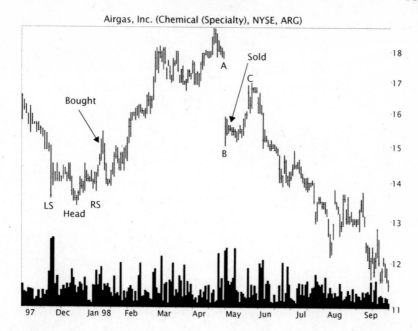

FIGURE 8.2 Jake bought after the head-and-shoulders bottom broke out upward and sold when it looked like the bounce phase of a dead-cat bounce was over.

The Inverted DCB

What happens to price when the company announces unexpectedly good news? Sometimes, the stock shoots up by 5%, 10%, 20%, or more *in one day*. Then the price tumbles. Figure 8.3 shows two examples. The first, at point A, happened when the company got news that banks extended a liquidity facility related to a receivables program. I have no idea what that means, but the market liked it. The stock shot up 26%, peaking at B. For a few days, the stock moved horizontally then began a swift decline to C. The drop measured 39%.

At F, the company said that quarterly sales slightly exceeded its earlier outlook. Up the stock went to D, peaking 47% above the close the day before the news. Then another decline set in, this time taking the stock down 59%.

I term this behavior—a rapid one- or two-day rise followed by a decline—an inverted dead-cat bounce, or iDCB.

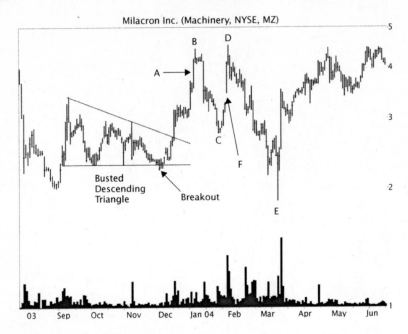

FIGURE 8.3 The announcement of good news sent the stock higher at A and F, but only for a short time.

Trading and Trading Tips

For swing traders, the choice to trade or not is easy. Consider selling after a large price jump (5% or more) when it occurs in one day. That means selling the day after the announcement sends price higher. According to my statistical review of nearly 31,000 samples where this occurred, selling was the smart move because price peaked the day after the announcement then retraced some or all of the gains.

For position traders and investors, the choice is not so clear. Why? Because price continues upward sometimes. Perhaps the general market or industry influences which way price will go, so be sure to check those when deciding to hold on or sell immediately. If the rise is vertical but takes longer than a day or two, then consider holding onto the stock. Chances are the stock will form a flag or pennant, signaling additional gains.

If a flag or pennant develops, trade in the direction of the breakout. If the breakout is upward, hold onto the stock. A downward breakout is the sell signal. One last thought: You never go broke taking a profit.

Case Study

Figure 8.4 shows how I made use of the iDCB information—a trade I've written about in another book, *Trading Classic Chart Patterns*—but I'm so proud of it that I just had to share it again! I bought an upward breakout from a head-and-shoulders chart pattern then sold two days later for a 25% gain. Here are the details.

With the stock trading near the yearly high, I expected the stock to rise back to 16 or 17, forming a double top. With luck, the stock would continue higher. When I saw the head-and-shoulders bottom forming, I decided to trade it. A buy signaled when price closed above the downsloping neckline, and I received a fill of 1,000 shares at an average price of 14.68. I placed a stop at 12.94, just below the 13 round number and slightly below the right shoulder low (RS).

In *Trading Classic Chart Patterns*, I describe how I scored the head-and-shoulders pattern for a +3 score. I usually won't trade a chart pattern having a minus score. A positive score meant that the stock had a good chance of rising to the 18.59 target predicted by the scoring system. That value comes from the median rise of 29.03% applied to the breakout price.

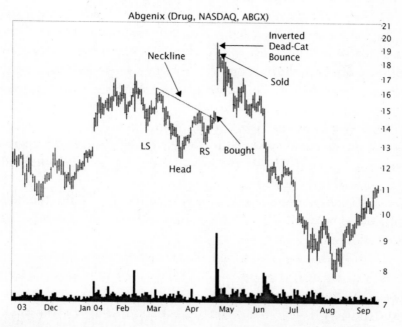

FIGURE 8.4 I bought the stock the day before good news and sold a day later.

The day after I bought the stock, it zipped up 20%, but I still don't know why. With such a tasty gain in just two days, I didn't want to take a chance and give it all back. So, I reviewed the situation and decided to sell. I sold my shares and received a fill at 18.308, for a three-day gain of 25% or $3,600. That day the company announced earnings.

What happened next amazes me even to this day. Look at Figure 8.4. The price tumbled, reaching a low of 7.76, or 60% below the peak the day before I sold. Wow!

Case Study

"What are you doing?" I asked Jake. He was sitting on a swing, not swinging, but just sitting there, holding a stack of papers.

"I'm reading your manuscript." He lifted the pages and they flapped in the late summer breeze. "The chapter on inverted DCBs. I just traded one."

Figure 8.5 shows his trade. The bottom of the large symmetrical triangle has a downward breakout in August. The rest of the triangle is off the screen and the lower trendline skirts the bottom of other valleys so even though the trendline looks drawn wrong, it is correct.

"The symmetrical triangle had a score of +1 and a price target of 18.46 (using my scoring system). Earnings were due in two weeks, so it was a gamble, but one I felt worth taking. I thought the stock would do well since others in the industry were going up gangbusters and the market was moving higher, too. I bought 1,000 shares at an average price of 14.60."

He placed a stop at 13.60, point A in Figure 8.5. If the trade were stopped out, he would lose about 7%. He thought the 18.46 target was aggressive and believed that the stock would stop at the January 2004 high at 16.70 (not shown).

"This looked like a busted symmetrical triangle." Since the triangle broke out downward but turned around and shot out the top, it suggested additional gains.

"When the company announced earnings, the stock took off," reaching an intraday high of 16.54, or up 15% from the prior close. "That was close to the January high, so I felt the stock had topped out. Five minutes before the close, I sold." The trade filled at 16.18. In two weeks, he made nearly $1,550 or 10%.

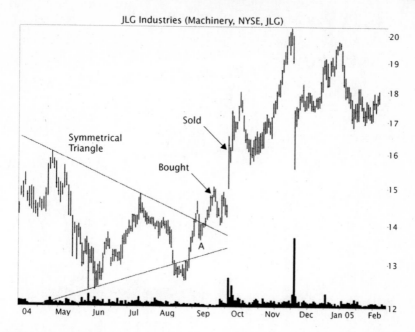

FIGURE 8.5 Jake bought after the breakout from a symmetrical triangle and sold the day prices took off.

Look what he could have made if he hung on. The stock peaked at 20.26. If he sold at that price, he would have made 39%, or about $6,000.

Bad Earnings Surprise

"I fell in love," Jake said as he walked into the office, a wide grin pasted on his face. His dimple made the requisite appearance.

"What's his name?"

"Funny. Real funny." He walked over to my computer and punched in a stock symbol then pointed at the screen. "I fell in love with Hughes Supply."

Before I get to his trade, let me tell you about bad earnings surprises. When a company announces earnings, the market can have one of three possible reactions. The stock might go up, go down, or do nothing. This section deals with those surprises that break out downward. By

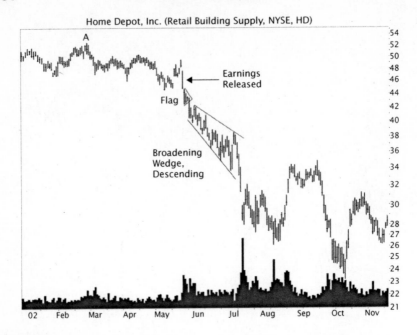

FIGURE 8.6　An earnings announcement sent shares cascading lower.

break out downward, I mean price closes below the low posted on the day of announced earnings. Figure 8.6 shows the two examples.

The first announcement happened at point A. The results beat the consensus estimate, but the stock dropped anyway, closing below the low posted on the announcement day two days later. Thus, the breakout was downward. The day after the announcement, an insider bought 10,000 shares, spending a cool half million. Even Jake doesn't have timing that bad. Over time, traders sawed the price of the stock in half.

Three months later, in May, the company was at it again, announcing quarterly earnings. The results were better than the consensus estimate, but the balance sheet did not show the kind of growth that Lowe's exhibited, according to the report. What happened to the stock? It gapped lower, making a large intraday price swing and closing near the low. The stock formed a small flag then a descending broadening wedge. Traders hammered the stock down to near 20 in January 2003 (not shown).

Identification

Here is what to look for when trying to identify a suitable trading candidate:

- The general market and industry should also be trending downward. Does it look like the downtrend will continue? If not, then avoid shorting the stock unless you have good reasons for doing so.

- Look for a falling price trend. Performance improves when you trade with the trend.

- The intraday high-low trading range on the announcement day should be taller than the 30-day average high-low range. The taller it is, the better. Earnings announcements with swings two or three times the average height perform much better than shorter ones.

- Price must close below the announcement day low, staging a downward breakout. The stock may bottom in a week and begin rebounding. If it does, close out the trade immediately.

Trading and Trading Tips

This pattern is not for the novice investor. Only experienced traders should attempt to short a stock showing a bad earnings surprise. The following trading information may prove useful:

- If you trade the stock perfectly, expect an average decline of 13% in a bull market, 17% in a bear market.

- It takes about a month for price to reach the ultimate low.

- Thirty-one percent of the patterns fail to drop more than 5%. Over half, 51%, fail to drop at least 10%. Those are not good numbers so you should be confident of your trading decision.

- Forty-seven percent of the patterns in a bull market will reach the ultimate low in a week, 48% in a bear market bottom during week one.

- The best performers have breakouts within a third of the yearly low.

- Pullbacks happen 41% of the time and when they do occur, performance suffers. Thus, avoid trading event patterns with nearby underlying support.
- Patterns taller than the median height divided by the breakout price of 5.01% perform best.
- To get a target price, compute the height (high-low) on the announcement day and subtract it from the low price. Prices hit the target 69% of the time.

Case Study

Figure 8.7 shows the setup for this case study. "I bought after the breakaway gap," Jake said. A breakaway gap occurs upon leaving a consolidation region, usually on high volume. The price gaps upward so that today's close is above yesterday's high, leaving a blank space on the price chart. Prices continue rising far enough that the gap does not close for a long time. What does that mean? Closing a gap means that price has

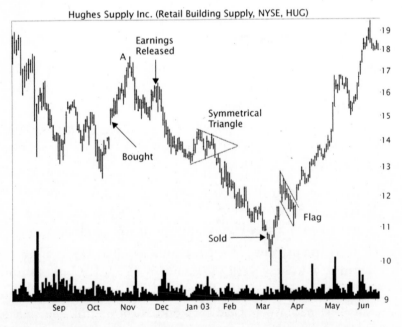

FIGURE 8.7 Jake bought the breakaway gap and hung on too long, well after bad earnings sent the stock plunging.

declined far enough to cover the gap left on the chart. Just 2% of breakaway gaps close in the first week, 23% close in the first month, 46% within three months, and 66% close within a year. That still leaves 34% open.

"You bought into a downtrend?" I asked. "Gutsy."

"Yeah," Jake replied. "I thought it represented a trend change, and for a while, I was right."

The stock peaked at A and when the company released earnings in November, the stock made a lower peak.

"You should have sold once the stock made a lower high. When price drops below the valley between them, it confirms a trend change."

"I know that now," Jake said. He didn't look happy talking about the trade. I'm sure visions of higher health insurance premiums filtered through his consciousness.

As Figure 8.7 shows, the stock tumbled after the second earnings announcement.

"When the stock broke out downward from the symmetrical triangle, why didn't you sell?"

He shrugged his shoulders and stared at his shoelaces. Then he looked up. "I sold just two days before the low. Can you believe that?"

"Everyone makes mistakes, Jake. The key question is, did you learn from your mistake?"

"Yeah. I'm not in love with Hughes Supply anymore."

Good Earnings Surprise

A good earnings announcement sends prices higher, sometimes gapping upward. The bad news is that 29% fail to rise at least 5%, and 48% fail to rise at least 10% after the breakout. Thus, only experienced traders should trade this one. Nevertheless, it pays to understand what might be waiting for you each quarter if you own a stock.

Figure 8.8 shows an earnings announcement that happened at the very bottom of a downtrend. The announcement acted as a reversal of fortunes. After the news release, the stock moved like a boy kissing a girl for the first time—a hesitant, shy, sideways move for a few days. A week after the announcement, the stock finally broke out upward then moved sideways and formed a symmetrical triangle. After the triangle breakout occurred, it was off to the races as price climbed in a measured move up fashion.

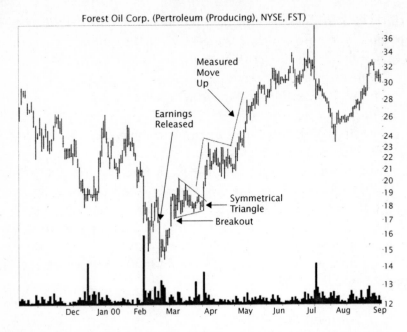

Forest Oil Corp. (Pertroleum (Producing), NYSE, FST)

FIGURE 8.8 Prices took a week to break out upward after an earnings release, and yet the rise was worth waiting for.

Identification

What should you look for when trying to pick good earnings announcements to trade? Here is a list:

- Look for a rising price trend. The best performance comes when you trade with the prevailing price trend, preferably in a rising general market (bull market with the appropriate index or average trending up).

- Trade announcements in a stock in which the industry is also doing well.

- On the announcement day or when the stock next trades, look for a tall intraday price range or for price to gap upward. The intraday price range should be taller than the 30-day average for the best performance. Taller is best. A gap shows buying enthusiasm.

- Wait for the breakout. That's a close above the intraday high on the announcement day.

Trading and Trading Tips

While researching this event pattern, I found some trading tips that might prove useful. Here they are:

- Price climbed an average of 24%.

- The best performers occur within a third of the yearly low, but they are rare, happening just 26% of the time.

- The worst performers are those in the middle third of the yearly price range.

- Throwbacks occur 41% of the time but when they do occur, performance suffers. Thus, look for overhead resistance and select event patterns with little or no cloud cover.

- Forty-one percent of the patterns reach the *ultimate high* in the first week.

- Tall patterns perform better than short ones. Tall means the high-low range is higher than the median height divided by the breakout price of 4.57%.

- To get a price target, measure the pattern height and add it to the intraday high on the announcement day. Prices reach the target 75% of the time.

days to ultimate high or low

the average time from the date of the breakout to the date of the ultimate high or low.

Case Study

Figure 8.9 shows the next case study. The stock made a symmetrical triangle that broke out upward, powered by an earnings announcement.

"I bought 400 shares at the market," Jake said, "filled at 31.75. I guessed that the triangle would support the price if the trade didn't work out right. You can see that it did, starting in May."

The price target was a measured move up of 34.09, call it 34. That's the measure from the base at 28.54 (A), the close the day before the earnings announcement, to 32, a day later when price peaked, and then projected upward from the low price the day before the buy.

"The measure rule worked for the October quarter surprise [target of 30] and I expected it would work for this one as well," Jake said. "Downside was the recent low of 28 and change." That would give a 12% loss, which he thought was a bit high.

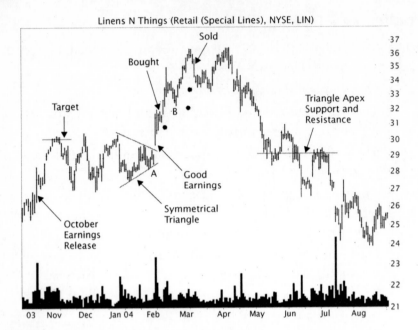

FIGURE 8.9 A good earnings announcement leads to a profitable trade. The black dots are the locations of stop-loss orders.

"I used a mental stop of 28 at first, just to allow the stock some breathing room. Then I raised it to 30.84, just below the prior valley (the first black dot in February)." A mental stop is one not placed with your broker. You monitor the stock and when it hits the price, you sell. Only professionals should use it because it requires commitment. If price hits the stop, you *have* to sell the stock.

The black dots on Figure 8.9 show where and when he placed the stops with his broker. He raised the stop to 32.13 or just below the nearby valley when price peaked. The next day, he raised it to 33.23 after the market closed.

Did the stop take him out? No. "I sold at the market because the CCI was diverging, the RSI was overbought, the market was down, and the stock was falling, piercing an up trendline."

The CCI is the commodity channel index, an indicator that shows short-term trading opportunities. Divergence occurred when the indicator was trending down even as the stock climbed from A. RSI is the relative strength index and the indicator peaked above 70, overbought. Indicators are beyond the scope of this book, but you can do your own research and evaluate them on this stock.

The S&P 500 made a triple top and was now heading down rapidly. The trendline Jake mentions connects points A and B and projects upward until it pierces price near the high. Collectively, the information told him to sell.

"The stock filled at 35.20." He made $1,350 or almost 11% and he handily beat the price target of 34.

Earnings Flag

If there is an event pattern to get excited about, it's this one: an earnings flag. Just 10% of earnings flags fail to climb more than 5% after the breakout, which is good for an event pattern. The average rise for flags is 34%, also good. Both numbers rank one (best) for performance among event patterns.

Figure 8.10 shows what an earnings flag looks like. Prices eased down from the broadening top and diamond bottom chart patterns leading to the September valley. Then prices bobbled up and formed an inverted and ascending scallop, bottoming at B. Even before the release of earnings in early November, the smart money was already in the stock, forcing the price up from the low at B. The earnings news was good as far as the market was concerned, and the stock continued higher until peaking at A. Then it moved sideways in a pennant pattern (shown as the earnings flag AC). An upward breakout from the pennant was the buy signal.

Notice that this earnings flag isn't a flag at all, but a pennant. The label *earnings flag* is a misnomer as the shape of the flag portion of the event pattern is often a random collection of squiggles. When the pattern takes the shape of a flag or pennant, then use a close above the top trendline as the buy signal. Otherwise, a close above the flagpole high serves as the buy signal. In Figure 8.10, the flagpole is the near vertical move from B to A. If the pennant were squiggles, then a close above A (the highest peak in the pattern) would be the buy signal.

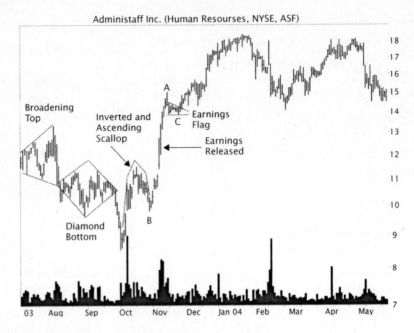

FIGURE 8.10   A steep rise precedes an earnings flag.

Identification

Look for the following when selecting an earnings flag:

- A large price move the day earnings are announced or the following trading day if the market is closed.

- A straight-line price run from the announcement to the flag forms the flagpole. The median flagpole length is five days.

- The flag portion of the pattern can be any shape. Look for prices to consolidate (move horizontally). It's an opportunity for traders to collect their breath, and check their pockets and couch cushions to see if they can scrape more money together to buy the stock.

- Wait for an upward breakout. That occurs when price pierces a flag trendline—or absent a trendline—a close above the high in the event pattern (usually the flagpole).

Perhaps most important of the guidelines is the straight-line price run. Like trading regular flags and pennants, a sharp run-up is almost mandatory. The rapid price rise shows unbridled enthusiasm for the stock. After the consolidation ends, the stock resumes the rise. Avoid earnings flags without a near vertical flagpole.

Trading and Trading Tips

Some trading tips and information that might increase your odds of a successful trade include the following:

- Most earnings flags are continuation patterns, but reversals perform better (a 38% average rise versus 33% for continuations).

- The average climb from the breakout to the ultimate high is 114 days (almost four months), so patience is required to capture the full gain.

- The flag width (excluding the flagpole) to the breakout averages 18 days.

- Most flags appear within a third of the yearly high, but those within a third of the yearly low perform best with rises averaging 48%.

- The worst performance comes from breakouts in the middle third of the yearly price range. Those are the ones to avoid.

- Throwbacks occur 63% of the time. When a throwback occurs, performance suffers so avoid patterns with nearby overhead resistance.

- Patterns taller than the median height divided by the breakout price of 13.56% do better than short ones. Measure the height from the bottom of the flagpole (where the rapid uptrend begins) to the top of the event pattern.

- Some patterns top out in the first week so be prepared to take profits.

- The measure rule predicts a price target. Find the height of the pattern from the base of the flagpole to the top of the pattern and add the difference to the flag low (the lowest price to the right of the flagpole). The result is the target and prices reach the target 86% of the time in a bull market.

Case Study

Jake pointed to the screen (see Figure 8.11). "Look at the trade I made. I'm particularly proud of this one."

He bought 500 shares, filled at 20.88, well after the release of earnings and even above the flag itself.

"Why so late getting in?"

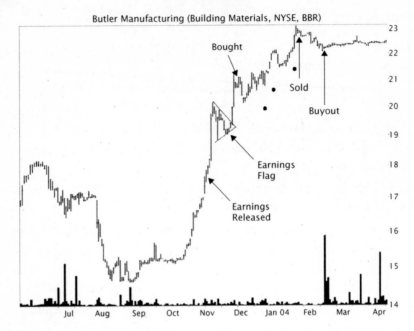

FIGURE 8.11 Jake was late buying after the earnings flag appeared, but his exit was almost perfect.

He shrugged his shoulders. "Better late than never." He predicted a slow uphill move with a target of 24, perhaps coasting as high as 25 or 26 before encountering overhead resistance.

If you consider that the base of the flagpole is near 15 and the top of the flag is about 20, that's a $5 spread. From the flag apex at 19, projected $5 upward, that's where Jake gets the 24 target. As you can see, the stock fell short of the target. A better target would be to use half the height projected upward for a closer target of 21.50.

The black dots on the chart show the stop locations and the days when he raised the stop. He likes to put his stops just below valleys (to the left and slightly above each dot).

Over the weekend, he reviewed the fundamentals of the company and didn't like what he read. "On the weekly chart, the stock peaked during January in four of the last five years. With a profit of almost $1,000 and an earnings release coming in February, I wasn't going to risk holding the stock."

The CCI and RSI indicators were both showing bearish divergence from October to December—predicting a downturn in the stock, but both turned up in January. The RSI was in overbought territory. The stock was just outside the top of the Bollinger band, a bearish signal even though price can slide along the band for days or weeks. Eventually, it will turn down and bounce off a lower band. The rate of change oscillator said that upward momentum was losing steam—another bearish divergence over the last two months. Jake considered all of those clues to make a trading decision.

He changed the most recent stop order to a market order and the stock sold at the open, filled at 22.88. He made $970 on the trade, or 9%.

A few weeks after he sold, the stock received a 22.50 buyout offer from BlueScope Steel.

Stock Downgrades

Few things are as upsetting as having a brokerage firm downgrade a stock I own and watch it tumble. The startling thing about stock downgrades is that price breaks out upward 39% of the time. What is probably an embarrassment for the people doing the downgrading, 48% issue their downgrades when the stock is trading within a third of the yearly low. Just 30% of the 691 downgrades I looked at occurred within a third of the yearly high when the warning would do the most good.

Figure 8.12 shows a litany of newsworthy items. First, a brokerage firm upgraded the stock in July. You can see what a great call that one was. If you followed their advice and bought the stock, you would have lost over 30% in five months. A week after the upgrade, the company announced earnings that missed the consensus estimate, starting price cascading downward like water over Niagara Falls.

At point A, a fund told a financial newspaper that the stock could reach $70 during the next year. The highest price the stock reached during that time was 54.30 (two days after the prediction). In fact, the stock closed a year later at 45.64, well short of 70.

Another poor earnings report sent the stock tumbling in mid-October. In mid-November, the company announced that a new cholesterol drug was showing promise for use in battling heart attacks. That sent the stock upward, but only for a few days.

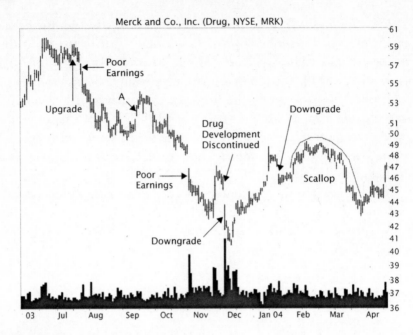

FIGURE 8.12 An upgrade occurs near the yearly high and the November downgrade comes near the yearly low.

Then came word that the company discontinued development of a diabetes drug. The next day, the stock gapped downward when two large brokerage firms downgraded the stock. The downgrade sounded like a good call, but you can see that it occurred near the yearly low. Clearly, the downgrade would have been much more effective if it happened in June near 60.

Another downgrade came in January as the stock was recovering. Price gapped lower on the news but soon rebounded. The stock rounded over in an inverted and descending scallop chart pattern. After that, and off the chart to the right, the stock moved horizontally before taking a big nosedive in October 2004 when the company pulled Vioxx from the shelves (see Figure 8.1).

Identification

Unless you are a favorite pet of the brokerage firm, you won't hear about a downgrade until after it happens. By then, the stock's price may be gapping downward. If you want to trade a downgrade, here's what to look for:

- A financial institution (brokerage firm, investment bank, and so on) announces the downgrade.
- Look for a large intraday trading range. The larger the better. It should be larger than the 30-day average intraday high-low trading range.
- A downward breakout occurs when price closes below the announcement day low. A downward breakout occurs 61% of the time, so that is the direction to trade.
- Heavy volume usually accompanies the downgrade.

Trading and Trading Tips

Consider the following trading tips and general information to help you avoid losing money or perhaps make some after a downgrade:

- If the breakout is upward, expect the stock to round over and then decline. An example of this is the January downgrade in Figure 8.12. In 37% of the cases, the stock begins tumbling within a week after the announcement. Within a month, half have peaked. Wait for the stock to peak and then consider selling a long holding or shorting the stock. The average decline of stocks once they peak (after a downgrade) is 30% in a bull market (but remember that the number is based on perfect trades).
- The average rise after an upward breakout is 27%. Downward breakouts drop an average of 14% in a bull market, 19% in a bear market.
- It takes price an average of 79 days to reach the ultimate high after an upward breakout and 26 days to drop to the ultimate low after a downward breakout.
- About 25% of the stocks showing an upward or downward breakout fail to move more than 5% in the direction of the breakout before reversing trend. Almost half don't clear a 10% (downward breakouts) or 15% (upward breakouts) hurdle.

- Both breakout directions do best when the breakout is within a third of the yearly low.

- Throwbacks and pullbacks occur 49% and 48% of the time, respectively. Pullbacks hurt performance so avoid trading downgrade announcements with a downward breakout and underlying support.

- Tall patterns perform better than short ones. In a bull market, use the height divided by the breakout price compared to the median 5.75%. In a bear market, a tall pattern is one taller than the median 6.52%.

- The measure rule works 71% of the time for upward breakouts and 69% of the time for downward ones. Compute the announcement day height and add/subtract it from the high/low for upward/downward breakouts to get a target price.

Case Study

Figure 8.13 shows the next trade. In December, a broker upgraded the stock and prices climbed for two days despite a warning that earnings would not live up to expectations. Then the stock plummeted in a straight-line run. Along the way, the company settled an asbestos related lawsuit, but the stock continued down. Three days later, a broker downgraded the stock and it dropped 11% in one day. Two days later, another broker downgraded the stock at the very bottom of its descent.

That's when Jake became interested. After a 36% decline in just eight trading days, he expected a bounce and decided to trade that bounce. The day the stock moved up, he bought.

"The straight-line price decline was key," he said. "Without that, I would have stayed away."

The release of earnings in late January was worse than expected, however the stock moved up sharply on the news. Jake drew a short-term trendline along the price lows as shown on Figure 8.13. He expected the stock to stall at point A, falling victim to overhead resistance stapled to the ceiling in October (see the dashed lines). When the stock closed below the trendline, he sold the next day.

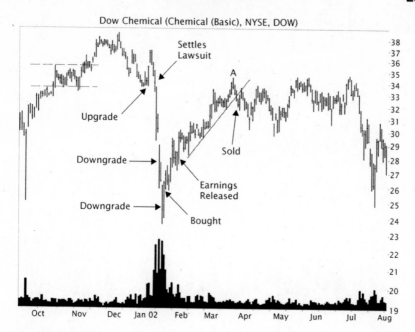

Dow Chemical (Chemical (Basic), NYSE, DOW)

Settles
Lawsuit

A

Upgrade

Downgrade

Sold

Earnings
Released

Downgrade

Bought

FIGURE 8.13 Jake bought after prices bottomed and exited when prices pierced a trendline.

Stock Upgrades

When I first looked at the study results of 698 stock rating upgrades, I had to recheck my work. The numbers said that regardless of the break-out direction, prices usually reversed course.

Figure 8.14 shows the first example. At the start of the New Year, a broker upgraded the stock and price gapped upward on the news. It coasted higher until peaking at point A. Then the buying enthusiasm powering the stock upward cooled and selling pressure took hold. The stock dropped, sinking to a low at B.

Another broker upgraded the stock the same day as the release of better than expected earnings. Again, the stock gapped upward on the news but this time, the stock did not make a higher peak. Prices rounded over and then tumbled from 17 and change to below 4 in October 2002, a massive decline of 80%.

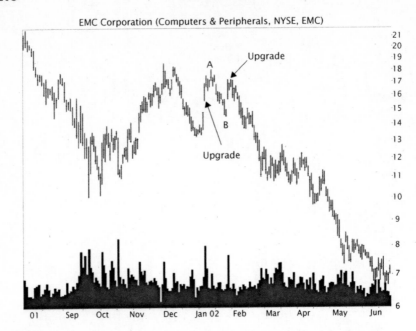

FIGURE 8.14 After an upward breakout from a rating upgrade, the stock curls over and heads down.

"And to think that there was at least one investor buying the stock at the very peak . . . " Jake said and stabbed his finger at point A. "I wonder if Trader Joe had the sense to sell before the stock bottomed."

Notice the price pattern in Figure 8.14. A rating upgrade and upward breakout followed by a decline a few days to a few weeks later. This hooking action is typical of stock upgrades. It doesn't happen all of the time. One measure indicates that in a bull market, over half are trending downward within three weeks. In a bear market, performance is even worse with 53% peaking within the first two weeks.

Figure 8.15 shows what a downward breakout looks like. A broker upgraded the stock from neutral to buy in late November. For a week, it looked like price was going to break out upward, but it never closed above the high posted on the announcement day. Instead, prices dropped, eventually closing below the announcement day's low and staging a downward breakout. Then look what happened. Two days later, in a daily pipe bottom at point A—pipe bottoms are more reliable on the weekly scale—the stock closed higher. Over the coming month, the stock continued moving upward, reaching a peak 53% above the low at point A.

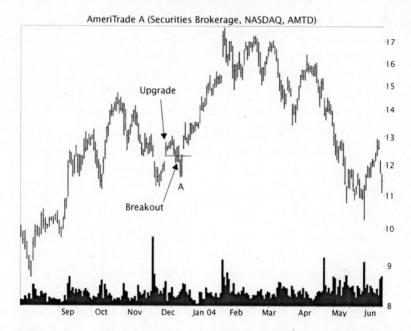

FIGURE 8.15 An upgrade has a downward breakout but prices soon rebound.

The breakout was downward but price soon moved up and posted a substantial gain. Over half the time, prices bottom in the first week after a downward breakout and then climb substantially.

Identification

Now that you know how upgrades behave, how do you recognize one worth trading? Here's a list of tips:

- A broker upgrades the stock, adds it to its recommended list, priority list, or focus list.

- On the announcement day, look for a large intraday (high-low) trading range that is above the 30-day average.

- An upward breakout occurs when price closes above the intraday high or below the intraday low (downward breakout) posted on the announcement day.

- Upward breakouts typically show heavy volume but downward breakouts usually have average volume.

Trading and Trading Tips

Once you have identified a possible trading candidate, here is how to trade it. Most of these tips assume that price continues rising for upward breakouts or continues tumbling for downward breakouts.

- For upward breakouts, prices rise from one to three weeks, on average, before cresting.

- For downward breakouts, prices drop for less than two weeks before starting to recover.

- For swing traders looking for a fast trade, trade in the direction of the breakout but expect price to reverse quickly.

- The average rise is 24% after an upward breakout. The average decline is 12% after a downward breakout in a bull market. Both numbers are based on perfect trades without fees.

- Once price reaches the ultimate high (upward breakout), it tumbles an average of 30%. After reaching the ultimate low (downward breakout), prices climb an average of 44%.

- It takes price an average of 61 days to reach the ultimate high and 25 days to hit the ultimate low.

- Eighteen percent of upgrades fail to rise more than 5%; 38% fail to drop more than 5% after a downward breakout. Be especially careful trading downward breakouts.

- The best upward breakouts occur within a third of the yearly high. Downward breakouts do best near the yearly low. If you want to short an upward breakout or go long a downward breakout, then do the opposite: Trade those with upward breakouts near the yearly low, downward breakouts near the yearly high. They move least before reversing.

- Throwbacks occur 63% of the time. Pullbacks happen 37% of the time in a bull market.

- Select tall patterns. Upward breakouts taller than the median 5.61% of the height divided by the breakout price perform best. Downward breakouts taller than the median 5.32% also do well.

Case Study

When I walked into the office before the market open, Jake was already there, pounding on the keyboard. "Take a look at this trade and tell me what you think."

Figure 8.16 shows the trade that Jake made. The day of the upgrade announcement, the stock made a large price swing but closed near the intraday low. It looked like a tail on the daily chart. Prices moved downward a few days later and the stock staged a downward breakout. When price bounced off the low at B, Jake bought.

"Was this a double bottom play?"

He nodded.

"Why didn't you wait for confirmation of the double bottom?"

"No need. The double bottom with a climbing price trend, coupled with the upgrade, it was a no-brainer. But I used a stop in case I was wrong."

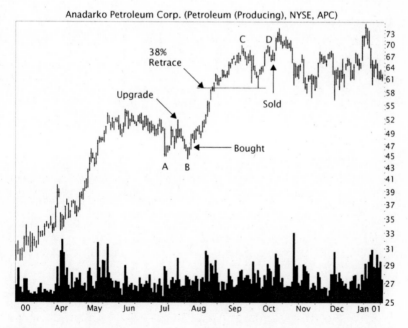

FIGURE 8.16 The stock formed a double bottom after an upgrade.

The stock made a beeline run until the nervous Nellies in September grabbed control of the stock. Prices peaked at C and rounded over. The stock retraced 38% of the gain from B before bottoming and rising up to D.

When price peaked at D, nearly the same as C, Jake suspected a trend change. "I sold once prices backed off the peak."

Chapter

Busted Patterns
Making Money by
Trading Failure

"See that?" I asked Jake as I pointed at the squiggles on the screen. "That's a *busted* head-and-shoulders. Buy it. It'll make you a bundle."

"Really?"

"Have I ever lied to you before?"

His eyebrow shot up for a moment then he turned to his computer and placed the trade. I smiled because I already owned the stock. I considered selling him my shares just as a famous mutual fund driver did a few years back. That guy hopped around the talk shows and played up a stock. Then the following week, his mutual fund started dumping the thing. When everyone found out about it, the story made quite a splash. Nevertheless, he's still out there running his mutt fund.

Traders have known about busted patterns for decades, but I consider them new. You never hear anything about trading a chart pattern that doesn't work as expected. I classify a busted chart pattern as one in which price moves less then 10% after the breakout before changing trend. This chapter takes a closer look at busted chart patterns.

Busted Broadening Patterns

Figure 9.1 shows the various busted broadening patterns. I'll be discussing them in clockwise order, starting from the upper left. Few broadening patterns busted in the database I used, so don't rely too heavily on the performance numbers. They are likely to change with additional samples. For reference, upward breakouts from the chart pattern types I looked at averaged price gains of 36% in a bull market. Downward breakouts averaged a decline of 18%. You can compare those numbers (from unbusted patterns) with the busted-pattern performance that I show in the below tables. In all of the performance numbers I cite, they are from many patterns traded perfectly, without commissions, so your results will vary.

FIGURE 9.1 Shown are some of the variations of busted broadening patterns.

Broadening Top

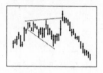 Broadening tops with upward breakouts bust when price exits the top but doesn't move far as the adjacent figure shows. Price then curls downward and drops out the bottom of the pattern, confirming the broadening top as a busted one.

Broadening tops have a throwback rate of 54% and a pullback rate of 48% (see Table.9.1). Why should you care about that? If the breakout is upward and prices throw back, you might think it's a busted pattern and try to trade it. That could squander several months worth of health insurance premiums, and everyone approaching retirement knows what that means. Wait for price to close below the lowest valley in the pattern before shorting the stock or selling a long position. If price drops that far, chances are it will continue downward. If the breakout is downward and pulls back, wait for price to soar out the top of the pattern before taking a long position.

TABLE 9.1

Description	Upward Breakouts	Downward Breakouts
Throwback or pullback rate	54%	48%
Busted-pattern performance	–31% (38 samples)	56% (54 samples)

I looked at 183 broadening tops with upward breakouts in a bull market and found that just 38 busted (21%). Downward breakouts had 182 qualifying and 54 busted (30%). Thus, busted broadening tops are somewhat rare.

Those that broke out downward then reversed climbed 56%. Those that broke out upward then plunged dropped an average of 31% as Table 9.1 shows.

Broadening Wedge, Ascending

The adjacent figure shows a downward breakout from the ascending broadening wedge in which price curls upward and will eventually close above the high in the chart pattern. When that happens, the pattern busts and it's worth taking a long position.

Ascending broadening wedges have a 50% throwback rate and a 57% pullback rate (see Table 9.2). I found 29 patterns with throwbacks and 95 with pullbacks in a bull market. When a pattern busts, prices climb 43% or sink 36%, depending on the final trend direction.

TABLE 9.2

Description	Upward Breakouts	Downward Breakouts
Throwback or pullback rate	50%	57%
Busted-pattern performance	−36% (5 samples)	43% (38 samples)

Trading an ascending broadening wedge is difficult for upward breakouts because determining when the price has broken out is the tough part. When the pattern with an upward breakout busts, price tumbles, hitting the upsloping bottom trendline. When price closes below the bottom trendline, that confirms the busted pattern and makes for a clean sell short signal. The bad news is that this pattern has prices that don't decline very far (slightly below average for all chart patterns with downward breakouts).

For downward breakouts like that shown in Figure 9.1, buy the stock when the price closes above the highest peak in the pattern. Watch for prices to reverse if they approach the top trendline.

Broadening Formation, Right-Angled and Ascending

Another downward breakout from a broadening pattern confirms the chart pattern as a busted one when price soars out the top. The same applies to upward breakouts when price peaks out the top, reverses, and then tumbles below the horizontal bottom trendline.

The throwback and pullback rates appear in Table 9.3. Notice that pullbacks occur 65% of the time, or two out of every three downward breakouts from a right-angled and ascending broadening formation. If price pulls back and you decide to jump in and buy the stock, chances are price will curl back down and drop. Wait for price to close above the highest peak in the pattern before buying the stock. That way, there is a good chance that price will continue moving up. For upward breakouts, wait for price to close below the bottom trendline before selling a long position or shorting the stock.

TABLE 9.3		
Description	Upward Breakouts	Downward Breakouts
Throwback or pullback rate	47%	65%
Busted-pattern performance	−26% (16 samples)	−50% (63 samples)

Busted patterns have prices that climb 50% or drop 26% once the new trend is established. The samples are few for downward breakouts, but they give you an indication of how well your trade might fare.

Broadening Bottom

 The adjacent figure shows a broadening bottom and it's similar to a broadening top, except prices enter the pattern from the top, moving down. In this example, price closes below the lower trendline boundary but doesn't move very far before reversing. Price crosses the pattern and pierces the upper trendline then continues higher. The pattern busts because the breakout is downward but fails to continue moving down. The same logic applies to upward breakouts that reverse and continue down, busting the pattern.

TABLE 9.4		
Description	Upward Breakouts	Downward Breakouts
Throwback or pullback rate	41%	42%
Busted-pattern performance	−31% (20 samples)	49% (18 samples)

Table 9.4 shows the throwback and pullback rates, which are similar; both occur just over 40% of the time. Busted patterns, based on few samples despite a database of nearly 250 in the study, show that rises average 49% and declines average 31%. The rises occur after a downward breakout and a trend reversal (busting the pattern). Declines happen after an upward breakout reverses.

As with many of the broadening patterns, take a position in the stock once price crosses the pattern and either closes beyond the prior peak/valley (for aggressive traders), or closes outside the trendline boundary (safest). Price may reverse as it nears the trendline, so expect that.

Broadening Wedge, Descending

The adjacent figure shows a busted descending broadening wedge. The breakout is upward but price falters, rounds over, and plunges. When price closes below the pattern's low, it confirms the busted pattern. A similar situation applies when price breaks out downward and reverses, soaring out the top of the wedge, busting it.

Descending broadening wedges are one of the better performers, but not as a busted pattern. How do I know? Because few patterns bust. I looked at 270 with upward breakouts and 47 with downward breakouts in a bull market, and just 51 patterns had price move less than 10% before reversing. Most reversals came from downward breakouts as Table 9.5 shows.

TABLE 9.5		
Description	Upward Breakouts	Downward Breakouts
Throwback or pullback rate	53%	53%
Busted-pattern performance	−26% (43 samples)	34% (8 samples)

Both upward and downward breakout directions have the same retrace rate: 53%. Those patterns that busted soared a weak 34% or dropped 26%, depending on the final trend direction. Because the sample size is so small, don't rely on the performance numbers.

For upward breakouts, sell a long holding or short the stock once price drops below the lowest valley. Watch for price to reverse once it nears the lower trendline.

For downward breakouts, buy when price closes above the top trendline. It may stall at the high posted by the start of the pattern, so be prepared, and consider tightening your stops as the target nears.

Figure 7.2 shows a busted descending wedge.

Broadening Formation, Right-Angled and Descending

 The last pattern of the six is the right-angled and descending broadening formation. In this example, price breaks out downward and then moves up haltingly before soaring in a straight-line attack. When price closes above the top horizontal trendline, it confirms a busted pattern. The breakout could have been upward followed by a downward plunge, forcing a bust.

After the breakout, prices return to the breakout price just over 50% of the time in a throwback or pullback as Table 9.6 shows. After the retrace, if price happens to continue moving in the same direction, it will bust the pattern and drop 26% or rise 52% on average. Again, the sample size is small despite having 191 patterns in which to choose.

TABLE 9.6		
Description	Upward Breakouts	Downward Breakouts
Throwback or pullback rate	52%	51%
Busted-pattern performance	−26% (28 samples)	52% (23 samples)

For upward breakouts, prices throw back and continue down, eventually dropping below the lowest valley and busting the chart pattern. Price need not pierce the lower trendline before you sell short the stock, but do make sure the industry and general market are also trending lower. If they are not trending downward, then wait for price to close below the lower trendline before shorting the stock.

With downward breakouts, wait for price to close above the top trendline before buying. The example in Figure 9.1 shows this scenario.

Case Study

"Are you going to use one of my trades, are yah?" Jake asked and put his open hand just inches from my face as I worked at the computer. He can be annoying sometimes.

"I've decided to use a trade in which you lost money."

His eyes lit up and he seemed buoyant, positively ecstatic. "The one where I lost ninety grand in JCB Enterprises?"

I laughed. "I sometimes brag about my losses, too." I punched a button on the keyboard and the result appears in Figure 9.2.

"When the stock broke out downward I took notice, but I wasn't in the mood to short the stock," Jake said. "So I just watched it."

A few days later, the stock vaulted to the top end of the broadening pattern. "That's when I bought." He placed a stop using a 38% Fibonacci retrace of the prior up move, which turned out to be near the bottom of

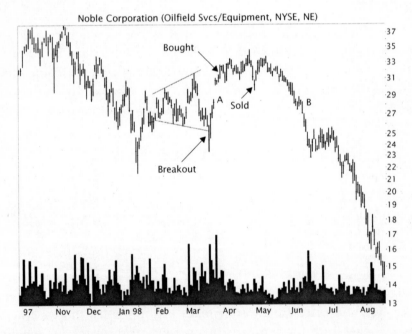

FIGURE 9.2 This busted broadening bottom broke out downward and zoomed higher, only to roll over and die.

the gap (point A). Gaps are common support or resistance areas and you can see how prices paused at B—even with the bottom of the gap.

The stock moved up marginally until late April when it tumbled four points in three days. "It looked like the start of a quick decline, and I wasn't going to stick around to see what happened. So, I sold the stock before it could hit the stop and saved myself some money." The stock could have dropped to the breakout price at 25 in short order, so selling was the wise choice. If he held on, look how big a loss he would have taken.

Diamonds, Doubles, and Head-and-Shoulders

Figure 9.3 shows the next batch of busted patterns, selected alphabetically and arranged with the tops above.

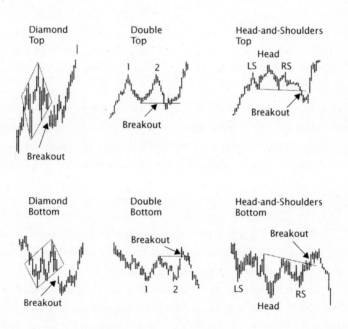

FIGURE 9.3 Shown are busted diamonds, double tops and bottoms, and head-and-shoulders.

Diamond Top

A diamond top busts when price breaks out in one direction and then returns to make an extended move in the opposite direction. In the diamond top shown in the adjacent figure, the breakout is downward but busts the pattern when price closes above the highest peak.

Throwbacks and pullbacks occur just short of 60% of the time (see Table 9.7). Wait for price to move above (after a downward breakout) the top of the diamond or below the bottom of the diamond (after an upward breakout) before taking a position. If you trade sooner, you may be buying into a throwback or pullback in which prices usually resume the original breakout direction.

TABLE 9.7

Description	Upward Breakouts	Downward Breakouts
Throwback or pullback rate	59%	57%
Busted-pattern performance	–23% (22 samples)	32% (28 samples)

The busted-pattern performance, based on few samples, is well below what it should be. The numbers are low enough that I would probably look for a different type of busted pattern to trade. (The inset in Figure 7.4 shows a busted diamond top with an upward breakout.)

Double Top

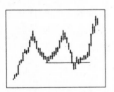

Double tops bust when the breakout is downward, but price doesn't fall far before rising above the top of the chart pattern. I used the Eve & Eve double top as the proxy for all double tops. Because a double top has only one breakout direction, I removed the upward breakout column. As Table 9.8 shows, pullbacks occur 59% of the time. The 74% performance is the rise from busted double tops. This is different from other patterns with up and down breakout directions. Those show a negative number for downward breakouts. A negative number for busted-pattern performance means that the breakout was upward then prices tumbled. The 74% rise is a mouthwatering gain in any trader's portfolio and the high sample count suggests the number is solid, but it's based on perfect trades without any fees.

TABLE 9.8	
Description	Downward Breakouts
Pullback rate	59%
Busted-pattern performance	74% (62 samples)

Trading a double top is simple. If the pattern confirms as a true double top, meaning that price has closed below the valley between the two tops, then wait for price to rise above the closest peak.

Try drawing a trendline connecting the peaks. If the trendline slopes downward, then buy when price closes above it. Ignore upsloping trendlines; just use a close above the closest peak.

If a double top does not confirm (the stock rises before closing below the valley floor), then you can also trade that pattern. The double top should qualify in all other respects (peak separation in both time and price, distance from peak to valley, and so on). Buy the stock when price rises above the nearest peak or above a downsloping trendline connecting the two peaks.

Head-and-Shoulders Top

A busted head-and-shoulders top looks like a pattern with an aggressive pullback except the pullback has price continuing up. It moves above the top of the chart pattern, confirming the bust.

A head and shoulders top breaks out downward and pulls back 50% of the time as Table 9.9 shows. If price continues moving in the same direction (upward), the average rise is 53%. That is a nice return for a busted pattern and the high sample count means the number is reliable.

TABLE 9.9	
Description	*Downward Breakouts*
Pullback rate	50%
Busted-pattern performance	53% (68 samples)

There are two ways to trade a head-and-shoulders top. One is to select patterns that confirm (price closes below the neckline or right valley low) and the other is to choose unconfirmed patterns. I show a confirmed head-and-shoulders top in Figure 9.3.

Place a trade once price closes above the right shoulder peak for aggressive traders. Price may stall as it approaches the price level of the top of the head, so keep that in mind. You can also draw a downsloping trendline connecting the head and right shoulder. Buy when price closes above the trendline. For investors, wait for price to close above the value of the head and then buy.

Diamond Bottom

I found almost 300 diamond bottoms but few that busted. The adjacent figure shows an example. Price breaks out downward but quickly recovers and will eventually rise above the chart pattern's high.

As shown in Table 9.10, throwbacks occur 53% of the time but pullbacks happen 71% of the time. After the pattern busts, prices climbed an average of 34% or dropped an average of 25%.

TABLE 9.10		
Description	*Upward Breakouts*	*Downward Breakouts*
Throwback or pullback rate	53%	71%
Busted-pattern performance	–25% (16 samples)	34% (15 samples)

Trade diamond bottoms as you do the top variety. Wait for price to climb above the highest peak in the pattern or below the lowest valley before taking a position. Entering earlier increases your risk of a failed trade.

Double Bottom

 A busted double bottom reminds me of a right-angled and ascending broadening pattern, one with a flat base and upsloping top trendline. Price breaks out upward before tumbling and closing below the twin bottoms, confirming a busted pattern.

Double bottoms break out in one direction, so Table 9.11 only shows the results for upward breakouts. Throwbacks happen 55% of the time so don't be fooled into taking a position in the stock until it closes below the lowest valley in the pattern.

	TABLE 9.11

Description	Upward Breakouts
Throwback rate	55%
Busted-pattern performance	–32% (58 samples)

Busted patterns have prices that drop an average of 32%, which I consider quite good. Like a double top, there are two ways to play a busted double bottom: You can buy an unconfirmed pattern or wait for confirmation. Figure 9.3 shows the confirmed variety.

The safest way to trade this pattern is to wait for price to close below the lowest valley in the double bottom. If you can draw an upsloping trendline below the two valleys, then a close below this line would also signal a trade. If you do short early using the trendline approach, price may stall at the twin bottoms, forming a triple bottom, so be prepared for that.

Head-and-Shoulders Bottom

A head-and-shoulders bottom busts when the breakout is upward and prices tumble. That's the situation Figure 9.3 shows.

The throwback rate from a head-and-shoulders bottom (HSB) is 45% (see Table 9.12). Busted patterns have prices that decline 28% on average.

Trading an HSB is similar to other busted patterns. After the breakout, price will curl downward. When it closes below the right shoulder low, sell a long position or short a new one. Less aggressive traders will want to wait for price to decline below the head before trading. Otherwise, expect price to pause or reverse either at the price level of the left shoulder valley or the head. Another early entry is to use a trendline connecting the head and right shoulder valley. When price closes below this trendline, short the stock or sell a long position. Again, watch for the decline to stall when it drops to the price level of the head.

TABLE 9.12

Description	Upward Breakouts
Throwback rate	45%
Busted-pattern performance	–28% (53 samples)

With an HSB, you need not wait for the pattern to confirm (price to close above the neckline) before trading it. If the three valleys conform to an HSB but prices drop after forming the right shoulder instead of confirming the HSB, then trade the stock according to the preceding guidelines.

Case Study

Sometimes you don't see a chart pattern soon enough to trade it. My experience suggests you should pass up a trade if you can't get in at a good price or if the price is running away from you. When I grab a quote on a stock, if the stock is down, I won't buy it. Why not? Because price is falling. In a few minutes, it will be cheaper.

I won't buy a stock if it is up too much intraday. Why not? Because I know that as soon as I buy, price will turn down, and I'll be stopped out for a loss. The comfort zone lies somewhere in between those two ranges. Like Goldilocks and the Three Bears, the stock has to be moving up but not too quickly.

Figure 9.4 is a case in point. When Jake found this head-and-shoulders top, the stock confirmed the pattern but prices climbed, rising above the head and producing a busted pattern.

"What should I do?" he asked.

"Wait for a throwback and then buy." I could tell that he really wanted to buy the stock right now. He started wringing his hands, pacing about the room, trying to decide. "Don't fall in love with the stock, Jake. There will be other stocks."

He looked up and me and knew that I was right. He returned to his computer and buried his head in the glow of the computer screen.

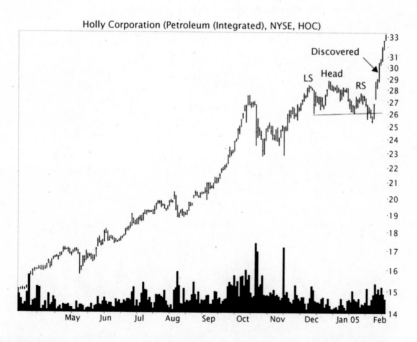

FIGURE 9.4 Jake missed this trade because he discovered it too late to take a position.

In the weeks since I took a snapshot of Figure 9.4, the pattern hasn't thrown back so he missed the trade. The stock has moved up to 45 and change. Did he miss a promising opportunity? You bet. Many stocks don't form straight-line runs like this one, so I think it pays to be cautious and pass up a late-entry trade.

If he had spotted the pattern sooner, he should have put a buy stop at the head 28.78 (a penny above the peak) or drawn a downsloping trendline along the head and right shoulder peaks. A close above the trendline at 27.28 would have gotten him in sooner, but was more risky. Pullbacks often rise to meet or slightly exceed the height of the right shoulder peak. If he had bought in at 27.28, he could have pulled $15 to $17 per share out of the market.

"Timing is everything," I told him.

He looked at his watch. "11 o'clock."

More Busted Patterns

Figure 9.5 shows the last spread of busted patterns.

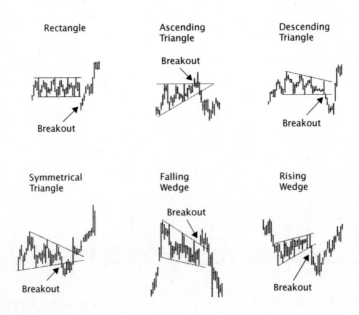

FIGURE 9.5 Here are another six busted chart patterns.

Rectangles

Rectangles can break out in any direction, but when price reverses and crosses the pattern to exit the opposite side, it confirms a busted pattern. That's the time to trade it. Figure 9.5 shows an example of this scenario.

I used a rectangle top as the proxy for all rectangles because it had the most samples (676), and Table 9.13 shows the numbers. Rectangles throw back 64% of the time and pull back 58% of the time. If price continues moving in the new direction, the rectangle busts and price rises an average of 52% or drops an average of 25%. Downward breakouts have few samples.

TABLE 9.13		
Description	*Upward Breakouts*	*Downward Breakouts*
Throwback or pullback rate	64%	58%
Busted-pattern performance	−25% (57 samples)	52% (22 samples)

The above figure shows a downward breakout from a rectangle top. Prices pull back and shoot out the top of the pattern. Only when they cross to the other side and close outside the trendline boundary should a trader consider the pattern busted and jump on the new trend.

After a downward breakout like that shown, if prices return to the rectangle pattern, then look for a partial decline. If one occurs inside the rectangle then that would be a buy signal with an assumed upward breakout.

Ascending Triangle

Ascending triangles can break out in either direction. The adjacent figure shows an upward breakout with prices throwing back and plunging through the bottom trendline, confirming a busted pattern.

Upward breakouts throw back 57% of the time as shown in Table 9.14, and if prices keep tumbling, they bust the pattern and decline an average of 24%. Downward breakouts pull back 49% of the time, and busted patterns have prices rising 45%. Again, these numbers may be averages, but they are from perfect trades without fees subtracted.

TABLE 9.14

Description	Upward Breakouts	Downward Breakouts
Throwback or pullback rate	57%	49%
Busted-pattern performance	–24% (149 samples)	45% (46 samples)

Figure 9.5 shows an ascending triangle with a busted upward breakout. For aggressive traders, short the stock or sell a long holding when price closes below the upsloping trendline. Watch for price to stall as it dips to the lowest valley in the pattern. For conservative traders, enter a new trade when price declines below the lowest valley in the busted pattern.

For downward breakouts that bust the triangle, take a position when price closes above the top trendline.

In Chapter 7, Figure 7.18 shows an ascending triangle that qualifies as a busted pattern because price drops 8%, just short of the 10% benchmark. Figure 5.1 in Chapter 5 shows another example of a busted ascending triangle. This one is treacherous because price breaks out upward and then moves down for just four days before gapping back into the triangle.

Descending Triangle

The adjacent figure shows a descending triangle with a downward breakout. When price closes above the downsloping trendline on the top, it busts the pattern.

Throwbacks and pullbacks occur at the rates shown in Table 9.15. Look at the performance of busted patterns. Those with downward breakouts that curl upward and shoot out the top rise an average of 60% and that is with 180 samples. Clearly, a busted descending triangle is one you will want to focus on. The other busted direction does well, with prices dropping 26% after a failed upward breakout.

TABLE 9.15		
Description	Upward Breakouts	Downward Breakouts
Throwback or pullback rate	37%	54%
Busted-pattern performance	–26% (77 samples)	60% (180 samples)

For aggressive traders in a busted downward breakout, take a position once price pierces or closes above the downsloping trendline. For conservative traders, wait for price to rise above the highest high in the pattern. That way, price is likely to continue moving up.

Be sure to check the market averages and other stocks in the same industry. If they are trending in the same direction, that improves your chances of a profitable trade.

Figure 8.3 in Chapter 8 shows an example of a busted descending triangle. Price barely closes below the lower trendline before moving up substantially. Another example appears in Chapter 6, Figure 6.12.

Symmetrical Triangle

 Symmetrical triangles are almost as common as aphids on my cucumber plants in summer, and the lower left of Figure 9.5 shows an example of a busted symmetrical. If price breaks out in one direction and shoots out the other side, then it's a busted pattern. That behavior often, but not always, leads to a large price move. Table 9.16 shows the results. Throwbacks complete 37% of the time and pullbacks are more frequent, 59% of the time. Prices that break out downward then reverse and punch through upward soar an average of 43%. Upward breakouts that bust show declines of 26%. Both directions have plenty of samples, so the results are solid.

TABLE 9.16		
Description	Upward Breakouts	Downward Breakouts
Throwback or pullback rate	37%	59%
Busted-pattern performance	–26% (97 samples)	43% (97 samples)

Once a symmetrical triangle breaks out and reverses, crossing both trendlines, trade in the direction of the new trend. Take a position once price closes outside the second trendline. Figure 8.5 in Chapter 8 shows an example of this scenario when price broke out downward, returned to breakout upward, and made a large gain. Figure 7.19 in Chapter 7 shows two busted symmetrical triangles; and Figure 7.18 shows a busted symmetrical in May.

If you are concerned about a reversal, especially if the industry or market is trending opposite your stock, then wait for price to move above the highest peak or below the lowest valley before trading. Price often stalls or reverses at prior peaks and valleys.

Falling Wedge

 I'm not keen on wedges, regardless of whether they are rising or falling. Other traders seek them out. I think the profit potential is meager compared to other patterns because price will often rise to the top of the pattern and then reverse. That doesn't leave much room for profit unless you are a talented swing trader aiming for those types of moves.

Figure 9.5 shows a busted falling wedge, one with an upward breakout but prices soon plunge.

Table 9.17 shows the numbers. A throwback happens over half the time and pullbacks occur over two thirds of the time. Based on few samples, downward breakouts bust then prices rise a sumptuous 51%. Upward breakouts drop and tumble 19%.

TABLE 9.17		
Description	Upward Breakouts	Downward Breakouts
Throwback or pullback rate	56%	69%
Busted-pattern performance	–19% (53 samples)	51% (21 samples)

Trade falling wedges like you would most other chart patterns. When prices break out in one direction, reverse and pierce the opposite trendline moving in the new direction, then take a position in the stock. If prices are moving upward, watch for them to stall near the top of the pattern—a common resistance zone.

For example, Figure 9.5 shows a falling wedge with an upward breakout. Sell a long holding or short the stock when price closes below the lower trendline.

Rising Wedge

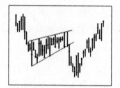 The rising wedge shown in the lower right of Figure 9.5 has a downward breakout in which price curls around and then moves above the highest peak in the chart pattern, confirming a busted pattern.

Table 9.18 shows that 73% of the rising wedges throw back and 63% pull back. Busted patterns show prices rising an average of 43% or dropping 26%. The upward move with 84 samples is particularly solid. Maybe that's why some traders like wedges. They have learned to search for busted ones.

TABLE 9.18		
Description	Upward Breakouts	Downward Breakouts
Throwback or pullback rate	73%	63%
Busted-pattern performance	–26% (25 samples)	43% (84 samples)

Figure 9.5 shows a rising wedge with a downward breakout. In such a situation, buy the stock once price closes above the top trendline. For upward breakouts, a close below the lower trendline is the trading signal. Expect support when price nears the lowest valley in the pattern.

Case Study

Figure 9.6 shows a trade Jake made on the weekly scale. He bought 200 shares, filled at the market for 65.33. "The company projected 20% annual growth through 2005," he said, "and I was foolish enough to believe them. The problem was their projections had nothing to do with the stock's price."

He bought the upward breakout from a symmetrical triangle. "I expected the price to stall at overhead resistance of 67 and again at 74 with support at 55 and 59–60." The 67 call was a good one even though price coasted to 69 during the week he bought. Below the symmetrical triangle, the stock dropped to a low of 53.28, with solid support showing in the 55 to 57 range, just as he predicted. The 59–60 support area only slowed the stock a bit.

"I wanted to hold the stock for the long term because it was trading near the yearly high," he explained. "A rise to 74 would only be a gain of 13%, and I wanted more which would take longer."

Ten days after he bought, the company announced that it was buying Immunex. That sent shares tumbling, causing a throwback and price to close below the lower trendline a few weeks later. A few days into the New Year, the stock pierced the 55 support zone.

"Although I wanted to hold it for the long term," he said, "I didn't want a massive loss on my hands." He received a fill at 54.20 for a huge loss of 17% or $2,250. "There was red ink all over my keyboard that morning. I expected the stock to pull back to the triangle bottom then continue its decline." The stock pulled back and continued rising, piercing the top trendline before heading back down again. The stock plunged to 30.57 in July, less than half what he paid for it.

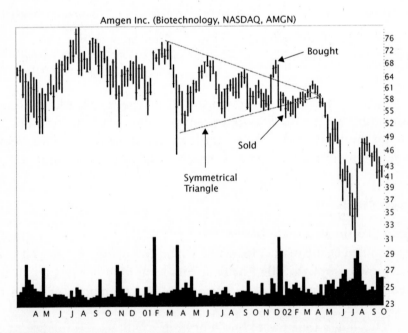

FIGURE 9.6 An upward breakout from a symmetrical triangle busts when prices drop to the other side of the triangle and close outside the lower trendline. Shown on the weekly scale.

Did Jake make a mistake selling? No, but he could have timed his entry better (by placing a buy order at the triangle trendline). That would have lowered his loss.

Look at Figure 9.6 again. Regardless of when you bought the stock, the upward breakout or the downward one, you would have likely taken a loss. A double turn like this happens occasionally, so do not be surprised when it happens to you. Keep trading those busted patterns for the big bucks.

Other Busted Patterns

In this chapter, I've covered 18 busted chart patterns that you are likely to see in your trading travels. I didn't cover all busted patterns. The safest way to trade a busted pattern is to buy when price closes above the peak in the pattern or short when price closes below the lowest valley. If trendlines shape the chart pattern, then a close outside those trendlines opposite the breakout direction also provides another trading signal. Watch for price to stall or reverse at support and resistance zones, especially the pattern's highest peak or lowest valley.

I think you'll find that trading a busted pattern is more profitable than trading non-busted ones. But remember that even busted patterns bust. The one shown in Figure 9.6 had an upward breakout, dropped down to breakout downward, and then returned to close above the top trendline before making the final plunge.

More Trades
Putting It All Together

This chapter gives you more trades that I made with my own money in the market. Use them as a quiz to test what you've learned.

For the most benefit, pull up each trade on your computer and view it on your trading setup. Decide whether there is a reason to trade each stock. Look at the general market and any trading indicators that you like to use. Search for chart patterns because that's the point of this book. I show each company twice, the first figure has little detail. Decide whether the trade is worth making. The second figure shows how I traded it. All figures use the logarithmic price scale.

IMC Global

Figure 10.1 shows a chart of IMC Global. In August 2004, the Justice Department cleared the merger of the company with a unit of Cargill, so it may be difficult to find the historical prices.

Gina's birthday is coming up and you want to buy her a new car. The problem is your petty cash is low so you go hunting for a trade and find the stock shown in Figure 10.1. At point A, do you buy the stock, hold it, sell it (assuming you already owned it), or sell it short (which suggests the stock will tumble so you can buy it back at a lower price)?

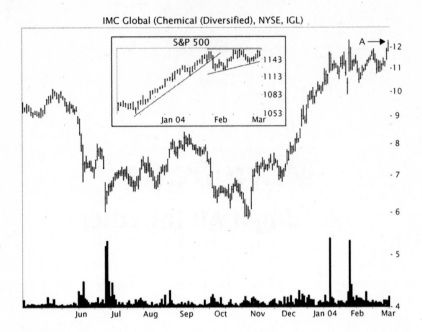

FIGURE 10.1 Do you buy, sell, hold, or sell short the stock at point A?

Doing nothing is always an option, but Gina would be upset at not receiving a gift, and she might tell your wife that you have been fooling around.

Trading out of desperation (you *need* the money for her gift) is often a way to the poor house. Those trades have a habit of going bad right when you need the income. Let's assume that money is no problem, it's just a question of whether to skip a week's stay at the bungalow in Hawaii this month. That will save fuel and other costs for running the Lear jet, especially if you hire a pilot to man the controls while you play games with Gina in back.

Because the stock's price is near the yearly high, you don't want to short the stock. Stocks making new highs have a tendency to continue making new highs. You also don't want to sell because the stock is rising. Why sell today if you can get a higher price for it tomorrow? That leaves buying the stock. Why would you want to buy it at such a high price? Answer: Momentum.

The inset in Figure 10.1 shows the S&P 500 index poised to make a new high when it breaks out upward from an ascending triangle.

Figure 10.2 shows how I traded the stock. The stock began rising from point A to B. Then the stock went horizontal in a high, tight flag (HTF). Of course, the outline of the move after B does not look like a flag or even a pennant. That's typical for HTFs; some have an irregular shape. The key is that the stock nearly doubled in two months from point A.

The low at point A is 5.82 and the high at B is 12.40. That means there is a 90% probability that price will rise to 13.14 in a bull market. How did I get that? Using the measure rule, compute the price difference between the trend low at the start (A) and the high in the flag (B), which is 6.58. Take half of this (3.29) and add it to the low in the flag (C at 9.85) to get the target. Since C is clearly an outlier, you might want to use a higher valley (like point D).

Where should you place a stop? Below the low at point E is a good choice because the tight pennant should help support the stock. The low at E is 10.76, so I would place a stop at 10.67, an oddball number (avoid round numbers) far enough away from the low.

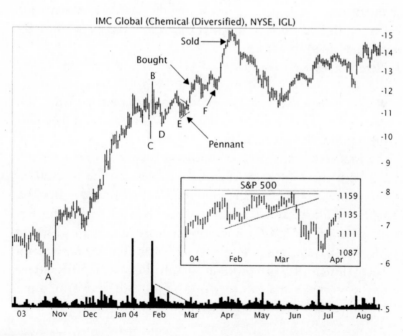

FIGURE 10.2 The stock moved up and was sold just days before it peaked.

With a target of 13.14 and a stop of 10.67, everything is in place for the trade. The stock is trading at 12.20. Do you take it? If you are wrong and the stock tumbles, that would represent a loss of 13%. Is that too high?

If the answer is yes, then compute a volatility stop using the average daily high-low difference over the prior month. That turns out to be 41 cents. Multiply this by 1.5 (62 cents) and subtract it from the current low of 11.80 for a stop of 11.18. That cuts the potential loss to 8%. Remember, low priced stocks (below $20) are more volatile than high priced ones. Placing the stop so close would have worked in this case, but I feel it's a bit close.

On March 2, 2004, I bought 1,000 shares at the market, filled at 12.20. My notebook entry for the trade used the 13.14 target and one at 14.36, found using the low on 2/27/04 at 11.07 (two days before I bought). The nearer target would be a gain of just 8%, but the farther one would be an 18% rise.

I placed a stop at 10.67, good till canceled. I raised the stop to 11.57 at point F because the general market was weak, and I wanted to close the distance. The price is just below the March 10 valley to the left of F. On 3/30, I raised the stop to 11.93 and a day later to 12.93. The next day, I decided to sell.

Here is my notebook entry:

> 4/1/04. I decided to sell my holdings because the market has been strong for the last several days, and I think it's still executing a pullback to formations (symmetrical triangles in some of the indexes). This stock is showing slowing momentum and has been moving up for the past six days. It's due to drop, so I'm taking my money and running. RSI says it's overbought. CCI will likely say sell tomorrow because CCI is dipping and about to hit the DCCI line. I looked at prior data and found four or five up moves in a row and looked at the aftermath. Since this stock has moved up sharply, I expect a 50% retrace of the up move and I don't want to give back $1,500 of a potential $2,100 profit, so I'm selling.

The CCI did signal a sale on the day I sold, but the stock closed higher.

Let me dissect the entry. A pullback to a chart pattern often means that price will turn down when the pullback completes. Holding a long position when the market turns downward is swimming against the current, something no trader wants to do. With momentum slowing in the stock, it also suggested a turn. The indicator, relative strength index (RSI with a 16-day lookback), was overbought, meaning traders had pushed up price to unsustainable levels. The stock could go higher and often does, but RSI was warning that things were pricy. The commodity channel index (CCI with a 20-day lookback) and the dual CCI (DCCI, a 5-day exponentially smoothed moving average of the CCI) said sell. It's a short-term indicator that confirmed my sell decision. I looked at the historical behavior of the stock when it moved up several days in a row and found that prices often reversed. All of this convinced me that it was time to sell. I sold the 1,000 shares at one time because selling half and holding half I think is like trying to rip a Band-Aid off slowly: It hurts longer. I've found that I earn more money selling all at once instead of scaling out.

The inset shows what the S&P did, ending on the day of the sale. The ascending triangle broke out downward in early March but the stock ignored the tug of the market current pulling at prices. Both the index and the stock moved higher in late March.

I made just over $2,000, or 17% on the trade. That's not enough for Gina's car, but it's a good start. Perhaps a plastic snap-together model would suffice. Make it a Corvette. You can brag that you bought your girl a 'vette and watch their jaws drop.

Giant Industries

Figure 10.3 shows the next potential trade. The stock moved up from the August low at a steady clip, trending upward at about 45 degrees, which usually makes for a powerful and long lasting rally—which it did. The stock peaked in March and backtracked, pausing to gather strength for the next move, whatever direction that may be. Volume followed price and made its own mountain peak. Would you buy, sell, hold, sell short, or avoid trading the stock?

The inset of the S&P 500 index gives a clue. Price broke out downward from the ascending triangle, piercing the upsloping bottom trendline.

Price pulled back to the trendline at A and eased lower then made a small broadening bottom pattern.

I think the pullback in the index was the key to this stock trade. When a stock or index pulls back, prices often continue moving in the direction of the breakout—downward in this case. Based on that, I would expect the index to move lower, just as it started to do. The question then becomes, would the stock follow the index down?

Figure 10.4 shows the trade. This is another high, tight flag (HTF), or really a high, loose flag. Loose flags have a tendency to fail more often and perform worse than tight ones. The difference is in their appearance. Tight flags seem compact, with highs and lows following straight trendlines. Loose flags have wild swings up and down. Figure 10.2, for example, shows a tight pennant, but the associated HTF is also a loose one.

Returning to Figure 10.4, the stock bottomed at A in December 2003, began the uptrend at C and peaked at B, almost tripling in price from A, an easy double in about a month from the January launch point at C.

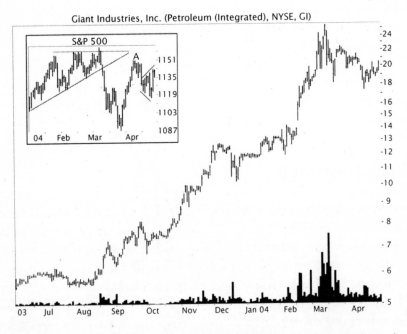

FIGURE 10.3 Is this stock a buy, sell, hold, sell short, or avoid altogether?

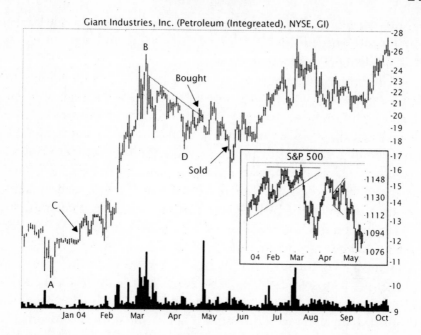

Giant Industries, Inc. (Petroleum (Integreated), NYSE, GI)

FIGURE 10.4 This high, tight flag failed to follow through on the upward breakout.

When price closed above the downsloping trendline, I thought the HTF was breaking out upward, so I bought 800 shares, filled at 20.38. The buy reason was a high, tight flag breakout in a hot industry.

The inset shows the direction of the general market. From the beginning of March (point B on the stock), the index trended downward and was moving lower on the day I bought. A declining market won't help a long trade.

I expected the market to rise for a few days until forming a large double top. The first top would combine as one the three peaks from January to March accompanied by the second peak now forming. The index was midway through creating a broadening bottom chart pattern at the time I bought.

The stop-loss point was at 17.30, or 15% away, "too far to place the stop with my broker," my trading notes say. That in itself is a warning. If the stop is too far away, then skip the trade. I chose the stop point because it was a nickel below the prior valley at D. Most of the stocks in the industry were near their yearly highs, ready to jump up, so maybe that's why I wasn't worried about the long drop to the stop. I was confident—overconfident—that this trade would work.

The upside target was 25.70, using half the height of the HTF (6.35) from where price started moving up at C to the high at B, projected upward from the closing price the day before the breakout.

The stock tumbled immediately then started to recover. Some say that a winning trade usually performs well right from the start. Bad ones go south quickly. I agree, and this trade is one example.

I did place the stop with my broker at 17.30, two days after I bought. Volatility was $1.01 over the past month, giving a volatility stop $1.50 below the current low. That would place the stop at 17.80, making it a bit closer than the one I used.

On May 19, the stock hit my stop and sold a nickel below it, filled at 17.25, for a loss of $2,500 or 16%. That's double the loss I like to see.

Prices collapsed in the S&P from the April high, sucking my trade down the drain along with the index. Look at the stock. I sold a day before prices bottomed. Had I held on, the stock would have fulfilled the measure rule and exceeded the 25.70 target.

Did I make the right decision to sell? Yes. Once you start second guessing and removing or lowering a stop, that's when your losses become uncontrollable. You'll find that the size of your wins diminish, too, because you'll be so paranoid about taking a loss that you'll sell as soon as the trade shows a profit.

An e-mail acquaintance has that problem now. He wrote asking if I could help him stop selling too soon. I told him he was probably checking his stock too often during the day, and he should place a stop with his broker and not worry about it. "Check it once a day, after the market closes," I told him. He wrote back and said he was checking his trade up to 20 times a day while working at his job. Employers don't like that behavior.

Lam Research

Figure 10.5 shows the next case study on the weekly scale. The inset shows the general market trending downward over the intermediate term. The NASDAQ composite looked similar to the S&P, a series of falling peaks with an uphill run leading to the end of the chart. The stock was also trending downward from the start of the New Year, but with slowing momentum. Do you trade the stock, and if so, what direction?

Let's discuss the index first. The chart pattern might be a measured move up. The low at 788 to the top of the chart would be the first leg. The corrective phase is the decline shown to the right of the peak near 1,157. The thinking is that when price leaves the corrective phase, price will rise, completing a nice run during creation of the second leg up.

Another interpretation is that the index shows a confirmed three falling peaks (3FP) chart pattern. What is different with this 3FP is that price has moved up since confirmation instead of down. Confirmation occurs when price closes below the lowest valley in the three-peak pattern. That happens as price drops to 1,075 before the last valley on the right.

One interpretation suggests price will rise and another says it will fall. Which is right? Since we're trading the stock and not the index, it doesn't matter, but that explanation doesn't wash with me. I think the market direction is important, and I vote for higher prices. Even though the 3FP confirmed, price has risen. Perhaps a closer look at the index on the daily scale would clarify the situation.

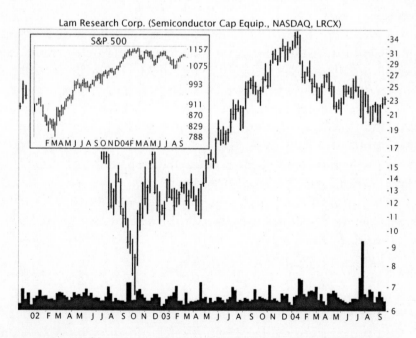

Lam Research Corp. (Semiconductor Cap Equip., NASDAQ, LRCX)

FIGURE 10.5 This stock appears on the weekly scale. Do you buy, sell, hold, sell short, or avoid it altogether?

Figure 10.6 shows how I handled it. The index did move higher (the inset chart ends on the day the stock sold).

As to the trade, five minutes before the close, I bought 700 shares at 23.10. Why? I wanted to trade the rounding bottom. Buying just after the halfway point I viewed as a wonderful profit opportunity. This is what I wrote in my notebook: "Fundamentals are good when compared to others in the semiconductor capital equipment business. A triple bottom (123 in Figure 10.6) and pipe bottom round out the base of the turn. This may take nine months to return to the old high, but it looks very promising. Expect price to blip up then return to the rounding bottom base as happens in some rounding turns. When it gets over 30, be prepared to sell. I feel confident about this trade."

The pipe bottom is the parallel price valley two weeks to the left of when I bought (point three on the chart). The triple bottom, 123, is the three prior valleys near the same price. The triple bottom did not confirm—price close above the highest peak in the pattern—until after I bought. The "blip up" in the rounding bottom is a jump in price just after price rounds from down to up. Price soon settles down at a slightly higher price before resuming the upward arc. That jump didn't happen during this trade.

I placed the stop at 19.64, for a potential 15% loss. The stop was 7 cents below the lowest valley in the rounding turn. "I am willing to sacrifice this drawdown to get to the old high of 33." I viewed this trade as a long-term one and was willing to take a larger loss to achieve my goal.

I put a 200-day moving average on the daily chart and found the NASDAQ was above its moving average. I expected the general market to rise and for the trade to reach the 33 target.

As the trade progressed, I raised the stop to 24.83 (11/17/04), 25.47 on 12/6, and 27.13 on 12/16.

On January 4, 2005, the stock hit my stop and filled at 27.131, suffering from the downturn that gripped the market at the turn of the New Year. I made $2,800, or 17%.

"I want to play," Jake said.

I hunched over the computer screen, but it was too late. He already read what I was writing.

"I want to tell them about the four million I made in KB Home."

I swung around and faced him. "This is a *Getting Started* book, not *How I Make Millions Trading.*"

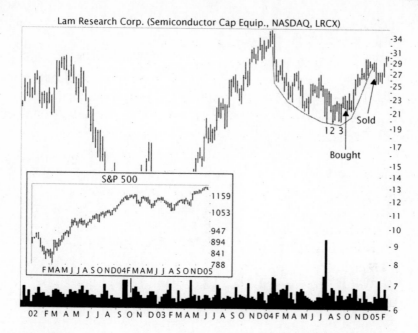

FIGURE 10.6 A rounding turn leads to a profitable trade. The S&P 500 index cooperated by moving higher between the buy and sell points.

"Why not just cut a few zeros off my numbers and use them anyway?" Then his eyes lit up. "That's what you're doing with your trades, isn't it?"

EMC

Figure 10.7 shows the next sample trade. Clearly, the stock is in a downtrend. Does that mean you should short the stock? The inset shows the S&P 500 index. Both charts are on the weekly scale, incidentally. The index bottoms in August 2004 and bumps up for a few weeks. The last week shown closes lower than the prior week, so the index might be turning down. Do you trade this stock?

What I saw on the chart was worth trading. The weekly scale gives you a hint as few patterns I discussed required that scale. The parallel downward spikes (far right) in the stock are a pipe bottom chart pattern. The pattern confirmed the following week when price closed above the higher of the two spikes.

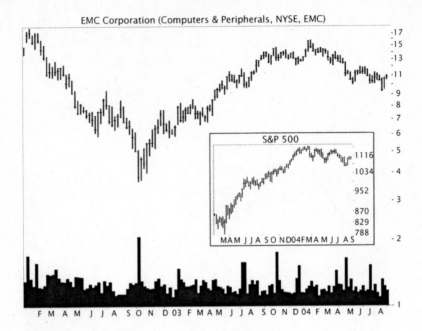

EMC Corporation (Computers & Peripherals, NYSE, EMC)

FIGURE 10.7 The stock is in a downtrend but the general market has been moving up for a few weeks. Do you trade this stock?

Figure 10.8 shows the chart on the daily scale. The inset shows the index until the day I sold. Point A is where the pipe occurs on the weekly scale. Here is my notebook entry for the trade:

> 8/26/04. I placed an order to buy 1,400 shares, at 11, stop. The stock is moving sideways, consolidating, and it's a shark-32 pattern [that's a three-day symmetrical triangle, with each succeeding day having a lower high and higher low]. I am hoping for an upward breakout from this congestion region. Fundamentals are with me as price has been climbing with brokers recommending the stock. The last earnings report was a good one. Buy reason: pipe bottom.

The buy stop at 11 wasn't filled because price failed to climb that far.

On August 30, I bought 1,400 shares at 10.53. I put a stop at 9.91 (below the 10 round number) for a potential loss of 6%. The target was 12, the site of overhead resistance. That was a good call as price stalled

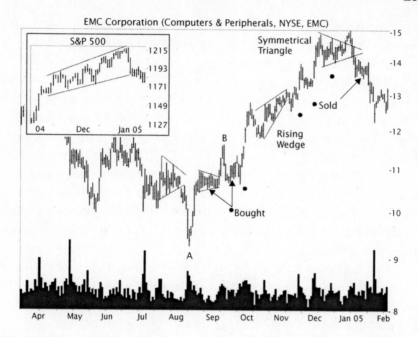

FIGURE 10.8 The chart shows the two buy and one sell orders. The black dots are stops.

near there in late September and found support at the base of the rising wedge. My notebook again:

> My guess was that the S&P would break out upward from a descending broadening wedge. It didn't as the inset shows. Buy reason: pipe bottom with lots of support at 10.50. Market may be choppy going into September, Dow Jones Industrials are down 20 points as is the NASDAQ. Large dip down (in August) washed out the sellers and a small shark-32 pattern/ symmetrical triangle suggests price is going to break out soon. Volume has been sloping down, supporting the coming break- out. Hope it's to the upside.

I raised the stop to breakeven, 10.53, on 9/14 but canceled it a week later because I felt it was too close: "This stock has thrown back and is searching for a reason to go higher. I may buy more and don't want to get stopped out on a brief dip." The throwback is the decline after point B.

That same day, I bought "1,100 shares, less than the 1,400 I would normally trade because this stock may confound me and move lower. It is having difficulty moving up, so it is not acting exactly as expected." The order filled at 10.96 and I place a stop at 9.91 on the 2,500 shares. "Buy reason: Buy after throwback. This is another opportunity to buy in. The Fibonacci retrace from 8/13/04 to 9/14/04, at 38%, supports the current price." That's the decline from B to the second buy point as a retrace of the move up from A.

I used a progressive or trailing stop as prices climbed. I raised it four times, with the final one being at 13.53. That was in mid-December and the black dots on the chart show the location and date. Notice that I placed the stops below the prior valley or round number—regions of support in each case.

I should have sold a few days sooner when the price broke out downward from the symmetrical triangle. On the trade, I made $7,000 or 26%. Since I sold, the stock has eased lower. Each buck that the stock declines means a loss of $2,500, so timely selling is important.

Rohm and Haas

Figure 10.9 shows the chart of Rohm and Haas, and the inset shows the S&P 500 index. The *index* formed a right-angled, descending broadening top—but did that give a clue to the direction the *stock* would take? For stocks, 51% of the time a stock breaks out upward from the chart pattern, so that was no help. Would you trade the stock?

The stock made a new high after the release of earnings even as the index moved horizontally. The twin peaks in May and June (A and B) confirmed a valid double top when price closed a penny below the valley between the two peaks. However, price busts the pattern when it rises above peak B and that leads to a strong rally.

Figure 10.10 shows how I traded the stock. Here is my notebook entry:

> 11/26/03. I bought 300 shares at market, filled at 40.12. This is an earnings flag trade. Quarterly report on 10/30 at 35.36 launched the flagpole. It topped out at 40.57 [A]. Thus, the measure is 5.21. From the flag low at 38.05 [B], that means a

rise to 43.26 [C]. I expect this to near 45 before stopping, just because of round number resistance and wishful thinking. Yesterday, the closing price pierced the flag's downsloping trendline, signaling a buy. Chemicals are strong in a weak market, so that is also good news. Volume is heavy on the flagpole rise then lower on the flag itself. Today is the day before Thanksgiving, so expect low volume and high volatility. Sell at 38.90 [a stop-loss point], otherwise set a sell order at 45. On the weekly chart, the flag low matches a long-term down trendline from peaks in late March and July.

The earnings flag comprises the flagpole (the near vertical rise from the earnings release, upward) to the flag itself at A to B. The long-term trendline I mention would serve to support the stock because prices in the flag were trading above the trendline. The black dots in Figure 10.10 show where and when I placed the stops. The first was at 38 on 12/22/2003. I moved it up to 39.90 on 12/31 and to 40.65 on 1/7/2004.

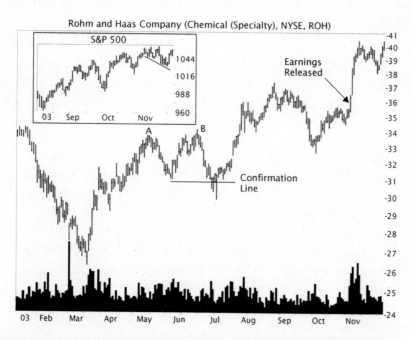

FIGURE 10.9 An earnings announcement gives a key to how the stock will perform. Do you trade this stock?

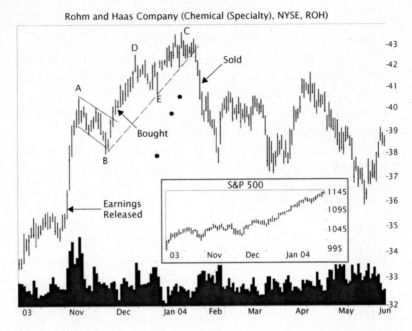

Rohm and Haas Company (Chemical (Specialty), NYSE, ROH)

FIGURE 10.10 Good entry but a poor exit cut a potential profit of $950 to $115.

For a time, the trade did well. The stock moved up after I bought and then continued higher in a small measured move up pattern (B to D is the first leg, the corrective phase is D to E, and the second leg is E to C). Here are the notes on the sale:

1/22/04. I was stopped out at 40.60 when prices blew through my stop at 40.65. Oil prices have been shooting up and natural gas prices as well. If I had to do this again, I would put an order to sell at the measured move up (MMU) profit target of 43.26. Prices topped out at 43.69. That would have made me $950 in about two months. I got worried when prices pierced the trendline, moving down. Maybe that was a sell signal, but I wanted to give the stock every opportunity to do well. I expect prices to rebound and move higher. I made about $115, net.

Higher oil and natural gas prices make producing chemicals more expensive because they are often used as feedstock. Specialty chemical companies are more immune to price changes than companies making basic chemicals.

The MMU I reference is the move from the earnings release to A, a corrective phase to B, and a second leg rise to C. In a well-behaved MMU, the move from the trend start to A is supposed to equal the move from B to C. In this case, it did almost exactly, but I used the earnings release and not the trend start in the measure.

The trendline I mentioned is the dashed line. When price closed below the line, it was a sell signal that I chose to ignore. If I sold the day after the trendline break, I would have made about $550 on the trade.

The inset shows the S&P 500 index climbing in a straight-line fashion even as the stock started tumbling. The market tide provided little support to the stock.

Looking back on this trade, placing a sell order at the predicted target of 43.26 would have worked out perfectly. Even selling when price pierced the trendline would have saved me some bucks. The good news is that I did sell, saving me from taking a pasting as prices dropped to a low of 35.90.

JLG Industries

Figure 10.11 shows price shooting up in late September on an earnings announcement. Before that, the stock confirmed an Eve & Eve double bottom (EEDB) when price closed above the highest peak between the twin bottoms. The EEDB suggested that price would rise and it does, peaking in early October. The rise exceeded the left side (W in the figure) of a Big W chart pattern. A Big W is a double bottom with tall sides.

The inset shows the S&P 500 index ending on the same day as the stock chart. Do you trade this stock? If so, how?

Figure 8.5 shows how I traded this stock a week earlier, but this time I bought 1,000 shares, filled at 16.43. Here are my notes from the trade shown in Figure 10.12:

> 10/11/2004. This is approaching the 62% retrace from the low at 14.21 [A] to the high at 17.98 [B]. I think, after three down days and perhaps another today, the stock will move up tomorrow. More traders will return from the Columbus Day

holiday and help the market move up. This may move horizontally, gathering strength for the next up move. I placed a stop at 14.43, below the gap, below the pennant apex, and below the 62% retrace, but the loss is large: 12%. Upside target: 17.45, just below the round number resistance of 17.50, and below the tail's high at 17.98.

The tail I mentioned is at point B. The black dots on Figure 10.12 are the stops positioned at the price and day of placement: "Future S&P direction (guess): Down but it might curl around in a partial decline from a broadening pattern. I actually think that's likely as the descending price falls on an upward supporting trendline. The S&P is up today by a minor amount."

I show the broadening chart pattern in the top inset of Figure 10.12, and how the S&P looked when I placed the trade in the inset of Figure 10.11. The Figure 10.11 inset gives you a better idea of where the partial decline would be—at the end of the figure if price rounded up. Instead, the index continued down, eventually touching the bottom broadening pattern trendline (see the top inset in Figure 10.12).

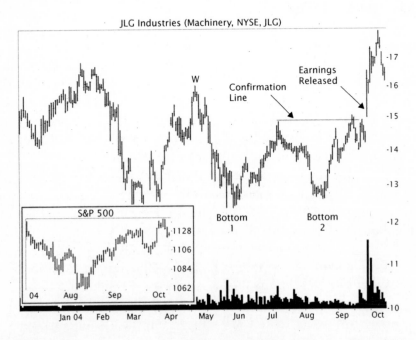

FIGURE 10.11 The stock is trending down after a quick rise. How do you trade this one, or do you?

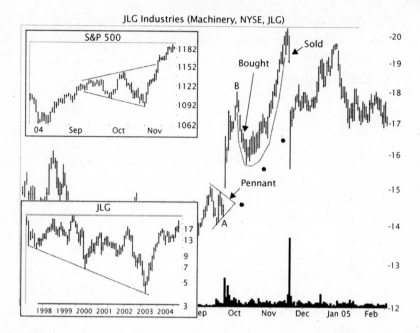

FIGURE 10.12 This swing trade turned out well, timing the sale almost perfectly in the ascending scallop chart pattern.

As prices climbed, I raised the stop to 15.48 and 16.43 as the dots show, positioned just below the prior valley low. The last stop was much too far away from the current price, 19.65 versus the stop at 16.43— 16% lower.

The stock traced a chart pattern called an ascending scallop. The day after prices peaked, I placed an order to sell 1,000 shares at the market open, filled at 19.85. Here is my notebook entry:

Sell reason: Hitting a round number [20]. On the monthly scale, it's at a horizontal trendline of a right-angled descending broadening pattern [see lower inset in Figure 10.12]. I anticipate a drop to 18 (50% retrace of prior up move) then a punch through the trendline. Buy on retrace bottom, at 18. This has been trending upward for too long without a retrace. Overhead resistance should prevent price from moving up much higher. Volume is dropping even as prices rise. This may coast up to 21 (site of old horizontal trendline) before collapsing. The ascending scallop will retrace, forming a handle. I want to sidestep the retrace and buy again after price drops.

The company announced earnings apparently after the close because the next day, price gapped lower, dropping below 18. With this trade, I got lucky by buying near the retrace low and selling near the peak, an almost perfect swing trade. I made $3,400 or 21%.

Southwest Airlines

Figure 10.13 shows the next trading scenario. A descending triangle tops the chart. The breakout is downward and a pullback at point A gives traders one last opportunity to sell or short the stock before the decline really begins. The airline stock hits an air pocket and drops rapidly for three days before consolidating—moving sideways in December—then price continues the decline but at a more leisurely pace.

The S&P 500 index shows a descending broadening wedge, but one with a hefty amount of white space—more than I like to see. The pattern would look better if the peak in early May rose up and touched the top trendline.

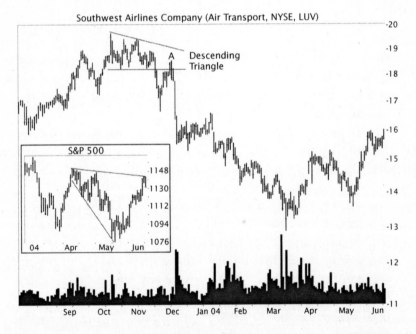

FIGURE 10.13   A descending triangle with a pullback at point A predicts a decline. Do you trade this stock in June?

Having reviewed the stock and index trends, do you trade the stock and if so, then how can you justify it?

Figure 10.14 shows how I traded the stock and what developed in the price action. In the inset, I replaced the descending broadening wedge with a broadening bottom pattern in April and a new symmetrical triangle in June. The triangle busted as price climbed little before the index plunged.

I show a right-angled, descending broadening formation (RABFD) in the stock during April and into May. The upward breakout threw back to the top trendline and had trouble lifting off the runway.

Here are my notes on the purchase:

> I bought 1,000 shares at 15.81, stop at 14.27, or 10% lower. This is just below the low on 4/21/04. Upside target: 17, using the measure rule for the RABFD: 15.30 + (15.30 − 13.56). Other airlines are moving lower, so I don't really trust this trade. Long term, I think the price is a good one. Short term, who knows? S&P direction over pattern lifetime: Down. Future market direction (guess): Dow transports will stall soon as it reaches old high in January. S&P: same. Buy reason: Throwback from RABFD completed and oil prices are trending down. Since most of the fuel is hedged, the price won't make much difference. If the airline can fly through the HCR in Dec 03 [shown in the inset], then this has a chance of moving up.

I show the stops as black dots on the chart. The measure rule for the RABFD uses the height from the horizontal top trendline to the lowest valley in the pattern added to the breakout price (the value of the top trendline). I show the horizontal consolidation region (HCR) as the zoom in December. The only time the stock paused at this region was during the weeks surrounding the purchase.

On June 25, the company announced a tentative accord with the flight attendants union after two years of negotiations, and the stock jumped nearly 8% on the news. I thought of selling as I was working on the inverted dead-cat bounce chart pattern for an article. My research showed that when prices rise 5% to 20%, they decline, giving back nearly all of their gains and sometimes more. However, I decided to hold on because I didn't view the 8% gain as very exciting when I was shooting for

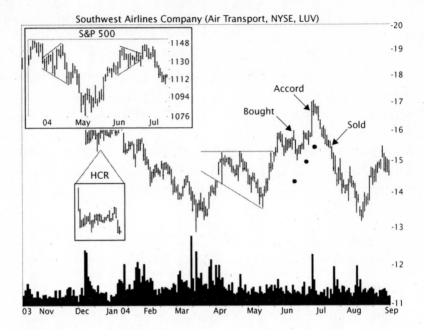

FIGURE 10.14 A throwback to the broadening pattern turned into an inverted dead-cat bounce with a late exit.

20%. Price did, however, touch my target of 17 exactly, and that should have been a selling cue. Had I sold then, I would have made over $1,100.

As my research predicted, the stock hit turbulence and dropped. I grabbed my parachute and pushed my way out the door on July 13, bailing out at a price of 15.41.

Fortunately the stock climbed enough for me to raise my stop and I lost only $430 or less than 3% on the trade.

The Art of Trading
Checklists

Before I get to the checklists, let me tell you about my trading day—I'll explain the details later. I'm an end-of-day trader, a position trader. I don't *day trade* stocks but hold them for weeks, months, and sometimes years. I review the stocks that I follow, and if I don't see anything interesting, I'm done for the day. I can go weeks without trading a stock, and I usually spend about one hour each day looking for trades or updating my database. The rest of the day is free time.

I start my day by reading the *Wall Street Journal,* which takes about 1.5 hours in itself because I'm a slow reader and I find much that interests me. I circle any significant news that happens in the companies that I follow. Those events include rating upgrades and downgrades, earnings reports, insider transactions, monthly sales data, explanations of large price moves (dead-cat bounces), and so on.

day trading
entering and exiting a trade usually within the same day.

After I finish reading, I head upstairs to my office where I update my database with the latest stock quotes and the newspaper news. My computer software that I wrote shows those events so I can watch how price develops over time.

When completed, I rank the 350 securities that I follow by industry performance. This is what I call "industry relative strength." The ranking tells me which industries are doing well and which ones are not.

I'll run my personal holdings through what I call "filters." Filters apply indicators to the stocks. Divergence and trading signals are what the filters tell me, but I don't get excited about them. I use the industry rank and indicator signals as *backstory*. They give me a feel for how the market and my stocks are shaping up. Sometimes I'll see a bearish divergence that suggests I'll have to sell a stock soon.

After that, I count my pennies, looking at the value of my holdings. Then, I review the charts on what I own looking for sell signals, checking on the stops (some may need to be raised), and occasionally a buying opportunity. Sometimes price will approach my stop and, instead of letting it hit, I'll just sell the stock. That cuts my loss.

The last thing I do is review every security that I follow. Each stock that appears does so by industry first, alphabetically second. That way, I get a feel for how each industry is behaving. If I see something interesting, I can page back and forth within the industry, checking how the other stocks are reacting to the news. Because many stocks may show the same chart pattern, I can select the most appealing one of the group using this method.

The 350 security review can be as short as 15 minutes or last an hour, sometimes longer. If the market is tumbling, I won't be enthusiastic about spending much time because I know trading would be throwing money away. When the market is moving up, I may spend more time looking for trading candidates and if I find one, then the exploration begins.

This is Jake. Tom doesn't know that I hacked into his computer and added this note, so don't tell him. With any luck, this will get printed. All I ask is for a chance to prove that money can't make me happy. Here he comes. Bye!

Before Buying

In the checklists that follow you'll see duplicate entries. The rules for not buying a stock are sometimes the same as for selling.

Here's what I look for before buying a stock:

✔ **Check the averages.** I review several each day: the S&P 500, the Dow Industrials, transports, utilities, and the NASDAQ composite. I use the S&P 500 as the proxy for the general market.

✔ **Check the market trend.** Trade in the direction of the market trend. For me, that means buying when the market is rising and sitting in cash or collecting dividends from utility stocks in a down market.

When reviewing the general market, I look for support and resistance zones then project price movement into the future. If I think the market will rise, then I'm more likely to buy. If I expect the market to drop, I'll avoid buying. However, I usually won't sell a stock just because I think that the general market or industry will go down.

✔ **Flip to the weekly scale (or the next highest period) and pay the most attention to the market trend.** This removes the day-to-day noise that clutters the screen and shows you tradable trends.

✔ **Check the industry.** Check other stocks in the same industry to get an idea of whether your trade will be successful.

- Are the other stocks showing signs of topping out? If so then consider skipping the trade.

- Are the other stocks bottoming? That may suggest a time to buy if prices reverse.

- If you can show several stocks on the same screen, find which one leads the pack and study it for clues to future price direction.

✔ **Look at the weekly scale.** I look for chart patterns on the daily scale so I switch to the next higher period to look for any threatening chart patterns in the stock I want to trade. Occasionally I'll use the monthly scale. If you trade intraday, then go to the next higher period.

- Is the stock trending in the same direction as on the shorter time scale? If yes, then that supports a buying decision.

- Do you see any existing chart patterns? My software shows all the patterns that I already found so I don't have to search for them.

- Do you see underlying support or overhead resistance? Those may cause pullbacks and throwbacks, respectively, which hurt performance.
- Draw trendlines to see where price may bounce off the trendline in the future.

✔ **Score the chart pattern.** I use my book, *Trading Classic Chart Patterns,* to score the chart pattern and gauge how likely the stock will reach the price target. If the score is negative, then I usually skip the trade. A surprising number of times a negative score has saved me from making a losing trade.

✔ **Review the current chart pattern history.** For the chart pattern you are about to trade, find one in the same stock and see how it performed in the past.

✔ **Check the indicators.** What are they telling you? I use the commodity channel index (CCI with 20-day lookback, DCCI with 5-day lookback). It gives short-term trading signals, which I usually ignore. I use it to check for divergence with the stock price. If the CCI shows lower peaks but the stock has higher ones, then the stock will likely turn down. It might not happen immediately, but that is the way to bet. The reverse is true for bullish divergence. If the CCI has higher valleys but the stock has lower ones, the stock will likely turn upward—eventually. I like to see peaks or valleys about a month to six weeks apart. Divergence using peaks or valleys farther apart tends to be less reliable. I use the following:

  - Relative strength index (RSI with 16-day lookback, 70/30 overbought/oversold threshold): I use this for divergence and as an indicator of overbought (too pricy) or oversold (too cheap). I don't use this indicator anymore. I get better divergence with CCI and a stock can remain overbought or oversold for months, or I never get a signal for a year or more with the default settings.

  - Bollinger bands (using a 20-day moving average): When the bands narrow (low volatility) that tells me price is going to make a big move. Price often bounces from one band to the other, especially when the band is horizontal and price touches it.

- Is the stock price diverging from the indicator?
- Is the indicator signaling a trade?
- Check for failure swings. These are little M- or W-shaped indicator patterns that may signal a short-term trend change.
- Figure 11.1 shows what I mean by divergence and failure swings between price and the RSI. The trendlines show price diverging with the indicator in July (bullish divergence) and November (bearish divergence). Failure swings appear in the circles and they show short-term turning points in the price trend. I've read that failure swings should span the horizontal indicator signal lines (30 or 70 for the RSI) and point in the direction price should take, but I don't know how important that is. Only the November failure swing obeys those constraints, and price changes from trending up to going horizontal. The W-failure swings show timely price trend changes.

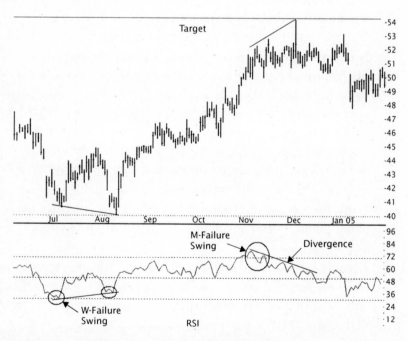

FIGURE 11.1 The stock diverges with the RSI indicator (trendlines) and failure swings appear at turning points (circles).

✔ **Review the industry relative strength.** This differs from the RSI. I measure the relative strength of the 35+ industries that I check on a daily basis, ranked for the price change over time. (I mostly use the difference between the current closing price and that of 6 months ago). I concentrate my trades on the top 10 performing industries and industries that are moving up the rankings at a good clip. You'll find that industries performing well will continue to do well, usually for months.

✔ **Get a quote before trading.** If the quote is lower than the last time you checked, delay buying. Why buy now when it will be cheaper later?

✔ **Is the stock trending up?** Wait for price to turn up before buying. Better yet, trade stocks moving up and don't wait for a reversal of the downtrend. View the stock on the weekly scale (or higher time scale) to help decide the trend.

✔ **If the stock is up a lot, skip the trade.** Don't chase a stock higher. After you buy, the stock will come tumbling down. How high is high? I usually skip trades in which a stock is 75 cents higher, but it depends on the stock. The stock has to be up over the prior day, but not by much, and trending higher to be a buy.

✔ **Is the stock trading near the yearly high?** I learned that buying stocks near the yearly low increases my losses because they invariably tumble. Instead, I buy stocks showing chart patterns near the yearly high, preferably breaking out to a new high. If they are making a new high, I don't have to worry about prior resistance zones (except for round numbers). When the breakout occurs, price coasts higher on momentum, allowing me to raise my stop and cut my potential loss.

✔ **Look for overhead resistance.** How high is the price likely to climb before hitting resistance? If the answer is not much, then skip the trade.

✔ **Look for underlying support.** If the stock drops, you will want to know how far down it's likely to go. Nearby support helps with selecting a stop-loss point. Place a stop below nearby underlying support.

✔ **Avoid mental stops.** Don't use a mental stop (one kept in your head) unless you are a seasoned professional.

✔ **How likely is a throwback or pull back?** Prices return to the breakout price usually in just a few days. Consider initiating or adding to your position once price resumes the original breakout direction. However, the statistics show that chart patterns with throwbacks or pullback have worse performance than those without throws or pulls.

✔ **Check for dead-cat bounces (DCBs).** I won't trade any stock showing a DCB within the last six months to a year. Those companies with earnings problems often have one DCB following another.

✔ **Prices don't trend forever.** If you are about to buy a stock that has been trending upward for several days in a row, the chances increase that you will be buying near a price peak. The same goes for consecutively declining prices. The trend may reverse soon after you sell. This, however, is not a license to hold onto a declining stock forever.

✔ **Price versus market divergence.** Intraday, if the stock is down when the market is up a lot, avoid the stock.

How to Sell?

I show this checklist item separately because it is so important:

✔ **Use stops.** In most of my trades, price stops me out. I raise the stop as price rises. That way, selling is easy. I let price take me out instead of relying on more esoteric indicators. If you can't make money in the markets, chances are you don't use stops. If you *do* make money, then it's a bull market where everything is going up. When the stocks stop going up, then what are you going to do? Place a stop on every trade.

When to Sell?

Each trading situation is different, but as your experience grows, you'll develop an inner voice that tells you when it is time to sell. Listen to that voice. Many of the trades that I've made within days of a high (and recounted in this book) are the result of listening to that voice coupled with supporting evidence. Since I can't lend you my voice, here is a checklist of the supporting evidence that may suggest a sale:

- ✔ **The stock is about to hit your stop.** Sell it immediately. Why wait for price to hit your stop if you *know* that it will? You *do* have a stop in place, don't you?

- ✔ **A bearish chart pattern has broken out downward.** This is the classic sell signal. Exit the stock immediately. Hoping price will rise won't turn it around, but if it does, it is a pullback and stock will soon head back down anyway. Sell it now!

- ✔ **The stock has closed below an upsloping trendline.** This is the first indication of a trend change, but I usually sell instead of waiting for additional evidence. Remember, the longer the trendline, the more reliable it is. Switch to the weekly (or higher time) scale and check the trendline again.

- ✔ **Stock falls more than 62% retrace.** Measure the retrace after an up move. Most will fall in the 38%, 50%, or 62% retrace amounts of the prior move. Anything more than that and expect price to continue down.

- ✔ **The 1-2-3 trend change method signals a trend change.** Review the discussion in the section 1-2-3 Trend Change Method in Chapter 3. If the trend changes, get out.

- ✔ **Price has hit the target.** In many of my trades, I accurately pick how far price is going to rise before it stalls or reverses. For swing trades (a short-term trade that rides the move from trough to crest or the reverse), place an order to sell at the target (or slightly below the nearest resistance zone). That will often get you out near the peak. For other trades, use a trailing stop. (Raise it as price rises.)

- ✔ **The averages are dropping.** The market is taking other stocks down along with yours, so it is time to get out. Flip to the weekly scale. If the trend is still down, then sell.

- ✔ **Stocks in the industry are topping out.** Any bearish chart patterns that appear in stocks in the same industry are warning bells. If other stocks are turning down then consider selling. Rare is the stock that can swim against the current for long.

- ✔ **Look at the weekly scale.** New chart patterns, trendlines, and support and resistance zones all appear on the weekly chart, so use them as sell signals.

✔ **The market is up but the stock is down.** When I get a stock quote, I also check the Dow industrials, NASDAQ composite, and S&P 500. If the Dow is up 100 points, but my stock is down, I will want to know why. This intraday price divergence I use as a warning, not as an automatic sell signal. Sometimes there's a good reason for the divergence. Currently, when the price of oil drops, my Exxon stock is going to go down and the market is going to soar. That's divergence, but it's not a sell signal unless oil keeps going down too.

✔ **Historical price review.** What happened the last time the stock made a new high, shot upward in a straight-line run, consolidated in a tight knot of price movement, dropped a few points in just days, or stalled at an old high? Past behavior can give you an indication of how well the stock will behave in the future. However, the more you rely on past behavior, the more likely the stock will surprise you. I remember looking at Schwab and seeing that price dropped after each of the last two stock splits. So I sold near the third split and watched from the sidelines as price soared.

✔ **Check the indicators.** Are your favorite indicators saying sell? Recognize that the more indicators you check, the more contradictions you'll have. Check a dozen indicators and some will say buy, some sell, and some hold. What does the best indicator—price—say? Is price rising or falling? Is price *trending* up or down? Don't know? Then switch to the weekly scale and ask if price is *rising or falling*. If it's falling, then sell.

✔ **Indicators are diverging from price.** This is usually a reliable sell signal, but not an automatic one. Price can diverge from indicators for months before the stock turns down, if it turns down at all.

✔ **Indicator failure swings.** These M- and W-shapes in the indicator can call short-term turning points accurately.

✔ **Overhead resistance.** Has the stock hit overhead resistance and is now heading down? Sell.

✔ **Is a throwback or pullback happening?** Review the section on those. Throws and pulls happen often after a breakout. Initiate or add to your position after a throwback once price resumes the move up. For a pullback, it's often your last chance to exit a stock before the decline resumes. Take the sell signal and get out.

General Trading Tips

Jake here. If you think no one cares if you're alive, try missing a few car payments. Bye!

Consider the following trading tips as well:

- ✔ **Tighten stops.** If other stocks in the same industry begin trending down, then tighten the stop in the stock you own in that industry. If your stock shoots up several points in a few days, then tighten the stop because price may reverse and retrace much of the gain. See the inverted dead-cat bounce in Chapter 8.

- ✔ **Trade tall patterns.** Tall patterns outperform short ones. This is the single best predictor of chart pattern performance. What is short and tall? It varies from pattern to pattern, so refer to my book, *Encyclopedia of Chart Patterns*, 2nd ed., for complete details.

- ✔ **Narrowing prices.** If the daily high-low range narrows over time, then expect a trend change. For example, a symmetrical triangle, with its narrowing price trend, shows this behavior. The breakout comes after the price range contracts and volume diminishes.

- ✔ **Don't forget busted patterns.** Chart patterns that break out downward then quickly reverse often soar higher than you expect. Jump aboard and ride the wave.

- ✔ **Trade with the trend.** If the market and industry are moving up, select stocks with upward breakouts. Avoid countertrend trades—the market or the industry is going down and your stock is moving up. The rise will be less than you expect unless the market or industry reverses. If you buy a stock even though the market is trending lower, that's fine providing you expect the market to reverse shortly. Just hope that you don't get stopped out while waiting.

- ✔ **Reversal chart patterns must have something to reverse.** For example, if a diamond top appears several points above a price plateau and the breakout is downward, expect prices to return to the plateau.

- ✔ **Don't average down.** If you buy and hold, then ignore this advice; you can likely ride out the downturn unless your stock is named Enron, WorldCom, Penn Central, United Airlines, or . . .

If a stock is declining, consider selling it. Don't add to your position hoping that it will eventually turn around. It may not, but, more likely, you'll get fed up and sell just days before it bottoms. Never try to prop up the price by buying more. Even Jake doesn't have that much money, and he's doing very well now.

✔ **Trade on the intraday scale.** Switch to the intraday scale or the next shorter period to place the trade. The shorter time scale will zoom into the price action and highlight support and resistance zones. I use the one- and five-minute scales to time my entry.

✔ **Raise that stop as price rises.** Check the volatility and place the stop no closer than 1.5 times the current price volatility. (See the volatility stop example in Chapter 5 for details.)

✔ **Never lower a stop.** If you feel a desire to lower a stop, sell the stock. Fall in love, just never with a stock.

✔ **Follow the same stocks each day.** Become familiar with them. Don't invest in unfamiliar stocks. Over time, you'll know when the stock is expensive and when it's cheap. That voice will tell you when to buy and sell.

✔ **Choose chart patterns that work for you.** Some chart patterns perform better than others. Be selective and become an expert in the patterns you trade. If you find a quirk that works, then tell me about it at tbul@hotmail.com.

✔ **Keep a trading diary and review it periodically.** I log each trade and review them periodically. I look for untimely entry and exits, bad habits that I've picked up, that sort of thing. It helps. In my notebook, I keep the date, trade time, number of shares traded, order type (stop, market, limit), price filled at, stop-loss price, price target, future S&P 500 index direction (a guess), buy or sell reason for the trade.

✔ **Explore.** Trading takes work. You have to believe the system you trade or you'll ignore the signals. Explore new techniques that add value to your system and prune the deadwood as it becomes less effective.

✔ **Diversify.** If you see a symmetrical triangle in an oil services company, chances are other stocks in the same industry show the same pattern. Don't buy them all. I choose the most promising to trade and then look at other industries.

✔ **Don't over diversify.** "At one time, I had over 40 stocks in my portfolio," Jake said. "I couldn't keep track of them all." No kidding. I usually have fewer than 10 stocks in my portfolio.

✔ **Check commodities.** I follow oil, copper, and natural gas because so many of the industries I track rely on them. If the price of oil is shooting up, the airlines, truckers, and chemicals may suffer but oil service companies, refiners, and drillers should prosper.

✔ **Tune your system.** The markets change over time and so should your system and your trading style. When the markets are choppy, directionless, I make short-term trades. When the market is trending, I relax and my hold time increases.

✔ **Ignore chat room chatter.** Some of the worst trades I've made come from scenario trading. I'd read that the price of oil was predicted to rise because of a production shortage. Then I'd buy a refiner and get cleaned out when the price of oil dropped instead. Don't restrict this advice to the Internet chat room. Apply it to newspaper articles and television news as well. Don't trade scenarios. Buy-and-hold investors may do well with scenarios, but they can wait years.

✔ **If you have to ask, you're making a mistake.** If you have doubts about a trade, such that you feel compelled to ask someone's opinion about it, then skip the trade. Don't let others spend your money.

✔ **Set price targets.** With experience, you'll be able to tell when price is about to turn. Use the measure rule for the chart pattern (usually the pattern's height added to the breakout price) to predict a price target. For more conservative targets, use half the formation height projected upward. If the target and overhead resistance are nearly the same, then you've struck gold. Place a sell order to dump the stock just below the resistance zone. You may be early, but you never go broke taking a profit.

✔ **Late entry.** If you find that you are consistently late getting into a trade, then place an order to buy the stock a penny above the breakout price. I use that strategy, and it works. Premature breakouts happen infrequently (between 3% and 22% of the time for triangles, for example), so don't worry about them.

✔ **Watch for a throwback or pullback.** Prices turn postbreakout in an average of 3 days and return to the breakout usually in 10 or 11 days, so watch for that. Have faith that prices will resume the original breakout direction—they do—86% of the time.

✔ **Don't short a stock.** If you can't make money on the long side, you won't make it on the short side either. Try it on paper first.

✔ **Prices drop faster than they rise.** I found this out when I reviewed the statistics measuring the time from the breakout to the ultimate high or low. Price trends after downward breakouts were quicker and steeper than their upward counterparts. This emphasizes the need to use stops to get out. If you can't sell, your losses will grow quickly.

✔ *Jake again. Always borrow money from a pessimist. He doesn't expect to be paid back. Bye!*

✔ **Price reverses one month after the breakout in a bear market.** This is also true in a bull market, but less often. The one-month benchmark also varies from pattern to pattern. It's rarely shorter, but often longer—five to seven weeks after the breakout. I found a *slight* rise in the number of patterns reaching the ultimate low a month after the breakout, so don't expect price to turn on a dime every time.

✔ **Price moves most in the first week after a breakout.** I discovered this when looking at failure rates. This emphasizes the need to get in early after a breakout. The best way is to have a buy order positioned a penny above the breakout price. That will get you in early and you won't have to worry as much about throwbacks taking you out.

Table 11.1 shows where in the yearly price range the chart pattern performs best. High means the pattern performs best when the breakout is within a third of the yearly high, low means within a third of the yearly low, and middle is the final third.

TABLE 11.1 Breakout Position in Yearly Price Range for Chart Patterns

Chart Pattern	Performs Best Where?
Broadening Bottoms, downward breakout	Low
Broadening Bottoms, upward breakout	High
Broadening Formations, Right-Angled and Ascending, downward breakout	Low
Broadening Formations, Right-Angled and Ascending, upward breakout	High
Broadening Formations, Right-Angled and Descending, downward breakout	Middle, High
Broadening Formations, Right-Angled and Descending, upward breakout	Middle
Broadening Tops, downward breakout	Low
Broadening Tops, upward breakout	High
Broadening Wedges, Ascending, downward breakout	Low
Broadening Wedges, Ascending, upward breakout	Middle, High
Broadening Wedges, Descending, downward breakout	Low
Broadening Wedges, Descending, upward breakout	Low, Middle, High
Diamond Bottoms, downward breakout	Low
Diamond Bottoms, upward breakout	Low
Diamond Tops, downward breakout	Low, Middle
Diamond Tops, upward breakout	Middle
Double Bottoms, Adam & Adam, upward breakout	Low
Double Bottoms, Adam & Eve, upward breakout	High
Double Bottoms, Eve & Adam, upward breakout	Low
Double Bottoms, Eve & Eve, upward breakout	Low
Double Tops, Adam & Adam, downward breakout	High
Double Tops, Adam & Eve, downward breakout	Middle
Double Tops, Eve & Adam, downward breakout	Low, High
Double Tops, Eve & Eve, downward breakout	High
Flags, downward breakout	Low
Flags, upward breakout	High

(continued)

TABLE 11.1 (Continued)

Chart Pattern	Performs Best Where?
Flags, High and Tight, upward breakout	Middle
Head-and-Shoulders Bottoms, upward breakout	High
Head-and-Shoulders Bottoms, Complex, upward breakout	Middle
Head-and-Shoulders Tops, downward breakout	Middle
Head-and-Shoulders Tops, Complex, downward breakout	Middle
Pennants, downward breakout	Low
Pennants, upward breakout	Low
Pipe Bottom, upward breakout	High
Pipe Tops, downward breakout	Low
Rounding Bottoms, upward breakout	High
Scallops, Ascending and Inverted, upward breakout	Low
Three Rising Valleys, upward breakout	High
Triangles, Ascending, downward breakout	Low, Middle
Triangles, Ascending, upward breakout	High
Triangles, Descending, downward breakout	Low
Triangles, Descending, upward breakout	Low, High
Triangles, Symmetrical, downward breakout	Low
Triangles, Symmetrical, upward breakout	Low
Triple Bottoms, upward breakout	Middle
Triple Tops, downward breakout	High

Totals for upward breakouts: high, 13; middle, 7; low, 9.

Totals for downward breakouts: high, 5; middle, 6; low, 14.

The numbers show that upward breakouts perform best within a third of the yearly high. Downward breakouts perform best within a third of the yearly low. What does this mean? Buy a stock making new highs and sell them short when they make new lows.

Table 11.2 shows where in the yearly price range the event pattern performs best. High means the pattern performs best when the breakout is within a third of the yearly high, low means within a third of the yearly low, and middle is the final third.

TABLE 11.2 Breakout Position in Yearly Price Range for Event Patterns	
Event Pattern	*Performs Best Where?*
Dead-Cat Bounce, downward breakout	High
Earnings Surprise, Bad, downward breakout	Low
Earnings Surprise, Good, upward breakout	Low
Flag, Earnings, upward breakout	Low
Stock Downgrade, downward breakout	Low
Stock Downgrade, upward breakout	Low
Stock Upgrade, downward breakout	Low
Stock Upgrade, upward breakout	High

Totals for upward breakouts: high, 1; middle, 0; low, 3.

Totals for downward breakouts: high, 1; middle, 0; low, 3.

Both breakout directions do best when the breakout is within a third of the yearly low.

Trading Psychology

In this checklist, I help you analyze your own trading psychology. You should also refer to Chapter 2 for more information.

✔ **Are you trading because you want to trade?** Sometimes I find myself hunting for chart patterns because the market is moving higher and I'm not in the market. At other times, I'll trade then make another trade a few days later with disastrous results.

✔ *Jake here. Tom's going to kill me if he finds these things, but if I plant enough of them, then maybe some will get printed. Anyway, did you know that research causes cancer in rats? Bye!*

✔ **Are you not trading?** This is the opposite of trading too often. You may be so scared of taking a loss than you avoid trading altogether. Do enough research that you are confident your trading system works. Then get back into the game.

✔ **If you get stopped out of several stocks, walk away.** At the start of 2005, I was stopped out of every one of my stocks. That told me the market was tumbling so I let it drop while I remained in cash. When I started seeing a plethora of bottoming patterns appear, then I started getting interested again. That's the beauty of chart patterns. Bullish ones appear when the market is poised to move up or is rallying. They disappear in falling markets so you get stopped out and remain on the sidelines as the market corrects.

✔ **Follow the system.** Would you be making more money if you followed your trading system? Understand why you're ignoring the trading signals you receive.

✔ **Don't overtrade.** When I first started trading, I discovered that the more often I traded, the worse I did. With experience, the more I trade, the more I make (but a bull market helps). This happens to inexperienced day traders. They think that if they can just pull $100 or $500 out of the market each day, they'll be set. I remember Jake telling me that "If I only make a buck on each of a million trades, I'd be a millionaire." If you cannot make money position trading or buying and holding, then it's unlikely you'll do well day trading or swing trading. Start with longer holding periods and move to the shorter ones as your trading experience grows.

✔ **Learn from your mistakes.** Are you making mistakes? If you don't review your trades periodically, you'll form bad habits that will lead to larger losses.

✔ **Focus on the positive.** The disaster you had today pales to the killing you made last week.

✔ **Push the comfort zone.** Make every trade seem rote. Don't let your losses bother you, and don't get too excited about your winners, either. An e-mail acquaintance wrote me that he was cutting his profits short. "Can you help?" I suggested that he might be holding on too tight. He was getting quotes too often instead of paying attention to his job, obsessing over every penny gained or lost. I suggested he check the stock once, at the end of the day, or flip to the weekly scale for his trades. He's trading much better now, and his stress level has gone down.

✔ **Ignore profits.** If you find yourself getting nervous about a winning trade or making too much money (believe me, it happens), then don't look at the bottom line. Concentrate not on the money but on improving your trading skills. Get used to making too much money.

✔ **Obey your trading signals.** Otherwise, what are you trading for? Plan your trade and trade your plan.

✔ **Don't trade when you're upset.** This also goes for being too excited. I find this happens to me in a bull market. All of my stocks are exploding upward; everything I pick is a winner. That's when I know a huge loss is coming. And it does when I place a stop too far away just as the market turns, sucking my stock down with it.

✔ **Abandoning a winning system.** In a bull market when everything you trade seems to hit gold, you become bored. You chuck a winning system for something more exciting. An acquaintance told me that he made money in 9 out of 10 chart pattern trades. He decided to abandon his system and invested the proceeds in a company called Bre-X. He lost most of it when the authorities discovered the stock was a scam.

✔ *Jake again. Keep this country beautiful. Swallow your beer cans. Bye, or is it buy?*

Chapter 12

Crunching the Numbers

The statistics shown in Tables 12.1 and 12.2 are from chart patterns in bull markets only. The numbers reflect hundreds and sometimes thousands of *perfect trades* without any trading costs deducted. Thus, don't expect your trading results to match them.

Not all chart and event patterns are shown, so the rankings may skip numbers. For a complete list of chart and event patterns in both bull and bear markets, consult my book, *Encyclopedia of Chart Patterns,* 2nd ed.

Chart Pattern Performance and Rank Table: Notes

The following notes apply to the tables:

The *average rise or decline* is the percentage price move from the breakout to the ultimate high or low.

The *breakeven failure rate* is the number of patterns with prices that fail to rise or fall at least 5% after the breakout.

Once price reaches the ultimate high or low, the *change after trend ends* measures the next price move until the trend changes again.

Throwbacks are for upward breakouts and *pullbacks* are for downward breakouts.

Rank is the sum of the individual ranks of the average rise or decline, breakeven failure rate, and change after the trend ends sorted and reranked. Two patterns can share the same rank, and patterns with downward breakouts are ranked separately from those with upward breakouts.

N/A means not applicable. The performance of some chart and event patterns are measured differently from most others (measured moves, flags, pennants, gaps, and so on) and are not ranked.

TABLE 12.1 Chart Pattern Performance and Rank

Chart Pattern	Average Rise or Decline (%)	Breakeven Failure Rate (%)	Change After Trend Ends (%)	Throwback Pullback (%)	Rank
Broadening Bottoms, downward breakout	−15	16	52	42	17
Broadening Bottoms, upward breakout	27	10	−34	41	17
Broadening Formations, Right-Angled and Ascending, downward breakout	−15	20	53	65	19
Broadening Formations, Right-Angled and Ascending, upward breakout	29	11	−31	47	19
Broadening Formations, Right-Angled and Descending, downward breakout	−15	14	55	51	13
Broadening Formations, Right-Angled and Descending, upward breakout	28	19	−26	52	23
Broadening Tops, downward breakout	−15	18	53	48	18
Broadening Tops, upward breakout	29	15	−33	54	19

TABLE 12.1 (Continued)

Chart Pattern	Average Rise or Decline (%)	Breakeven Failure Rate (%)	Change After Trend Ends (%)	Throwback Pullback (%)	Rank
Broadening Wedges, Ascending, downward breakout	−17	11	49	57	14
Broadening Wedges, Ascending, upward breakout	38	2	−31	50	6
Broadening Wedges, Descending, downward breakout	−20	9	47	53	11
Broadening Wedges, Descending, upward breakout	33	6	−33	53	12
Diamond Bottoms, downward breakout	−21	10	59	71	1
Diamond Bottoms, upward breakout	36	4	−33	53	8
Diamond Tops, downward breakout	−21	6	47	57	7
Diamond Tops, upward breakout	27	10	−29	59	21
Double Bottoms, Adam & Adam, upward breakout	35	5	−33	64	10
Double Bottoms, Adam & Eve, upward breakout	37	5	−33	59	8
Double Bottoms, Eve & Adam, upward breakout	35	4	−31	57	11
Double Bottoms, Eve & Eve, upward breakout	40	4	−31	55	6
Double Tops, Adam & Adam, downward breakout	−19	8	54	61	4

(continued)

TABLE 12.1 (Continued)

Chart Pattern	Average Rise or Decline (%)	Breakeven Failure Rate (%)	Change After Trend Ends (%)	Throwback Pullback (%)	Rank
Double Tops, Adam & Eve, downward breakout	−18	14	50	59	15
Double Tops, Eve & Adam, downward breakout	−15	13	54	64	13
Double Tops, Eve & Eve, downward breakout	−18	11	63	59	2
Flags, downward breakout	N/A	2	41	46	N/A
Flags, upward breakout	N/A	4	−22	43	N/A
Flags, High and Tight, upward breakout	69	0	−36	54	1
Gaps	N/A	N/A	N/A	N/A	N/A
Head-and-Shoulders Bottoms, upward breakout	38	3	−31	45	7
Head-and-Shoulders Bottoms, Complex, upward breakout	39	4	−29	63	9
Head-and-Shoulders Tops, downward breakout	−22	4	51	50	1
Head-and-Shoulders Tops, Complex, downward breakout	−23	4	48	67	3
Measured Move Downward	N/A	N/A	46	N/A	N/A
Measured Move Upward	N/A	N/A	−26	N/A	N/A
Pennants, downward breakout	N/A	4	40	31	N/A

TABLE 12.1   (Continued)

Chart Pattern	Average Rise or Decline (%)	Breakeven Failure Rate (%)	Change After Trend Ends (%)	Throwback Pullback (%)	Rank
Pennants, upward breakout	N/A	2	−25	47	N/A
Pipe Bottoms, upward breakout	45	5	−33	44	2
Pipe Tops, downward breakout	−20	11	56	41	4
Rounding Bottoms, upward breakout	43	5	−31	40	5
Rounding Tops, downward breakout	−19	12	57	48	5
Rounding Tops, upward breakout	37	9	−31	53	13
Scallops, Ascending and Inverted, upward breakout	43	4	−32	61	3
Three Rising Valleys, upward breakout	41	5	−33	60	4
Triangles, Ascending, downward breakout	−19	11	52	49	9
Triangles, Ascending, upward breakout	35	13	−29	57	17
Triangles, Descending, downward breakout	−16	16	60	54	10
Triangles, Descending, upward breakout	47	7	−30	37	5
Triangles, Symmetrical, downward breakout	−17	13	50	59	15
Triangles, Symmetrical, upward breakout	31	9	−31	37	16
Triple Bottoms, upward breakout	37	4	−33	64	7
Triple Tops, downward breakout	−19	10	53	61	7

Event Pattern Performance and Rank Table

I rank event patterns separately from chart patterns. However, I use the same methods to gauge performance.

TABLE 12.2 Event Pattern Performance and Rank

Event Pattern	Average Rise or Decline (%)	Breakeven Failure Rate (%)	Change After Trend Ends (%)	Throwback Pullback (%)	Rank
Dead-Cat Bounce	N/A	N/A	N/A	N/A	N/A
Dead-Cat Bounce, Inverted	N/A	N/A	N/A	N/A	N/A
Earnings Surprise, Bad, downward breakout	−13	31	51	41	3
Earnings Surprise, Good, upward breakout	24	29	−27	41	5
Flag, Earnings, upward breakout	34	10	−33	63	1
Stock Downgrade, downward breakout	−14	26	50	48	2
Stock Downgrade, upward breakout	27	25	−30	49	3
Stock Upgrade, downward breakout	−12	38	44	37	5
Stock Upgrade, upward breakout	24	18	−30	63	2

Epilogue/Closing Position

The whoop, whoop, whoop of the approaching helicopter disturbed the tranquility. Looking out over a rolling carpet of pines etched between hills, I sat in the gazebo with my feet propped up on the railing. With each splash, my eyes dropped to the pond just beyond the railing, to the expanding ripples. From my hilltop perch, the pond served as an infinity-edge pool framing the hills and valley beyond. This was my favorite spot, my refuge.

Jake bounded out of the helicopter carrying a bottle of champagne in one hand and glasses in the other. "I thought I'd find you here," he said.

For a moment, I imagined that he was going to break the bottle against the gazebo and announce the launching of another phase of his life. Instead, he peeled the foil wrapper from the bottle.

As I expected, the explosion shot the cork to the rafters, bounced off, and struck me on the shoulder before spinning like crazy on the floor. Just like in movies, the bubbly careened over the sides and water-falled onto the cedar floor, soaking Jake's hands.

"When I first met you," I said, "I thought you were going to rob me."

"That's what traders do. We steal from others. Thanks for teaching me the ropes."

We clinked glasses and the chirp of leaded crystal caused a cardinal to stare at us. The Dom Perignon was a delightful surprise that blended with spring's spices flavoring the wind.

I pointed to the chopper, its blades still spinning. "Is that new?"

"Yeah," he said, "But it doesn't belong to me. The company I bought owns it, but I'm going to sell it. You once suggested I take over my health insurance company as a way to lower my premiums. I did. I hired attorneys to shred the golden parachutes of the executives, can-celled their health insurance coverage, and then fired them all."

"You should have kept their coverage in place and then jacked up their premiums every quarter, just like they did to you."

"Yeah. Now you tell me. How's the book coming?"

"It's at the printer even as we speak."

"Then you can't change anything?"

"Nope. Not even if I wanted to."

"Did you find those jokes I inserted into the manuscript?"

Glossary

Average   The sum of the scores divided by the number of scores.

Average rise or decline (ARD)   I measure the rise from the breakout price to the ultimate high, or the decline from the breakout price to the ultimate low, for each stock, and then compute the average.

Bear market   I used the peak in the Standard & Poor's 500 index on March 24, 2000, and the low on October 10, 2002, as the start and end of a bear market.

Breakout   Table G.1 shows the breakout location for each pattern.

TABLE G.1   Breakout Location for Chart Patterns

Chart Pattern	Breakout Location
Broadening patterns, all types	A close outside the trendline boundary
Diamond Tops and Bottoms	A close outside the trendline boundary
Double Bottoms, all types	A close above the highest peak between the two valleys
Double Tops, all types	A close below the lowest valley between the two peaks
Flags	A close outside the trendline boundary
Flags, High and Tight	A close outside the trendline boundary or highest peak in the pattern
Head-and-Shoulders Tops and Complex Tops	A close below the upsloping neckline, or a close below the low between the head and right shoulder for downsloping necklines
Measured Move Down or Up	Not applicable
Pennants	A close outside the trendline boundary
Pipe Bottoms	A close above the highest spike in the pattern
Pipe Tops	A close below the lowest spike in the pattern
Rounding Bottoms	A close above the right lip
Scallops, Ascending and Inverted	A close above the highest peak in the pattern
Three Rising Valleys	A close above the highest peak in the pattern

(continued)

TABLE G.1 (Continued)	
Chart Pattern	*Breakout Location*
Triangles, Ascending	A close outside the trendline boundary
Triangles, Descending	A close outside the trendline boundary
Triangles, Symmetrical	A close outside the trendline boundary
Triple Bottoms	A close above the highest peak in the pattern
Triple Tops	A close below the lowest valley in the pattern

Breakout volume   The volume level on the breakout day.

Bull market   Every date outside of the bear market from March 24, 2000, to October 10, 2002, as posted by the Standard & Poor's 500 Index.

Busted pattern performance   A chart pattern that reaches the ultimate high or low less than 10% away from the breakout and then reverses direction. The performance measures how far prices move in the new direction (the direction opposite the breakout) before reaching a new ultimate high or low.

CCI   The commodity channel index, a price momentum oscillator that compares the current mean price with the average of its mean price. I use a 20-day lookback with a five-day DCCI signal line. I use it most for spotting divergences between the indicator and price.

Confirmation point, price, level, or line   Also known as the breakout point, price, level, or line—a price or location that validates a chart pattern.

Consolidation   See *Continuation*. Also, when prices move horizontally instead of trending upward or downward. A consolidation is an area of price congestion.

Consolidation region   A solid block of prices or a region in which prices switch from trending to moving sideways.

Continuation   For chart patterns, I use this term as a synonym for consolidation. For a continuation, prices must break out in the same direction as they entered the pattern. For example, if price enters the pattern from the bottom and exits out the top, the pattern acts as a continuation. Contrast with reversal.

Countertrend pattern   A pattern with an upward breakout in a bear market or a downward breakout in a bull market. The breakout direction is against the prevailing market trend.

Corrective phase   Part of a measured move up or down, a region where prices retrace a portion of the prior move.

Day trading   Entering and exiting a trade usually within the same day.

Days to ultimate high or low   The average time from the date of the breakout to the date of the ultimate high or low.

DCCI   Dual CCI, a five-day exponentially smoothed moving average of the CCI.

Fibonacci retrace   See *Retrace*.

Flat base   A consolidation region in which prices touch or near the same price multiple times over several weeks or months, and identification is usually easiest on the weekly scale. The bottom of this region appears flat and sometimes forms the base of an impending up-move, hence the name, flat base.

Some chart patterns (such as double and triple bottoms, or head and shoulders) form after a flat base, the bottom of the chart pattern will usually reside slightly below the flat base level.

Gaps   When today's high is below yesterday's low, or today's low is above yesterday's high, a gap appears on the price chart. A gap closes when price later retraces and covers the gap.

Half-staff formation   Chart patterns such as flags, pennants, and even members of the triangle family (ascending, descending, or symmetrical) sometimes appear midway in the price move.

Horizontal consolidation region   A horizontal, or almost horizontal, congestion area where prices share a common value for an extended time (usually weeks to months). Flat price tops or flat bottoms are the preferred appearance.

Intermediate term   Between three and six months.

Intraday   Within a single trading day.

Limit order   An order to buy for no more or to sell for no less than a specified price.

Linear regression   A mathematical method to fit a straight line to a series of numbers; the slope of the resulting line gives the trend.

Long term   Lasting over six months.

Measure rule   Varies from pattern to pattern but is usually the pattern height added to (upward breakouts) or subtracted from (downward breakouts) the breakout price. The result is the predicted price target. Price often falls short of the target, so use half the height in the measure rule computation.

Median   Median value is the middle one in a sorted list of values such that half the values are below the median and half above. If no middle value exists, the average of the two closest values is used. For example, in the list 10, 15, 30, 41, and 52, the median is 30 because there are two values on either side of it.

Neckline   A trendline joining the valleys (head-and-shoulders top) or peaks (head-and-shoulders bottom). A close below or above the neckline, respectively, means a breakout.

Partial decline   After price touches a top trendline, it declines but does not touch (or come that close to) a lower trendline before forming a distinct valley and usually staging an immediate upward breakout. Partial declines must begin before the actual breakout and form after a valid chart pattern appears (in other words, after the minimum number of trendline touches, usually two, and any other criteria needed to establish a valid pattern). Applies to broadening patterns and rectangles.

Partial rise   After price touches a lower trendline, it rises but doesn't touch (or come that close to) the upper trendline before forming a distinct peak and usually staging an immediate downward breakout. The partial rise must begin before the breakout and form near the end of a valid chart pattern (in other words, after the minimum number of trendline touches, usually two, and any other criteria needed to establish a valid pattern). A partial rise applies to broadening patterns and rectangles.

Position trading   Trading that holds a security overnight, sometimes maintaining a position for weeks, months, or longer, but not buy-and-hold forever.

Pullback   Occurs after a *downward* breakout when price returns to, or comes very close to, the breakout price or trendline within 30 days. There must be white space between the breakout point and the pullback low. The white space rule prevents the pullback term being applied to prices clustering near the breakout price. Contrast with throwback.

Retrace   After trending, prices give back some of their gains. That movement is called a retrace of the prior move.

Reversal   A price reversal occurs when price enters and exits the chart pattern from the same direction.

RSI   The Welles Wilder relative strength index, a price momentum indicator.

Short   When a stock is sold with the expectation that a trader can buy it back at a lower price.

Short term   Lasts up to three months.

Stop or **stop-loss order**   An order to sell at a price below or to buy at a price above the current price.

Swing trading   Short-term trading that takes advantage of price swings from retrace low to crest high or the reverse.

Tall or short patterns   I measure the formation height by taking the difference between the highest peak and the lowest valley in the chart pattern, and then dividing the difference by the breakout price to get a percentage of height to price. I use the median value as the difference between short (values below the median) or tall (values above the median).

Throwback   Occurs after an *upward* breakout when price declines to, or comes very close to, the breakout price or the chart pattern trendline within 30 days. There must be white space between the hooking price action of the throwback and the breakout price. Contrast with pullback.

Trend change   When price goes from trending up to down or horizontal, or horizontal to up or down.

Trend start   Where the trend begins. To find the trend start, begin at the formation start and move backward in time. If prices *climb* leading away from the formation, find the highest peak before price closes 20% or more below and before the highest peak. When this occurs, the highest peak marks the trend start.

If prices drop leading away from the chart pattern (working backward in time), find the lowest valley before price closes 20% or more above and before the lowest valley. When that occurs, the lowest valley marks the trend start. In many cases, I ignored brief price price overshoot or undershoot just before the chart pattern begins.

For flags and pennants, the peak (swing high) or valley (swing low) closest to the start of the trend leading to the flag or pennant is used (not a 20% trend change).

Ultimate high   I determine the ultimate high by looking after the breakout for the highest peak before prices decline by 20% or more, measured from the highest peak to the *close*. I stopped looking if price *closed* below the formation low, assuming that a stop-loss order would be placed at that location.

Ultimate low   I determine the ultimate low by looking after the breakout for the lowest valley before a minimum 20% price rise, measured from the lowest valley to the *close*. I stopped looking if price closed above the formation high, assuming that an investor would have placed a stop-loss order at that price.

Volatility stop   A method of stop placement such that normal price volatility will not result in the triggering of a stop-loss order. I use the average of the high-low price difference of 30 days multiplied by 1.5. A stop should not be placed closer than the result subtracted from the current low price.

Yearly price range or yearly trading range   The price range that the security traded over the prior 12 months. To determine the yearly trading range, start from the day before the breakout and find the highest peak and lowest valley over the prior 12 months. I divided the yearly price range into thirds and compared the breakout price with each third.

Index of Chart and Event Patterns

Broadening Bottoms, page 124

Broadening Formations, Right-Angled and Ascending, page 133

Broadening Formations, Right-Angled and Descending, page 133

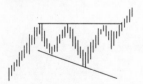

Broadening Tops, page 124

Broadening Wedges, Ascending, page 102

Broadening Wedges, Descending, page 129

Bump-and-Run Reversal Bottoms

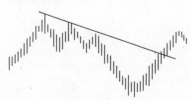

Bump-and-Run Reversal Tops

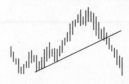

Closing Price Reversal

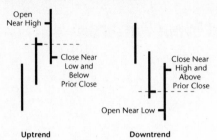

Uptrend Downtrend

Cup with Handle

Cup with Handle, Inverted

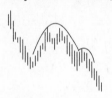

Dead-Cat Bounce, page 185

Dead-Cat Bounce, Inverted, page 189

Diamond Bottoms, page 138

Diamond Tops, page 138

Double Bottoms, Adam & Adam, page 109

Double Bottoms, Adam & Eve, page 109

Double Bottoms, Eve & Adam, page 109

Double Bottoms, Eve & Eve, page 107

Double Tops, Adam & Adam, page 144

Double Tops, Adam & Eve, page 144

Double Tops, Eve & Adam, page 144

Double Tops, Eve & Eve, page 144

Flags, page 151; Flag, Earnings, page 201

Flags, High and Tight, page 74

Gaps

Head-and-Shoulders Bottoms, page 119

Head-and-Shoulders Bottoms, Complex

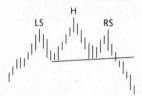

Head-and-Shoulders Tops

Head-and-Shoulders Tops, Complex, page 157

Hook Reversal

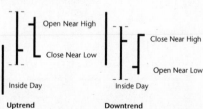

Horn Bottoms

Horn Tops

Inside Days

Island Reversals, Bottoms

Island Reversals, Tops

Islands, Long

Key Reversal

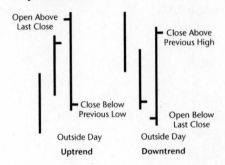

Measured Move Down, page 162

Measured Move Up, page 162

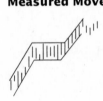

One-Day Reversals, Bottoms

One-Day Reversals, Tops

Open-Close Reversal

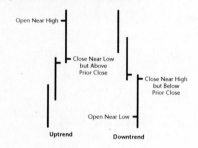

Open Near High

Close Near Low
but Above
Prior Close

Close Near High
but Below
Prior Close

Open Near Low

Uptrend   Downtrend

Outside Days

Pennants, page 151

Pipe Bottoms, page 80

P   P

Pipe Tops, page 169

P   P

Pivot Point Reversal

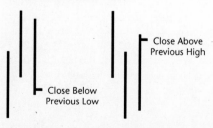

Close Above
Previous High

Close Below
Previous Low

Uptrend   Downtrend

Rectangle Bottoms

Rectangle Tops

Rounding Bottoms, page 92

Rounding Tops

Scallops, Ascending

Scallops, Ascending and Inverted, page 84

Scallops, Descending

Scallops, Descending and Inverted

Shark-32

Spikes or Tails

Uptrend
Spike High

Downtrend
Spike Low

Three Falling Peaks

Three Rising Valleys, page 88

Triangles, Ascending, page 173

Triangles, Descending, page 97

Triangles, Symmetrical, page 173

Triple Bottoms, page 113

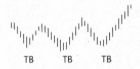

TB   TB   TB

Triple Tops, page 179

TT   TT   TT

Wedges, Falling

Wedges, Rising

Weekly Reversals, Downside

Weekly Reversals, Upside

Wide-Ranging Days

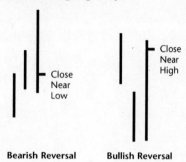

Bearish Reversal   Bullish Reversal

Index

Page numbers in *italics* refer to illustrations.